# POP CITY

# POP CITY

*Korean Popular Culture and
the Selling of Place*

YOUJEONG OH

CORNELL UNIVERSITY PRESS
ITHACA AND LONDON

306.095195
036

First published 2018 by Cornell University Press

Printed in the United States of America

Library of Congress Cataloging-in-Publication Data

Names: Oh, Youjeong, author.
Title: Pop city : Korean popular culture and the selling of place /
    Youjeong Oh.
Description: Ithaca : Cornell University Press, 2018. |
    Includes bibliographical references and index.
Identifiers: LCCN 2018015853 (print) | LCCN 2018017112 (ebook) |
    ISBN 9781501730733 (pdf) | ISBN 9781501730740 (epub/mobi) |
    ISBN 9781501730719 | ISBN 9781501730719 (cloth ; alk. paper)
Subjects: LCSH: Popular culture—Korea (South)—History—
    21st century. | Place marketing—Korea (South)—History—
    21st century. | Television plays, Korean—History and criticism. |
    Popular music—Korea (South)—History and criticism.
Classification: LCC DS923.23 (ebook) | LCC DS923.23 .O35 2018 (print) |
    DDC 306.095195—dc23
LC record available at https://lccn.loc.gov/2018015853

For Hyun-Jin

# CONTENTS

# Acknowledgments

I would like to thank my teachers at the University of California, Berkeley. The Berkeley Geography Department is where my dramatic transition from an engineer to a social scientist began. Professor You-tien Hsing has been a scholar and a teacher I admire, having shaped my ideas about urban geography. Richard Walker provided lasting intellectual stimulus for my work. I also thank Paul Gorth, Michael Watts, and Kurt Cuffey for their teaching and kind advice. Although this book does not discuss much about gender, I received intellectual inspiration and professional guidance from Barrie Thorne. I was fortunate to have great teachers throughout the campus, including Margaret Crawford, Marco Cenzatti, Hong Yung Lee, and Clare You.

At the University of Texas at Austin, I have been very fortunate to benefit from the most encouraging groups of scholars. My greatest thanks go to Robert Oppenheim for his professional leadership and generous support. I would also like to thank Heather Hindman, Martha Selby, Kirsten Cather, Mark Metzler, Huaiyin Li, Sharmila Rudrappa, Chien-hsin Tsai, Kyung Park,

Sang-Hoon Park, Eunjoo Kim, Boyoung Kim, Grace MyHyun Kim, Yvonne Chang, Oliver Freiberger, Donald Davis, Chiu-Mi Lai, Nancy Stalker, Patricia Maclachlan, Jeanette Chen, Joel Brereton, Rupert Snell, and Yi-Chun Lin.

I have received both intellectual and emotional support from amazing scholars who have worked together to discuss developmentalism and urban Korea. My special thanks go to Professor Jesook Song, who has stimulated me to grow into an independent scholar. I have learned a lot from intellectual dialogues with Laam Hae, Hyun Bang Shin, Bae-Gyoon Park, Mun Young Cho, Hyeseon Jeong, Seo Young Park, and Sujin Eom. Thanks so much for each of them.

I am greatly indebted to professional and moral support from the Korean studies community. My sincere thanks go to Namhee Lee, Dal Yong Jin, Hae Yeon Choo, Yoonkyung Lee, Eleana Kim, Jaeeun Kim, Ju Hui Judy Han, Nan Kim, Suzy Kim, Seungsook Moon, Kyung Hyun Kim, Jiyeon Kang, Young-Gyung Paik, Laura Nelson, Suk-Young Kim, and Sangjoon Lee. I have enjoyed talking with my longtime friends, all of whom are amazing scholars as well, including Sunghoon Oh, Yumin Joo, Jee-Eun Regina Song, Yuri Jang, Sung-Heui Bae, Ari Kang, HyungKyoo Kim, and Seungnam Kim. The intellectual and personal communications with my students at UT Austin also helped me a lot: thanks to Chuyun Oh, Jean Young Kim, Zachary Adamz, Jennifer Kang, and Jinsook Kim.

I am very grateful to Gabriella Lukács and Hyun Bang Shin for reading the manuscript draft and providing helpful comments. I had the privilege of participating in the Social Sciences Research Council (SSRC) Korean Studies Workshop for Junior Faculty. I am thankful to those who read an earlier version of my book prospectus and offered comments to me: Theodore Jun Yoo, John Lie, Jinsoo An, John (Sung Bae) Cho, Olga Fedorenko, Maya Stiller, and Masato Hasegawa. Portions of chapter 5 were previously printed in Oh 2017, used by permission.

I sincerely appreciate the work of the good people at Cornell University Press. Thanks especially to my acquisitions editor, Jim Lance, for his support and professional guidance. The field research for this book was conducted with generous support from POSCO Endowment, an AAS (Association for Asian Studies) NEAC (Northeast Asia Council) Travel Grant, a College Research Fellowship at UT Austin, a UC Pacific Rim Research Program Advanced Graduate Research Fellowship, and a Koret Foundation Fellowship. I also thank Kwanjeong Educational Foundation.

This book would not have come to fruition without my family's support. My mother's everyday prayer and my mother-in-law's dedication keep me going. My biggest thanks go to my husband, Jihoon Kim, who has always been with me. My dearest thanks go to my son, Joshua Hyun-Jin Kim, who patiently allowed me to spend time to travel and write this book. I love you, Hyun-Jin and Jihoon.

# Pop City

# Introduction

Most Korean[1] television dramas end with a still screen image, designed to act as a cliff-hanger to each episode. The tension is left to linger for a while; then the credits start to run, accompanied by background music against the still screen frame, revealing the names of the drama series sponsors one by one. Since the mid-2000s, the names of Korean municipalities have started appearing in the first few credits, implying that they are the production's biggest sponsors. My inquiry into cities' drama sponsorships began with a very brief discovery of one small city's name in the list of fast-rolling credits of a 2006 megabudget historical drama. Initially, like most other viewers, I did not notice or pay much attention to the credit lists. My accidental recognition that one day, however, caused me to formulate questions about the logistics of these arrangements. Municipalities sponsor drama productions not only to garner public recognition of their areas, but more important, to promote their respective places. In return, Korean television dramas strategically reveal these cities' landscapes, iconic places, and popular attractions by blending them with stories and characters' experiences, as well as by including them in the textual notices at the end of each episode. The underlying logic is that the audiences for television dramas represent potential visitors to the sponsoring areas. The rise of K-pop (Korean pop music) since 2011 has offered another medium for Korean municipalities to employ in their place marketing. Korean cities, counties, and districts increasingly try to project K-pop images in their locales by inviting K-pop groups to their local festivals, employing K-pop idols as their public relations ambassadors, or holding K-pop concerts. These strategies intend to deliberately cultivate a K-pop–evoking ambiance in their physical places to help boost the tourism industry. This book explores cases of place promotion as mediated through Korean popular culture since the early 2000s, specifically television dramas and K-pop music. Arrangements for mutual employment between popular culture and cities are now a common phenomenon, one that more than sixty South Korean municipalities have engaged in since the beginning of the new millennium.

The alliance between cultural production and urban policies reveals the untold stories about *Hallyu*, or the so-called Korean Wave, referring to the overseas popularity of Korean entertainment products, including films, television dramas, pop music (K-pop), and online games. The Korean Wave emerged and swept East Asia beginning in the mid-2000s, and has continued to enjoy international visibility in the United States, Latin America, the Middle East, and parts of Europe. The unexpected and unprecedented international attention given to Korean media has given rise to nationalistic celebrations to mark South Korea's becoming a culture-exporting country after many years of being a culture importer. Various scholarly works have aimed to understand what aspects of Korean culture appeal to foreign audiences, mainly focusing on content analyses of television dramas, K-pop music (videos), or ethnography-based reception studies.[2] The rise of the Korean Wave is undoubtedly an important phenomenon that helps us understand contemporary global Korea; however, I contend that the question should be shifted from "How has Hallyu been possible?" to "How is Hallyu reconfiguring the country?" Since the 2000s, Hallyu has significantly transformed South Korea, so that everybody now seems to be riding the Korean Wave. Korean manufacturers, the beauty, fashion, and tourism industries, culinary services, and even medical services, are trying to use the power of Hallyu to sell their products and services. With the meteoric rise of K-pop in particular, everything seems to be prefixed with a *K*, a letter that brands made-in-Korea products and culture: for example, K-drama, K-pop, K-food, K-beauty, K-style, and K-culture. What I wish to call attention to in this book is that *K*-prefixed products and services are not abstract but manifested in and associated with specific places, thus engendering "K-places." Korean television dramas and pop music not only project an international image of Korean consumer goods and services but brand Korean cities by cultivating and displaying their images and meanings therein. The global spread of Korean entertainment has extended beyond the cultural arena, reconfiguring Korea's multiple regions and locations as well by attracting its audience as tourists. This book reinterprets the Korean Wave by casting new light on the influence of Korean pop culture not only on commercial and economic life but also on the transformation of cities.

By focusing on the spatial aspects and impacts of Hallyu, this book explores the ways Korean municipalities commodify and sell their urban and rural spaces to potential tourists by being represented in and associated with popular culture. First, I discuss why Korean cities are desperate to promote their specific locations. I focus particularly on the reasons Korean municipalities have needed to use popular culture, rather than other tools, in their place-promotion strategies. Beyond the obvious benefits of circulating Korean entertainment globally, this book discusses the historical, material, and political conditions in Korean cities and their urgent need for the affective and sensational power wielded by popular culture. Second, I examine the nature of popular culture–mediated urban promotion. Urban spaces, as I shall demonstrate, are produced and sold in exactly the same way that television dramas and pop idols are: by promoting spectacular images of them rather than developing their substantial physical and cultural qualities, and by capturing and capitalizing on consumers' emotional engagement. By revealing how the speculative, image-based, and consumer-harnessing nature of popular culture shapes the commodification of urban space, I argue that pop culture–associated place promotion entails capital's domination of urban space in more sophisticated and fetishized ways than in the past. In addition to the synergies between abstract popular culture and physical urban spaces, however, this book also delves into the inherent contradictions between them, emphasizing the limits of a form of promotion in which the latter make use of the former.

## Why Selling Places?

The concept of "selling places" emerged with the changing conditions of capitalism that occurred during the 1970s, that is, the demise of Fordism and
the emergence of flexible accumulation strategies (Harvey 1989b). Since then,
many once-thriving Western cities have experienced deindustrialization as
increasingly mobile capital movements abandon previous industrial bases in
search of new geographies where labor costs less and its organization is
weaker. Reacting to the erosion of industrial bases, the practices of urban governance shifted from the provision of public services to those concerned
with urban (re)development, what David Harvey (1989a, 4) calls a move from
"boosterism" to "entrepreneurialism." According to Harvey, urban entrepreneurialism is marked by the public sector's assumption of risk in development projects conducted through public–private partnerships. By attracting
private investment, urban governments initiate various development projects,
such as creating festival marketplaces, renovated waterfronts, shopping malls,
convention centers, sports stadia, aquariums, theme parks, museums, and
other cultural places. The construction of spectacular places and the themed
built environment is designed to sell the experiences of leisure and entertainment. That is, a strategy to attenuate capital flight and lure residents and
tourists entails creating and selling the consumption experiences offered by
cities. What should be noticed here is the mutual construction, commodification, and marketing of urban places and the place-based consumption experiences. The postindustrial strategies to revive urban economies involves
the making of place as a marketable commodity packaged with goods,
services, and experiences that can be consumed in many different ways, sig-
naling a relative transformation of cities from sites of production to sites
of consumption. With the changing conditions of capitalism, selling places
through the commodification of urban space has emerged and functioned
as a new accumulation strategy in cities such as New York, London, Boston,
Baltimore, Barcelona, and Glasgow, among many others (Harvey 1990; Paddison 1993; Zukin 1995).

Place selling is not limited to deindustrialized Western cities, however. Aspiring megacities in Asia, Latin America, and the Middle East
such as Beijing, Shanghai, Dubai, and Brasilia are also active participants
in consumption-oriented place promotion and practicing the "art of being
global" through the construction of urban spectacles such as iconic land-

marks or Olympic stadia (Roy and Ong 2011). For these aspiring cities, deindustrialization is not necessarily a prerequisite for carrying out place selling. In the tough struggles against increasingly fluid capital mobility, the creation and selling of distinctive places is an obligatory survival strategy within contemporary capitalism. Building and selling the spectacular places also works as a political strategy to assert power, boost global recognition, or pacify social discontent (Broudehoux 2007; Shin 2012). The display of urban spectacles can also represent a postcolonial imperative to practice self-determination by combining local heritages and indigenous cultures with cutting-edge forms of architectural innovation (Yeoh 2005).

Rather than deindustrialization or the search for global status, the central driver of widespread place selling in Korea has been the administrative decentralization that has brought drastic changes in urban governance since the mid-1990s. Previously, the country's military regimes[3] governed through a centralized bureaucratic system by which the central government appointed local governors and mayors in a rotational system with four-year terms. During the developmental period from the 1960s to the 1980s, local areas were mere utilizable parts with which the central government orchestrated the nation's economic development. Due to the centrally appointed local leaders' compliance with the administrative center's requests, local interests were muted in favor of the more urgent and bigger task of national development. Since the late 1980s, when the country's democratization movements burgeoned, Korea has been taking steps to decentralize public administration. In 1988, the Sixth Republic made sweeping revisions to the Local Autonomy Act to revive local control and grassroots democracy, which had been suppressed under the military regimes. In 1991, local elections were carried out to establish local councils, and in 1995 South Koreans had their first experience of electing their own local governors and mayors.[4] The newly introduced popular election system has created an environment in which the local state and society envision self-determined futures for their hometowns and energetically design projects for their own interests.

Taking local interests into account is directly connected with accumulating political assets for elected local officials. The elected politicians' top priority is to be reelected, so they are under pressure to amass a number of visible achievements quickly, that is, within their limited tenure of four years. Elected leaders have two types of local audience that pay attention to their performance: first, local residents within their administrative territories, that is, those who vote them into or out of office; second, residents within the next-level administrative boundaries, that is, in provinces for cities and counties, and in metropolitan cities for districts. From my field research, I observed how elected officials had strong political aspirations not only to be reelected at their present level but also to become leaders of a higher-level administration. Given their determined political ambitions, local politicians need their administrative performances to be highly visible so that the public can easily recognize them. How, then, to impress the local audience with their work? In the field, I asked the same question to all mayors, governors, and civil officials I met: "What is the local government's priority?" Surprisingly, most of the interviewees gave similar answers: "To *develop* our areas" (emphasis added). The word *develop* can be translated into Korean in two ways: *baljeon*, meaning "bringing advancement," and *gaebal*, meaning "improving the economy" or "the built environment," or both. The conventional understanding of development in the post–Korean War developmentalist period is that *gaebal* (the urban/industrial infrastructure construction for economic development) brings *baljeon* (betterment).[5] For those local politicians in the decentralized era, however, development means realizing *baljeon* by increasing publicity. Publicity entails both enhancing the recognition status of municipalities (and thereby that of their leaders) and attracting tourists. There are critical factors that drive elected local leaders to pursue *baljeon* only by boosting publicity rather than through *gaebal*, which appears to be more tangible and visible.

Before examining local governments' recent practices of publicity-oriented place marketing, I would like to briefly overview South Korea's urbanization process, which mainly focuses on achieving *baljeon* by carrying out *gaebal*. The country's urbanization in the post–Korean War period went hand in hand with its industrialization. The developmental state poured a huge amount of investment into the installation of infrastructure such as expressways, railways, bridges, ports, dams, and industrial parks that became the basis for economic development.[6] The construction of large-scale industrial complexes (*gongdan*) located in the greater Seoul area and across southeastern Korea drove the development of labor-intensive light industries (such as plywood products, shoe manufacturing, textiles, and food processing) in the 1960s and capital-intensive heavy industries (such as steel, petrochemicals, automobiles, machinery, metals, and shipbuilding) in the 1970s. The first industrial complex was built in Ulsan in 1962 and several more appeared in the 1960s and 1970s in places such as Kuro (Seoul), Po-hang, Kwangyang, Kumi, Yeochun, and Changwon. To initiate new high-tech industries such as computers, semiconductors, new materials, tele-communications equipment, and biotechnology, the central government continued to develop new industrial sites throughout the 1980s in Suwon, Namdong (in Incheon), Sihwa, and Ansan. The construction of major expressways (Seoul–Busan, Seoul–Incheon, Honam, and Yeongdong) facili-tated logistics and transportation between industrial parks and major ports, which contributed to export-oriented industrialization. The state orchestrated the urbanization associated with industrialization through site allocation, land acquisition, and legal regulations in the three rounds of the Comprehensive National Physical Plan (*gukto jonghap gyehoek*).[7]

Housing construction is another kind of fixed-asset promotion that was guided by the central government. The "enclosure" process that released ru-ral labor from agriculture through a ruthless cutting of the price of rice caused rural-to-urban migration on a massive scale beginning in the 1960s. The extraordinary concentration of the country's population in Seoul, in particular, catalyzed sociospatial restructuring of the capital city through multiple rounds of creative destruction in residential areas. To solve the chronic housing shortage, the central government initiated massive residen-tial development through Land Adjustment Development (*toji guhoek jeongri*) between the 1960s and 1980s.[8] Beginning in the 1970s, state policy focused on constructing mass-produced apartment complexes (*apateu danji*), most of which were developed in Seoul during the 1980s and 1990s, containing more than 310,000 housing units. These large-scale, high-rise standardized apartment complexes signified a growth ideology of massive quantity and high speed on the one hand, and contributed to producing an urban middle class by bringing its members modern living conditions and home ownership on the other (Gelézeau 2007).

State-led, megascale housing construction reached its zenith in the devel-opment of five new towns (*odae sindosi*) between 1989 and 1993. The Five New Towns (FNT) project aimed to build new cities on the outskirts of Seoul as a way of implementing the Roh Tae-woo administration's (1987–1993) am-bitious Two Million Housing Units Construction Plan (*jutaek ibaengmanho geonseol gyehoek*), according to which the government promised to produce two million housing units within five years. Coming to power within the new democratic presidential election system,[9] the Roh Tae-woo administration was required to focus not only on achieving economic growth but also a fairer distribution of that growth. While housing was at the center of distributive politics, property values were skyrocketing in the late-1980s[10] and the unfettered rising prices were aggravated by the chronic housing shortage in Seoul. Under the pressure of this political, social, and economic situation, yet wielding the state's enormous managerial powers, the Roh Tae-woo administration completed the construction of five new towns—Ilsan, Bundang, Pyungchon, Sanbon, and Jungdong—where a grand total of 2,720,000 housing units were established in just five years.[11]

Even after the demise of the developmental state in the 1990s, state-centered developmentalism did not disappear in Korea. Rather, it was revived in the form of the "neodevelopmentalism" associated with neoliberalism in the wake of the financial crisis of the late 1990s. Myung-rae Cho (2004) conceptualizes "neodevelopmentalism" as the way neoliberalism has caused a new developmental boom, invading everyday spaces and environments. While developmentalism in the 1970s and 1980s placed a heavy emphasis on the economic sector and its requisite spatial interventions, neodevelopmentalism has operated through the commodification of (urban) space. A series of urban development projects since the 1990s—the Five New Towns project; the Cheonggyecheon Restoration; new redevelopment-oriented town projects in Seoul; the Multifunctional Administrative City; Innovation Cities;[12] and the Four Rivers Project—indicates how neodevelopmentalism has controlled the spaces of people's daily lives, extracting the maximum degree of exchange value from urban spaces. In contrast to the developmental state's proactive role in governing the market, capital now drives neodevelopmentalism. Yet it is still mediated by the state, particularly the central state, in the sense that state urban projects facilitate the movement of capital.

The practices of *gaebal*, particularly in the developmental era and to some extent in the postdevelopmental period, are concerned with the transformation of the built environment on a massive scale. The primary driver of *gaebal* is the central state, with its previous authoritarian and still dominant power. Contrary to such central state–dominated, fixed asset–focused forms of developmental urbanization, recent local municipalities' urban policies mainly focus on culture-mediated place promotion. These new trends, however, do not signal the abandonment of infrastructure-oriented urbanization; on the contrary, major development projects in Korea still mainly

Table 0.1. South Korean self-reliance ratio of local finance (%)

| | Year | | | | | | | | | |
|---|---|---|---|---|---|---|---|---|---|---|
| | 1997 | 1998 | 1999 | 2000 | 2001 | 2002 | 2003 | 2004 | 2005 | 2006 |
| National average | 63.0 | 63.4 | 59.6 | 59.4 | 57.6 | 54.8 | 56.3 | 57.2 | 56.2 | 54.4 |
| Metropolitan cities | 89.4 | 90.0 | 81.8 | 84.8 | 82.9 | 79.8 | 82.2 | 81.4 | 80.3 | 78.5 |
| Provinces | 42.5 | 42.1 | 38.3 | 37.9 | 35.6 | 34.6 | 39.4 | 41.3 | 36.6 | 36.1 |
| Cities | 53.3 | 54.1 | 52.0 | 50.6 | 43.4 | 40.2 | 38.0 | 38.8 | 40.6 | 39.4 |
| Counties | 21.2 | 22.9 | 23.4 | 22.0 | 18.1 | 17.4 | 16.3 | 16.6 | 16.5 | 16.1 |
| Districts | 51.6 | 49.7 | 52.3 | 46.9 | 45.0 | 45.1 | 42.3 | 42.6 | 44.3 | 40.5 |
| | 2007 | 2008 | 2009 | 2010 | 2011 | 2012 | 2013 | 2014 | 2015 | 2016 |
| National average | 53.6 | 53.9 | 53.6 | 52.2 | 51.9 | 52.3 | 51.1 | 50.3 | 50.6 | 52.5 |
| Metropolitan cities | 73.9 | 73.8 | 72.7 | 68.3 | 68.6 | 69.1 | 66.8 | 64.8 | 65.8 | 66.6 |
| Provinces | 34.9 | 39.5 | 33.3 | 31.6 | 33.0 | 34.8 | 34.1 | 33.2 | 34.8 | 35.9 |
| Cities | 39.5 | 40.7 | 40.7 | 40.0 | 38.0 | 37.1 | 36.8 | 36.5 | 35.9 | 37.4 |
| Counties | 16.6 | 17.2 | 17.8 | 18.0 | 17.1 | 16.4 | 16.1 | 16.6 | 17.0 | 18.0 |
| Districts | 37.5 | 37.1 | 37.3 | 35.4 | 36.6 | 36.0 | 33.9 | 31.1 | 29.2 | 29.7 |

*Source:* South Korean Ministry of Public Administration and Security (2016).

embody accumulation through the (re)construction of the built environment. When the primary developer is shifted from the central to local governments, however, the nature of development is inevitably changed because local municipalities lack sufficient material bases and discretional capacities to initiate hardware-driven megadevelopment projects. Despite the political devolution of power, local fiscal autonomy remains extremely weak even after decentralization. As shown in table 0.1, the level of fiscal independence of local states has hovered around 50 percent during the past two decades. What should be carefully scrutinized, however, is the degree of local fiscal independence possessed by small-sized cities, counties, and districts, which is generally less than 40 percent.[13] The overall average was boosted due solely to the metropolitan-level municipalities. The figures express local governments' continuing dependency on the central government, on the one hand, and their weak material foundation for launching development projects, on the other. Attracting industries or launching megaurban projects, therefore, is far beyond local governments' capabilities.

Moreover, due to the chronic regional disparity between the center and periphery caused by uneven development (discussed below), it would hardly be an exaggeration to say that there is no substantial demand for mega-development in local areas.

With immense developmental desires yet limited political and financial resources, what can local leaders do to develop their areas, that is, to achieve *baljeon* in a situation in which they cannot carry out *gaebal?* Selling place, or place marketing, emerged in this context as a promising strategy to attract tourists as a means of raising publicity and boosting local economies. Compensating for material deficiencies, renewed attention has been given to local cultural assets such as unique artifacts, art forms, histories, traditions, vernacular cuisines, or certain features of the natural environment that aim to act as tourism magnets (Hae 2017).[14] Pushing such a culture-oriented paradigm were intellectuals and Western-educated urbanists who planted the notion that place marketing provides locals with the power to foster endogenous development and actualize practices of participatory democracy in the era of local autonomy (Hae 2017). As decentralization itself was promoted by the central state's policy drive, however, it was the central government that actively sparked the proliferation of place marketing in the form of local cultural festivals (*jiyeok chukje*) since the mid-1990s. When the tourism[15] sector was transferred from the Ministry of Transportation to the Ministry of Culture and Tourism in 1995, the central government pushed for the integration of culture and tourism by introducing a system to support promising local cultural festivals. The Ministry of Culture and Tourism, first, selected 8 cultural tourism festivals in 1996 and gradually increased the number to 21 in 1999, 25 in 2000, 30 in 2001, and 29 in 2002 (Korea Culture and Tourism Institute 2006). The selected municipalities receive not only forms of financial aid but also support for publicity directed at both domestic and international audiences. As of 2006, a total of 1,176 local festivals were counted, a number that indicates that central state support has kindled fierce competition among local municipalities. While the central subsidy system contributed to the mushrooming of local festivals, at the same time, it also caused financial and public relations problems among those that did not receive assistance.

To summarize the discussion thus far, the country's political decentralization and the weak fiscal capabilities of local governments triggered the rise of place selling as a feasible local development strategy. Municipalities at all levels—provinces, cities, counties, and districts—are engaging in place promotion. Thus, the scope of place selling in this book covers both urban and rural places, although I draw on scholarly works on the commodification of *urban* space. Decentralization prompted strong developmental aspirations in municipalities, but at the same time revealed their lack of the fiscal recourses needed to initiate large-scale infrastructure projects. Given their deficiency of material bases, their methods of pursuing *baljeon* do not necessarily involve engaging in raw, material competition to attract more capital investment; rather, they undertake tourism-oriented development by promoting distinct local cultural assets. Patrick Mullins (1991, 331) defines "tourism urbanization" as "urbanization based on the sale and consumption of pleasure." As discussed above, the sale of urban consumption experiences is usually accompanied by the spectacular construction of place. While resource-poor Korean municipalities also resort to tourism urbanization as a development strategy (Hoffman, Fainstein, and Judd 2003), they do not carry out the physical construction of dazzling forms of tourist infrastructure such as upscale consumption places and megaevent venues. Instead, those hidden assets that were once treated as "indigenous," "primitive," or even "backward" are reinterpreted as profitable source materials for holding local festivals that primarily target tourists rather than local residents. Without a central subsidy, however, there are financial and publicity problems that arise when presenting local festivals, while the competition among municipalities increases.

Since the mid-2000s, Korean municipalities have attempted to capitalize on the overseas popularity of the Korean entertainment industry. As globally circulating popular culture functions as a window through which audiences come to know Korea,[16] specific places within the country have emerged as physical sites through which K-culture experiences can be extended: sites where television shows or films were made; K-pop concert venues; areas where entertainment agencies are aggregated; shops selling celebrity merchandise; and places associated with K-stars' personal memories. Sites represented in or linked to popular culture have become fantasy places that audience-tourists aspire to visit, and such desires have actually been materialized through a boom in culture-driven tourism.[17] Both central and local governments have made various efforts to attract (foreign) tourists by marketing places through their associations with dramas and K-pop. The Korea Tourism Organization, a state corporation supervised by the Ministry of

Culture, Sports and Tourism, has employed top Hallyu stars as advertisement ambassadors since the mid-2000s. Its recent slogan, "Imagine Your Korea," which has replaced the previous "Dynamic Korea" and "Korea Sparkling," particularly showcases the country's cultural appeal to foreigners, portraying Korea as "a trendy and creative tourist destination that leads global pop-culture."[18] What should be noticed here is not merely the deployment of culture to attract overseas tourists. The new motto, "Imagine *Your* Korea" (emphasis added), highlights the value of personal experiences, motivating individuals to discover the various charms of Korea for themselves. Tourist-centered and experience-focused visits mark a departure from previous guided sightseeing tours to areas noted for their natural or historical value. It is important to recognize that the "must-see" destinations in these guided tours include the tourism complexes developed by the central state, such as Bomun Tourist Complex (*gyeongju bomun gwangwang danji*) and Jungmun Tourist Complex (*jungmun gwangwang danji*). When tourists themselves act as agents who design their own travel experiences, their destinations are diversified, leading to the discovery of *jibang* (regional districts) beyond Seoul and already famous attractions. The transition in the mode of development from infrastructure-driven megaconstruction to small-scale culture-focused place selling has neatly dovetailed with changes in the tourism industry from directed tours of some renowned places to agent- and experience-oriented tours of diverse areas. Korean popular culture publicizes Korea, brings international audiences to the country, and acts as a specific tool through which foreign tourists discover and experience various places in Korea.

The concurrence of the globalization of Korean popular culture, political decentralization, and the boom in transnational tourism created a perfect environment through which pop culture–based place marketing has become one of the most viable methods for enhancing elected local leaders' visibility. Tourist destinations are not necessarily the sites with preexisting historical, cultural, or natural resources; they can be "created" by giving cities a new image. Television dramas and K-pop music can instantly provide entirely new images to certain places through their stories and characters, regardless of the area's preexisting identities. Due to the quick and easy creation of pop culture–amalgamated places, municipalities that are poorly endowed with material and cultural resources now have new opportunities to promote tourism. With the rise of new tourism patterns that emphasize individual tourists' experiences in exploring hidden corners of the country, even previously unmarketable places can be rendered appealing to (foreign) tourists. Yet even traditional tourist destinations such as Jeju and Kyungju are active practitioners of culture-mediated place marketing and tourism promotion because they act as powerful mechanisms to create publicity.

Popular culture possesses some enticing attributes that fiscally weak but entrepreneurial local states cannot resist harnessing. First, popular culture has an affective power that lures audiences. The blooming of emotions in television dramas and idol performances represents an intrinsically different method of attracting tourists than more traditional print media such as brochures. Relying on the affective appeal of pop culture via characters, story lines, idols, and so forth, place promotion strategically targets emotionally susceptible audience groups with the aim of igniting a desire to actually visit the featured sites. Emotionally motivated fan-tourists take the branding of media-associated places one step further by spreading their affective engagement with them among fan communities. Second, popular culture has the power to cause a sensation. As mentioned above, local policies in the era of decentralization are almost entirely designed to showcase the political performance of elected mayors and governors. Urban policies aim to grab the attention of the media and local audiences as much as to actually enhance the living conditions of local communities. Globally rising K-dramas, K-pop, and K-stars are, in that sense, effective channels for advertising local leaders' urban projects widely and sensationally. Local leaders love to release press reports that put the names of the top stars they are working with on the front page to garner immediate media attention. That is, reports in secondary media additionally publicize any municipalities linked with drama stories and idol imagery. Once municipalities reveal their locales in the cultural content, they do not need to be overly concerned with enhancing publicity; the commercial entertainment yields a multiplied promotion system across diverse media and by the audiences themselves.

In sum, within the context of the globalization of Korean entertainment and the country's decentralization, Korean municipalities that are developmental and entrepreneurial but financially and politically weak are attempting to render their locales more noticeable and seductive to tourists through popular culture. As Hallyu and Hallyu tourism have become targets of urban development projects, this seemingly cultural phenomenon has manifested itself in the urban environment. As local governments try to revive local areas by attracting foreign tourists by capitalizing on Korean entertainment's global popularity, their ways of solving local (subnational) problems—such as underdevelopment, poverty, or lack of recognition—are transnational.

## How Does Popular Culture Help Sell Places?

I have discussed the recent global hype surrounding Korean entertainment and the political and economic reasons that Korean municipalities have chosen popular culture as a dominant element in their urban policies. In this section, I will provide a detailed discussion of how popular culture facilitates the selling of place. The primary aim of this section is to illustrate the crucial difference between place marketing pursued predominantly through thematic motifs versus via pop culture methods. There is also a perfect match between the selling mechanism of popular culture–featured places and the weak material conditions of Korean municipalities.

In response to cities' entrepreneurial turn under late capitalism (Hall 1998), urban governments are increasingly compelled to practice the marketing of cities to attract incoming capital investment, boost local economic development, and improve their cities' images. As the commodification of urban space to attract capital, investment, residents, and tourists has become a critical part of capitalist accumulation, rampant place-making strategies emerge in which distinct images of places are created via the following methods: (1) the transformation of public spaces into privatized consumption areas characterized by a thematic and spectacular built environment; (2) the commodification of local festivals, histories, traditions, and culture in an attempt to attract tourists; (3) the promotion of cultural spaces, cultural institutions, and cultural policies in association with the creative and cultural industries; and (4) the active incorporation of natural elements, landscapes, and eco-designs (Paddison 1993; Zukin 1995; Gottdiener 2001; Harvey 2001a; Hannigan 1998; Gotham 2005; Oh 2014). As Mark Gottdiener (2001) contends, the political economy of place making hinges on endowing a place with symbolic value as a vehicle for profit realization. Thematic designs, eco-concepts, commodified history and traditions, and cultural forms generate additional value—symbolic value—in the built environment by conferring onto it associations with style, quality, or cosmopolitanism that cater to consumers' desires for status, fashion, sex appeal, or power. In line with Bourdieu's concept of "symbolic capital," defined as "the collection of luxury goods attesting to the taste and distinction of the owner," (1977, 188) symbolic value functions as a means of social distinction that often exceeds and replaces the use-value of a commodity or place. Harvey (2002) explains the creation of collective symbolic capital wherein special marks of distinction attach to some place to help yield monopoly rent. As rent is based on exclusive control over tradable items, some special qualities enable owners to extract rents from those desiring to use them. The creation of symbolic value by accumulating marks of distinction, therefore, facilitates marketing a place, guaranteeing fast and stable rates of return. What becomes critical in place making, therefore, is deciding which *themes* (distinguishable marks) to employ to produce symbolic value. Over time, more diversified themes have been employed—from nature, culture, history, sports, and heritage, to even traumatic memories of disaster.

The cases in this book focus on the deployment of popular culture in creating unique images of place. At a superficial level, the places' meanings and values are created by linking them to distinctive themes drawn from television dramas or K-pop music, as in conventional place making. Pop culture–channeled place promotion, however, exercises a very distinct selling mechanism because the urban/rural places are blended with cultural content. It is not the remarkable themes but the places' affective qualities and consumers' emotional attachments to them that enhance the value of the places. Operation of the entertainment industry is based on the ability to manipulate affect within the audience. Affect becomes a source of value by bringing emotions into the relationship between cultural products and viewers, thereby transforming commodities into emotionalized communication tools (Lukács 2010a). The success of the pop culture industry therefore hinges on the formation of affective relations with consumers. In this book, I argue that pop idols and drama characters are human agents used to build an affective intimacy with audiences. The same principle applies to entertainment-based place marketing. The power of commercial entertainment lies in its ability to turn a physical space into an affective place. The media presentation of stories, characters, dramatic scenes, performances, and idol images reconstructs a televised space not merely as a themed place but as an affective place filled with emotion, imagination, desire, and fantasy.

For many scholars of affect, the difference between affect and emotion is critical (Massumi 2002). Emotions involve specific feelings such as "anger, anxiety, comfort, depression, desire, desperation, envy, exclusion, fear, guilt, happiness, hardship, joy, longing, love, pain, romance, suffering, or worry" (Pile 2010, 6). Affect is a bodily function that arises in a particular context; it is something that is difficult to represent in linguistic terms and lies beyond consciousness. Whereas emotions are cognitive, representable, and personal, affect is precognitive, nonrepresentable, and interpersonal (ibid.). The body matters for both, but in different ways: while the body is a site of feeling and experience for emotion, it is also a device that enables the transpersonal in affect (ibid.). Scholars of affect argue that although experiences and feelings are embedded in social relations, they are ultimately personal and are thus nontransmittable. Affect, on the other hand, is transmittable because it is un-formed and unstructured (abstract), which is why it can be such a powerful social force. Due to its capacity to bypass the discussion of intention, mean-ing, or interpretation, affect is often used in discussions of social, political, and cultural domains (Trigg 2014). The theorization of the difference be-tween emotion and affect is certainly not the focus of this book. Rather, I use *emotion* and *affect* as interchangeable terms,[19] as they share multiple qual-ities, drawing on Sara Ahmed's theorization: "The distinction between affect/ emotion can under-describe the work of emotions, which *involve* forms of intensity, bodily orientation, and direction that are not simply about 'subjec-tive content' or qualification of intensity. Emotions are not 'after-thoughts' but shape bodies are moved by the worlds they inhabit" (2010, 230–231n1).

Both emotion and affect matter in studying the ways popular culture pro-vides places with emotional qualities and the ways people feel, enact, and extend the cultural experience in a physical place. I call attention to all types of affect/emotions associated with popular culture: the emotions represented in television dramas or K-pop music; the emotions and affect generated in the process of appreciating popular culture; and the affect and emotions de-veloped in audiences as they experience places associated with pop culture. Drama characters and K-pop idols not only exist as images but can affect people through their affective labor, encouraging them to engage in other types of affective labor such as transmitting the appreciation of media content throughout diverse media. Some deeply immersed fans talked about their experience of affect (although they did not use that specific term) by describing the ways "the intense sensation and emotions acted and impinged upon the body" (Choe 2008, 114; Choe 2016) while viewing the television dramas and visiting the drama-filmed sites. The intense bodily emo-tional sensations that are triggered by both pop culture and pop culture–

featured sites, but are not discursively representable, speak to the approaches of "affective geography." Yet, in both my physical and virtual ethnography of Korean pop culture fans, I was able to recognize such experiences of affect and associated emotions and communicate them through interviewees' proactive expressions in verbal, bodily, textual, and visual forms. Taking such emotional expressions seriously, this book also follows the perspectives of "emotional geography"[20] that investigate the quality/capacity of place to evoke emotions and the bodily experiences of such places.

I argue that popular culture confers affective values on place through its intense displays of emotions such as tension, love, longing, and desire. An affective place is distinct from a merely themed place in the way it attracts visitors. An emotion-laden place draws prospective tourists by stimulating their interest, yearning, and empathy. Because the audience-tourists have already developed a certain level of emotional attachment with dramas or pop idols—albeit to varying degrees among different groups and individuals[21]—their consumption of a culture-related place transcends mere appreciation of the site and entails developing empathetic bonds with it. Particularly the so-called pop culture–induced pilgrims, who are serious devotees of television series or K-pop idols, do not seek the touristic consumption of place but rather wish to deepen their personal or shared connections with the drama plot, characters, or idols.[22] Through the self-motivated tourists' bodily, haptic, and affective consumption of places associated with dramas and K-pop, they amplify, deepen, and sometimes challenge and negotiate the affective values of places, constructing a new place identity that transcends the reality of the place and culture-depicted images. Such emotional engagement with a place turns visitors into agents of value creation on its behalf—that is, into facilitators of place selling.

In media studies, it is now commonplace to see audiences as active agents, rather than as passive objects trapped in "cultural determinism" (Adorno 1991; Adorno and Horkheimer 2002), in producing their own meanings and pleasure through the consumption of media content (Hall 1980; De Certeau 1984; Fiske 1989; Du Gay 1997). More recent discussions acknowledge the role of the audience as "a collective of active agents whose labor may generate alternative forms of market value" (Jenkins, Ford, and Green 2014, 116). The consumption of media content, unlike other commodities, does not diminish the value of goods. Rather, the collective aggregation of consumption generates greater value, such as when more viewership leads to greater ratings and the selling of more advertisements. Elsewhere, I have explored the ways the collaborative and discursive consumption of Korean television dramas cultivates additional pleasures (beyond the pleasures from the original content) and facilitates interactions between people via social media (Oh 2015). The amplified pleasures in the discursive consumption of popular culture can also be translated into both cultural and material values because the highly engaged audiences pass along the cultural content (both original and secondary fan-made content) across diverse media. Such fan activities help to retain the size of fandom, recruit new members, or further fuel audience fascination. For those reasons, anthropologist Grant McCracken (2005) has proposed shifting the description of people away from "consumers," as the term locates people at the end of a chain of value creation, to "multipliers" as an alternative that acknowledges the ways audience members generate value through their activities. An audience is not a one-time commodity whose viewership is sold to advertisers but can also be a labor whose engagement and activities can produce renewable values. The media industry has already acknowledged and tapped into passionate fans' investments in the media content by promoting secondary products such as video on demand, DVDs, electronic rentals, or media merchandise.

Within the disciplines of urban studies and geography, there have been few efforts to identify consumers as value generators. In conventional place making, a commodified urban space decorated with motifs from culture, history, and spectacular events is sold to investors, tourists, and potential residents. Here, the presumed users of the place are seen as passive objects and outsiders to be invited in and encouraged to consume preproduced urban environments such as shopping malls, upscale restaurants, and gated communities. In pop culture–based place making, the audience-tourists are active participants, as well as consumers, in enriching the meanings and values of a place through their development of an affective attachment to it. Visitors to the place broaden, deepen, materialize, and challenge the images and meanings presented in popular culture. Thus, pop culture–mediated place marketing goes through a dual process of value generation. First, the original entertainment content of the kind found in television dramas or popular music imparts affective values to the built environment. Second, visitors' appreciation of and engagement with the place amplify these affective values, further branding the place. As popular cultural products require a certain level of consumer involvement (e.g., longing, loyalty, and fandom), the commodification of urban space via popular culture similarly harnesses audience groups' (particularly fans') emotional investments as free but dedicated labor to facilitate its selling. The "affective economics" (Jenkins 2006, 61) can be extended into the selling of place by commodifying passionate fans' desires, commitment, and their social power. Exploitation, however, might not be an adequate descriptor of this mechanism because audience members themselves benefit from their willing participation in such arrangements. Fans' "labor of love" (Galbraith 2016, 234) can be rewarded by increased enjoyment and deepened emotional fulfillment. The affective economy both commercializes and satisfies fans, but "in asymmetrical ways" (Takeyama 2010, 238) between place marketers and consumers.

The utilization of users' emotional engagement in selling places speaks to the severe disinvestment by both public and private marketers of place. Because dramatizing the urban environment relies on images from television dramas or of K-pop idols, place-based extravaganzas do very little to improve cities' actual physical qualities or to resolve community issues. Harvey (1989a) points out that entrepreneurialism focuses much more closely on the political economy of place than on territory. In other words, the construction of places such as new civic centers, privatized public spaces, or dazzling new entertainment complexes has a limited spatial impact and concerns only the actual place itself, whereas welfare projects such as housing, education, and health care work to improve living or working conditions within a particular jurisdiction. The construction of place embodies elitism in action; it has a much smaller impact on a territory as a whole, and thus raises issues of spatial injustice (MacLeod 2002). What I wish to point out is the further narrowing of the public's role in image-dominated and user-harnessed place construction through popular culture, although the public sector (i.e., local government) hypes place promotion at the policy and publicity level. As entertainment-oriented place marketing taps into consumers' emotional resources and engagement in enriching the values of places and advertising them, the place marketers' investment is even further diminished. The spectacular cultural images projected onto the urban landscape obfuscate this continuing disinvestment. The process is a sophisticated mechanism in the commodification of urban space: pop culture fetishes confer dramatized images on urban space and lure affective consumers to engage with and further advertise the place in question. By drawing on consumer agency to both consume and sell place, place marketers can reap returns without significant investments. Korean place marketers' utilization of fan-tourists' emotional investment to rebrand and promote places reveals their resource-strained condition, which, ironically, leads them to rely more on consumer engagement.

Such a refined and instant commodification process creates tensions for local residents, who are almost invisible in the urban image construction process. Popular culture and media create pseudo local histories that do not engage with the community, but simply elicit audience affection that will smooth the marketing and selling of places. Flamboyant urban spectacles mediated through commercial entertainment have nothing to do with the lived experiences of local residents; instead they conceal and distort the existing local reality, local demands, and local politics. Although newly generated meanings are not necessarily related to preexisting local history, municipalities remain eager to utilize the instant, pseudohistory created by popular culture to boost their recognition and entice tourists. Scholars point out the dual effects of urban spectacles in relation to the state: image construction serves political ends as an instrument of state legitimation and as a means of popular pacification, on the one hand, and urban beautification also has a depoliticizing effect by distracting society's attention from social and economic inequities and reducing a city to a transparent and unproblematic surface, on the other (see, e.g., Debord 1994; Broudehoux 2004; Shin 2012). Nevertheless, another critical function of spectacles is to render such discrepancies and tensions even more visible (Gotham 2005; Broudehoux 2007). The exaggerated representation of a place can cause local residents to recognize how they have been detached from the process and thereby spark their political will to combat the conflicts and struggles that arise when converting cities into tourist spectacles. Place marketers, who are mostly local leaders and civil officials, face a contradictory situation in which the accumulation of political capital through the sort of instant publicity that popular culture can furnish clashes with their imperative of maintaining legitimacy to enable them to manage the local community.

## Speculative Venture

Harvey (1989a) argues that the place marketing practices of urban entrepreneurialism are speculative because they involve risk-bearing scenarios for the deployment of local fiscal resources, as opposed to rationally planned and coordinated forms of development. Interpreting entrepreneurialism as a type of innovation in which urban entrepreneurs devise new ways of doing urban governance to be as competitive as possible, Jessop agrees that an entrepreneurial function involves uncertainty "since innovation means venturing into the unknown" (1998, 82).[23] Cities cannot predict whether their investments in property-oriented development will be successful. Moreover, only a few cities can enjoy competitive advantages within the ever-intensifying interurban competition, because holding iconic events (such as the Olympic Games and world fair) as a place promoter, for example, is a rare and fleeting opportunity. The recent pop culture–featured place marketing practices in Korea—the central focus of this book—are extremely speculative not only because the public sector (i.e., local governments) assumes the risks involved in the place projects, but more important, because the practices are associated with popular culture. I will outline the ways both the Korean pop culture industry and Korean local municipalities are venturing into speculative business. Their speculative character has been intensified due to the mutual reliance between the two speculative players: the entertainment industry and local municipalities.

I would like to first examine the speculative features of the culture industry by outlining the industrial changes that have occurred since the beginning of the Korean Wave. All business is risky, but the culture industry is particularly risky because it is centered on the production and selling of texts and symbolic goods that depend on subjective judgment at the point of consumption (Bilton 1999). The accidental and unexpected formation of the Korean Wave, I argue, has aggravated speculation in the Korean pop culture industry to the point that it has spiraled out of control. The reason for this lies in the characteristics of cultural products. According to Nicholas Garnham (1990), cultural commodities have special features,[24] one of which is their relatively low reproduction cost.

> Because one of the use-values of culture is novelty or difference, there is a constant need to create new products which are all in a sense prototypes. This drive for novelty within cultural production means that in general the costs of reproduction are marginal in relation to the cost of production. Thus the marginal returns from each extra sale tend to grow, leading in turn to a powerful thrust towards audience maximization as the preferred profit maximization strategy. (160)

Therefore, once a television drama has been filmed and edited, and an accompanying music album has been recorded, the production of an additional physical copy costs relatively little. In the current era of digitization, which Bolin describes as "the process whereby media texts are broken down into digits, and are hence reproducible without a loss of quality" (2009, 347), the marginal returns from each extra sale are relatively high because the reproduction costs are negligible.[25] The high ratio of fixed to variable costs means that big hits are extremely profitable because the surplus rises without any increase in the production cost. This point has been critical to the Korean culture industry since Hallyu began because the unexpected overseas popularity of Korean pop culture has led to the acquisition of additional markets, meaning pure profits without extra production costs.[26] In contrast to the finite domestic market, the number of overseas markets is vast. For example, *Jewel in the Palace* (2003), one of the drama series that drove the formation of the Korean Series, has been exported to more than sixty countries. The focus therefore becomes the search for export markets that might yield profit jackpots.

The sudden and accidental formation of the Korean Wave sparked expectations about overseas markets among previously domestic-focused cultural producers. Anticipation caused a sudden increase in the number of industry players—drama producers, entertainment management agencies, record labels, and idol wannabes—who hoped to take advantage of potentially lucrative export opportunities. Yet the Korean Wave does not necessarily indicate a rise in actual overseas demand for Korean entertainment. Rather, there has been an increase in potential demand initiated by the success of some pioneering shows, and the industry has advanced only far enough to see the latent opportunities. The proliferation of industrial players driven more by expectations than by actual demand has rendered the industry highly speculative, because competition is heightened among nascent players whose capabilities have not yet been verified. Moreover, most anticipation-driven industrial newcomers lack financial power, driving them to search for funding sources. While financial struggles drive industrial players to be even more speculative, as chapter 1 and 3 will elaborate, Korean cities (and, to some extent, other East Asian cities) emerge as one of the sources of funding, opening up a marriage between the culture industry and cities, and thus between culture and place.

The global popularity of Korean entertainment has generated a great sense of anticipation among place marketers, in particular because overseas audiences are seen as potential tourists. Attracting foreign tourists certainly boosts local economies due to the high number of visitors and their strong purchasing power. Yet a more critical role of overseas tourists is to create sensations. The gaze of foreigners has been a persistent theme in South Korean development. In pursuing export-oriented economic development, the developmental state cultivated a mentality of consciousness of the foreign gaze: an outlook that emphasizes the extent to which the international community is paying attention to the performance of South Korea, a postcolonial latecomer on the world stage. To verify the extent of this gaze, domestic media have competed with one another to deliver overseas responses to major sporting events such as the Seoul Olympic Games in 1988 and the Korea–Japan World Cup in 2002. The developmental state harnessed the imaginary but powerful idea of overseas attention paid to Korea to mobilize the population, increasing the amount of both exports and labor, and forcing individuals to make sacrifices for the greater cause of national development. The foreign gaze stimulated the country to speed up development and hasten modernization, implanting the normative notion of national progress. Now, in an effort to transform urban space from a production to a consumption space, the presence of foreign bodies is celebrated to make these cities appear global, truly attractive, and worthy to visit. As the presence of foreign tourists has become the central promotional asset, chapter 2, 4, and 5 will recount the ways municipalities pay attention to the number of foreign tourists that visit their areas and capitalize on these numbers in their second-round advertisements. But how are foreign tourists allured to every corner of Korea? The instant popularity of entertainment content does not lead to constant inflows of tourists; consequently, intermunicipal rivalry for attracting foreign tourists is intense. Moreover, other political and diplomatic matters significantly affect the number of tourists. For example, when the sinking of the ROKS (Republic of Korea Ship) *Cheonan* occurred in 2010, the number of inbound Japanese tourists dropped significantly for a while, and the deployment of the antimissile Terminal High Altitude Area Defense (THAAD) in 2016 virtually stopped the previously high influx of Chinese tourists.[27] Drawing overseas travelers to local places is therefore also speculative because there is never any guarantee of steady streams of tourists.

Both the Korean pop culture industry and Korean municipalities are engaging in speculative ventures to penetrate overseas markets and draw overseas tourists. Both groups may be well aware that the Hallyu-driven hype is more or less supply-driven rather than demand-driven. Despite the risks involved in the oversupplied race, both the cultural producers and place marketers appear confident because of the sheer amount of uncertainty involved. That is, nobody knows whether a play, show, song, and so forth, will be a hit or not; therefore, it is never clear whether the place selling packaged within particular entertainment content will be successful or not. Due to the Korean Wave, or more precisely due to the megasuccess of some pioneering shows such as *Winter Sonata* and places like Chuncheon (the spatial setting of the drama series), Korean cultural producers and local governments consider such unpredictability to be an opportunity. Because some former successful cases enjoyed huge fortunes through just one megahit, small independent producers, minor music labels, and poor local municipalities keep engaging in the venture despite several failures they have experienced. Due to this uncertainty, they believe one big hit *will* come and compensate for the past losses. The practices of gambling on unpredictability aggravate their speculative tendencies.

Another factor contributing to the speculative character of the Korean culture industry and urban governance is their increasing financialization. The critical problem of contemporary financialized capitalism (or rentier capitalism) is that it seeks capital gains without producing any tangible benefits to society. In industrial capitalism, the surplus value that is created is reinvested to expand markets, invest in new production techniques, or produce future manufacturing bases. Financialized capitalism, by contrast, seeks profits through rents accrued by monopolizing access to physical, financial, cultural, or intellectual properties (Hudson 1998). Place marketers' search for short-term profits by generating buzz via popular culture without tangible long-term investment resembles the practices of financialized capitalism. The mechanism of culture-mediated place marketing that costs relatively little and extracts surplus value through the audience's emotional dedication mirrors rentier capitalism's speculative proclivities—that is, aiming for instant returns without solid resources.

Intriguingly enough, the highly speculative nature of Korean cultural industries and cities has spawned culture–place associations based on the groups' mutual needs. The cultural producers in search of funds have found Korean cities to be both financial and spatial sponsors that are willing to both cover the production costs and provide the filming sites. The buzz-seeking municipalities reap multiple advantages from their employment of popular culture, that is, spontaneous publicity, relative inexpensiveness, and the ability to inspire users' loyalty. The linkage between cities and pop culture, however, does not always produce synergies. In fact, the dynamics between the two are quite complicated. Television dramas and music, as abstract media, are different from physical urban spaces in the ways they operate through time: the instant nature of commercial entertainment quickly generates dramatic promotional results for cities, but its unpredictability and subordination to current fashions render the benefits unstable and volatile. While popular cultural industries simply leave particular urban places after receiving sponsorship from them, local authorities are forced to deal with any material and physical problems that they leave behind. Although municipalities are already familiar with such instability after witnessing many failure cases, many of them still venture into projects nonetheless in the hope of being part of a megahit. Two critical questions arise. First, could the mobilization of local finance and resources for such speculative projects be justified? By channeling public resources into the image-making project, local governments often forgo other opportunities concerning welfare and social well-being in general. Although place selling is, of course, place-specific— that is, the creation of superficial seductive images only focuses on limited places—its impacts exceed the place boundary and affect local communities at large. Thus, a second question emerges regarding who is responsible for the lingering challenges that the pursuit of a faster return imposes on urban communities and how to deal with them.

## Unevenness

Unevenness is a key critical concept discussed throughout this book. While virtually all municipalities at every level display a similar desire to promote their areas, there are stark contrasts between players in Seoul and those in other parts of the country in the strategies and channels they choose, and in the outcomes of their place-promotion efforts. Unevenness operates in multiple realms and at multiple levels in spatial, cultural, and socioeconomic processes. First, I tackle the spatial disparities created by the country's unbalanced development (*bulgyunhyeong baljeon*) among regional cities and districts in Seoul in terms of their development, power, and wealth. Second,

I underscore the fact that this very spatial unevenness makes it inevitable that regional cities and Seoul's districts will choose different promotional media: television dramas for regional cities and K-pop idols for Gangnam and Myeong-dong, two affluent central districts in Seoul. Third, this book shows how the different promotional media have brought about different outcomes and challenges to the two groups of actors.

The multilevel asymmetries referred to above originate from the country's uneven development. Scholars argue that the concept of uneven development provides a sound basis for understanding the shifting geographies of capital accumulation and social inequality (see, e.g., Smith 1994; Harvey 1978, 1996, 2001a). Capitalism requires continual growth and is subject to periodic crises of overaccumulation in such forms as idle productive capacity or augmented labor power. One solution to both problems is geographical relocation, what David Harvey labels a "spatial fix." Excess capital may find alternative places for production, property development, or other speculative investment (Harvey 2001b). The incorporation of East Asia into the world industrial production system—as a site to absorb surplus capital in the form of foreign aid, as a new export market, and as a provider of inexpensive manufactured goods—can be understood as a spatial fix for the potential crises in the West in the 1950s and 1960s. When the country was about to initiate industrialization after the Korean War, the Korean state was forced to start from scratch on war-torn land. The Korean developmental state adopted strategies to mobilize national resources and people, then concentrate them in a few selected sectors or areas as an effective means of initiating development. In other words, South Korea's international competitiveness was created and maintained through uneven development at the national level.

The state's so-called picking winners policy favored capital, men, and the greater Seoul area over labor, women, and local regions in the name of expediting economic development. For example, the developmental state preferred export-targeted industries and, therefore, actively promoted labor-intensive light industries such as textiles, shoes, and wigs in the 1960s and heavy and chemical industries in the 1970s. In light of the country's resource constraints, spatial selectivity and concentration were also evident in the channeling of investments for infrastructure into a few designated areas to maximize efficiency. Strategic spatial selection favored the Seoul Metropolitan Area (SMA; *sudogwon*) and the southeast coast, which turned into major industrial sites as a result of the state's investment (Park 2008). While Marxist geographers discuss uneven development as characteristic of and functional to capitalism by bringing wealth to the center and exploiting the peripheries,[28] uneven development in South Korea was brought about by state policies that controlled the operation of capital. But planned concentration likewise created center–periphery unevenness.

Within such a context, the SMA was a primary destination for resource distribution, capital investment, and population movement. The outcome of such spatial selectivity has been an extraordinary degree of concentration of capital, people, and power in the greater Seoul area, which can be expressed in multiple numerical indicators. For instance, more than half of the Korean population lives in the Seoul metropolitan region, despite the fact that the area comprises a mere 11.8 percent of South Korea's territory. As of 2010, the greater Seoul area was home to approximately 55 percent of the country's manufacturing firms, 66 percent of universities offering regular four-year degrees, 73 percent of the research and development institutions, and 77 percent of Korean venture businesses. As of 2000, the SMA was said to have 46.5 percent of the working population and to be responsible for 48 percent of the total gross domestic product. Not surprisingly, the headquarters of 95 of the 100 largest enterprises, all 27 central ministries, and 87.6 percent of their affiliated organizations are also located in the SMA.[29] As a result, the SMA has commanded hegemony in all aspects, while the rest of the country has held merely a peripheral status.[30] The trend implies that the benefits gained from already established agglomeration economies and relatively abundant employment opportunities outweigh the negative congestion that accompanies extreme concentration.

Many regional cities located outside of the greater Seoul area, and even some cities and counties within the SMA, mostly those designated as greenbelt or nature preservation areas, have been neglected by national development and have suffered from economic stagnation, poverty, and underdevelopment. "Regional city" is an English translation of the Korean word *jibang dosi*, used as an opposite concept to *sudogwon*, meaning the Capital Region, the greater Seoul area, or the SMA. In this book, "regional city" refers to a small, local, peripheral, and marginalized city, county, or district, shaped by South Korea's uneven development trajectories of the post–Korean War era. I argue that the legacy of uneven development relegated

Korean regional cities to marginal status, thereby creating within them strong aspirations toward betterment. In the decentralized era, regional cities have tried to transcend their marginal position by boosting self-motivated development.

Intriguingly, however, the underdeveloped conditions of regional cities can be capitalized on by portraying them as exotic, lyrical, and imaginary elements in popular culture. For television drama producers who require spacious nonurban land to build drama sets or provide exotic visual elements to be integrated into drama stories, regional cities emerge as the perfect spatial backgrounds for television dramas and also attract eager financial sponsors. Thus, during the First Korean Wave (2003–2011), which was driven by dramas, mutual needs and synergies were formed between regional cities and drama producers. By dramatically displaying places in regional cities, television programs, on the one hand, conferred new meanings and identities on them and, on the other, allowed audience members (who were potential tourists) to get to know the *jibang*. The 2000s witnessed the formation of critical interconnections between the transnational buzz of Korean television dramas and the political decentralization of Korea itself. Thus, television dramas have been used in regional cities' recent efforts to turn the trajectories of uneven development around by actively promoting their areas.

The Second Korean Wave (since 2011) led by K-pop music has engaged in a very different kind of spatial development. While the global K-pop boom has also drawn on international fans' interest in K-pop–associated places, their destinations are not nationwide but are concentrated only in the Seoul districts where entertainment agencies and music labels are clustered. Thanks again to the country's uneven course of development, Seoul, particularly the Gangnam area, boasts rich cultural resources, including in particular companies that produce dramas, films, music, animation, and commercials. For those ardent fans who wish to meet their favorite K-pop idols in person, Seoul is the place where they can extend their experience of K-pop from the visual and virtual, via online music videos, to the corporeal and physical. Under the local election system, some ambitious district governors in Seoul began tapping into the already established cultural infrastructure to promote their areas. Without any tangible investments, Seoul districts have fortunately "found" and utilized historically formed popular culture resources in their areas. Two representative districts are discussed in this book: Gangnam and

Myeong-dong, whose meanings, landscapes, and identities have shifted in recent years because of K-pop images.

Many cities, counties, and districts are vigorously promoting their areas using K-dramas and K-pop. Local states cannot ignore the sensational publicity effects that popular culture can bring. Yet the different forms of media—television dramas and K-pop music—that the center and margins are able to utilize in their place marketing reveal the continuing legacy of uneven development. Regional cities with limited material and cultural assets are associated with television dramas that target their less urban landscapes. Yet one-off sponsorships of a drama production without providing a stable cultural infrastructure to support it have their limits in terms of stability and sustainability, leaving regional cities with long-term revitalization problems. Affluent districts in Seoul, the fortunate beneficiaries of unbalanced development, on the contrary, can easily take advantage of the cultural infrastructure they already possess. Although both players engage in short-term, publicity-seeking speculative investment, thanks to their concentration of resources, districts in Seoul are able to devise more renewable and diversified cultural strategies through the cooperation of entertainment firms. Unevenness, therefore, still permeates the country, as shown by the different media and outcomes of pop culture–mediated place promotions in different areas.

The discussion of unevenness reveals the spatial aspects of Hallyu by identifying how the cultural phenomenon constructs and is constructed by the urban changes in Korea. The spatial impacts of the Korean Wave that alter local places complicate the conventional understanding of Hallyu as a vehicle for outward expansion in tune with Korea's global aspirations. The outward circulation of Korean entertainment has spawned inbound global flows by drawing in its audience as tourists and shoppers. Specific places in South Korea, particularly those in local areas that have been historically overshadowed by the hegemonic power of Seoul, have recently emerged as sites of consumption for both domestic and foreign tourists. The actual influx of visitors has caused "friction" (Tsing 2005) in specific localities, transforming their economies, landscapes, and politics. The preexisting uneven historical, political, and economic geographies turn such frictions into uneven flows. Hallyu is not just a cultural phenomenon but an amalgam of multiple domains, including popular imaginaries, cultural desires, consumer markets, tourism, and local development. The changes in cultural production and consumption, tourism, and urban places that has been driven by the Korean Wave show how global, national, and subnational flows are intertwined. This book identifies the correlation between culture and space by clarifying the Korean Wave as a multisphere, multiscalar, and multidirectional phenomenon.

## Organization of the Book

*Pop City* is organized around the two different waves of Korean media entertainment that have engendered distinct types of place marketing: the drama-driven First Korean Wave from 2003 until 2011, and the pop music–led Second Korean Wave since 2011. The year 2011 was the turning point when the Korean media started to circulate the term *shinhallyu*, meaning New Korean Wave. The third generation of K-pop idols, including Girls' Generation and KARA, made successful inroads into Japan in 2011. SM entertainment held the SM TOWN Concert in Paris that year, signifying the true globalization of K-pop beyond Asia. Since 2011, Korean popular music and pop idols have emerged as front-runners in attracting international audiences to consume South Korean culture. The periodization does not necessarily signal a downturn in Korean dramas' performance overseas. China has replaced Japan as the main importer of television dramas since 2013, so the export markets for Korean dramas have broadened recently, driving production to even higher levels. Nevertheless, the preferred medium for municipalities' place promotion has certainly transitioned from television dramas to K-pop music, particularly in areas associated with K-pop idols.

Moreover, the two different waves are associated with two distinct geographies: the First Korean Wave is tied with regional cities (part 1) and the Second Korean Wave, with districts in Seoul (part 2). The two parts of the book have a parallel structure. Each pairs an analysis of a Korean pop culture industry with an examination of place-promotion cases featuring that culture and demonstrates how the profit-seeking practices of the culture industry have neatly dovetailed with Korean cities' branding schemes. Part 1 examines how the speculative nature of Korean drama production has been projected onto drama-themed place marketing practices that are short term and high risk. Part 2 shows how place marketing cases using K-pop reflect the visually oriented and affective qualities of K-pop production and consumption. In sum, I examine how place-promotion strategies mirror precisely the speculative, image-dominated, and consumer-exploitative popular cultural industry, on the one hand, and how the ways their cooperation with the cultural industry[31] bring both short-term opportunities and long-term managerial challenges to cities, on the other.

# PART I

# The Speculative Production of Dramas and Drama Sites

This first section of the book examines the drama-driven First Korean Wave (2003–2011) together with drama-themed urban promotion practices mainly in Korea and partly in Japan. Based on the ethnography of the Korean drama industry, chapter 1 discusses how Korean television dramas are produced, covering funding channels, sponsorship practices, and the ways the dramas cater to their export markets. Focusing on Korean cities' marketing strategies, chapter 2 analyzes how cities create the sites that are used as settings for dramas and then reuse them to attract tourists. The linkage between the two chapters lies in the cooperation between "marginal drama producers" and "marginal cities." By marginal drama producers, I mean those independent drama producers who jumped into the industry only after witnessing the unexpected overseas popularity of pioneering dramas such as *Winter Sonata* and *Jewel in the Palace* in the early 2000s. They were motivated by romantic fantasies about the higher rates of return obtainable in foreign markets. Despite their great expectations, however, their actual industrial position is marginal because they suffer from insufficient financial resources and weak production capabilities, and are at a disadvantage vis-à-vis broadcasters in the redistribution of profits. Their financially marginal condition, combined with the spatiality of drama production, has driven these independent producers to resort to Korean cities that could be both financial and spatial sponsors. By "marginal" cities, I am referring mainly to the Korean regional cities, discussed in the introduction, that have persistently aspired to develop themselves but have been deprived of the necessary material and cultural resources.

Collaboration between marginal drama producers and marginal cities results in the simultaneous production of drama and place. Cities deliver funding to cover part of a drama's production costs; sometimes they also provide land on which a set will be built. In return, television shows dramatically depict landmark places in the sponsoring cities, integrating them into their story lines. While drama sponsorship rebrands city places, place placement in dramas also reconfigures dramas' story lines, leading to a mutual construction of drama and place. What I wish to emphasize is the speculative nature of both the drama production and the drama-associated city promotion. Both players seek instant short-term success. Local leaders use drama sponsorship as a sensational tool for bringing flash publicity to their municipalities. Drama producers insert significant sponsoring city sites into drama story lines and backgrounds as a means to secure immediate funding. The two chapters in this section show how the very marginality of both drama producers and regional municipalities shapes their speculative ventures; the level of uncertainty is very high, but the rewards for success are correspondingly great.

I collected the data presented in this section during my fieldwork, from January to July of 2011 and from May to July of 2014. I would like to talk briefly about the data collection process because it reveals both the speculative and marginal characteristics of the drama producers and aspiring cities.

Having neither previous experience of it nor connections with it, the ethnography of the Korean drama industry itself presented me with difficulties. I had to spend a lot of time making contact with industry insiders and scheduling appointments with them because many of them simply refused to meet an "outsider." These hard-won opportunities to meet with industrial players, however, did not necessarily lead to smooth interviews. Many of my interview questions received no clear answers due to the interviewees' surprisingly conservative attitudes. Independent drama producers were reluctant to disclose the costs of drama production, the amount of sponsorship they received, and the nature of the financial flows. As discussed in chapter 1, the Korean drama industry operates amid tensions and conflicts between two major players within it: broadcasters and independent producers. My interviews with both parties often ended in harsh and emotionally charged criticism by the one of the other, pushing me to examine the contradictions within the industry in my research. Most of the data used in this book come from each side's offensive descriptions of the other, because I eventually found it easier to gather correct information about certain players from their counterparts rather than from themselves. In addition, I was helped to understand the practices within the industry not only by the data and explanations people provided but also by the manner in which they answered or evaded my questions.

The dominant impression I received in the field was of the stark contrast between the media celebration of the East Asian, or even global success, of Korean television dramas and the producers' actual situation. Many of their offices were surprisingly humble. An interview with a male informant at a small-sized production firm in a small, dark room was a scary experience. The interviewee, who looked like a mobster rather than a cultural creator, even threatened to sue me "if this interview content is ever revealed in any printed material," adding "we never have enough time to shoot dramas, but we do have enough time to file lawsuits."[1] This precarious situation was no exception for majors either. One weekday morning, I met a key staff member at one of the major drama production firms. Despite the meeting being prescheduled, we were unable to continue our conversation due to incessant incoming phone calls. The staff member told me that the firm was involved in more than twelve lawsuits at that moment and one of the trials was scheduled for that afternoon. Overhearing the phone conversations, I was able to gauge the financial and legal situation the firm faced, despite its industrial position as a major. For sensitive reasons such as these, the names of the drama production firms are not specifically identified in this book unless they are officially mentioned in other sources. Based on those fieldwork experiences, I examine how Korean drama producers can be characterized as marginal despite their ostensible position at the forefront of the Korean Wave.

The ethnography of the sponsoring cities was relatively easier to deal with because local officials did not send the curious researcher away. Instead, many of them considered meeting me to be an extension of their promotional activities. The priority for most municipalities I visited was raising their recognition status. The ambiance I mostly witnessed in provincial cities and counties was calmness, entirely the opposite of the bustling and over-crowded urban experience of Seoul. The absence of busyness and activity in these serene landscapes and atmospheres highlighted their desperate need to boost their publicity. Chapter 2 will deal with the historically and socioeconomically conditioned marginality of local municipalities—a different kind of marginality from that of drama producers—which led to their tying themselves to the broader reach and sensational representations of television dramas.

Nevertheless, the sponsoring cities were also sensitive about how much sponsorship they provided and did not reveal the exact amounts. I have therefore left many blank spaces regarding who paid how much to whom, only presenting the figures for production cost and sponsorship amount.[2] Most of the cases in which specific sponsors and amounts of sponsorship are revealed are cited from news articles. Personal collection/overview of media reports since 2000 has, therefore, significantly helped me to understand the development of the drama industry and the practices of drama sponsorship over the past fifteen years. News articles about the entertainment business, viewer ratings, behind-the-scenes stories about drama productions, and star gossip have assisted me in figuring out matters that I could not make complete sense of from interviews alone—in particular, the differences between superficial and actual causes and outcomes within the processes of drama production and consumption. Yet many Korean news articles, particularly those covering entertainment issues, are published by simply drawing other sources through news-buying practices; that is why authors are not particularly identified in many Korean entertainment news articles. For such reasons, in my citation of the news articles, I identify the news titles, the published individual newspapers, and the published date only without mentioning authors (reporters).

Once, in the late 2000s, members of the South Korean National Assembly competitively reported on budget-wasting cases in which local government had poured tax money into sponsoring television dramas. Official and unofficial reports released then enabled me to identify detailed statistics and stories that had previously been concealed from the public.

To observe and interview drama-inspired tourists, I accompanied three Japanese tour groups with a translator to visit sites featured in television dramas. I also visited another five different drama locations and engaged in on-site observation and conducted interviews with the tourists I happened to meet there. In May 2011, I visited Shin-Ōkubo in Japan, where souvenir shops and cafés selling Hallyu-associated products are clustered, and conducted semistructured, in-depth interviews with more than twenty Japanese women about their consumption of Korean dramas. During the same visit, my on-the-spot interpreter led me to "Korean schools" in which mostly female fans of K-drama were learning Korean language to be able to enjoy K-culture more. Those extremely engaged and highly vocal interviewees recounted their personal experiences of drama tours in detail.

In this book, only prime-time drama series (i.e., those aired during the 10–11 p.m. slot) broadcast via terrestrial stations are discussed because they both reflect and are constructed by the speculative nature of drama production. Since at least until the early 2010s, overseas markets could be accessed almost exclusively through the domestic airing of programs on terrestrial stations, causing independent producers to bet everything on winning one of the three prime-time slots.[3] Terrestrial prime-time series (*jisangpa deurama*), where vested interests regarding exports, and thus further profits, are concentrated, garner the most intense speculation.

Chapter 1

# SPECULATIVE PRODUCERS

## The Production of Korean Drama

Korean television dramas are known for a typical narrative structure that appeals to a primarily East Asian audience, but also, more recently, a global audience. Thus, textual analyses to examine "the kind of stories that are told in Korean TV dramas" have dominated Hallyu studies. This chapter redirects attention to the industrial arena and analyzes "why such stories are told in particular ways." More important, rather than accounting for the popularity of Korean dramas, I examine how Hallyu has reconfigured their industrial dynamics and production practices. I argue that the Korean Wave has turned the Korean drama industry into a speculative field in which the industrial players have vested interests in export. The unexpected performance of some Korean television dramas in foreign markets in the early 2000s caused a sudden proliferation of independent drama producers. Despite their sizable numbers and mounting expectations of achieving a megahit in foreign markets, the independent producers' industrial positions are marginal on account of their being exploited by the broadcasters' monopolistic power. Their suppressed status causes independent producers to engage in even more speculative practices, pushing them to seek more and more sponsors. This chapter illustrates how the speculative nature of their business has, in turn, affected the production practices, forms of sponsorship, and storytelling methods typical of Korean television dramas. The focus of the analyses will be to show how K-drama narratives are commercially crafted to attract sponsors and do well in export markets.

## Hallyu and the Growth of Independent Producers

Under the military dictatorship that ruled South Korea until the 1980s, the central state monopolized the country's broadcasting system through the direct control of two broadcasting channels, KBS (Korean Broadcasting System) and MBC (Munhwa Broadcasting Corporation). As public networks, the two stations produced virtually all television dramas and their in-house crews constituted the labor force in drama production. The country's democratization in the late 1980s, albeit superficial in nature, fostered a growing societal interest in mass culture that allowed the private sector to establish commercial stations. Korea's first commercial channel, SBS (Seoul Broadcasting System), was launched in 1991. As a newcomer to the industry, SBS's market position was weak compared with its two already established competitors.[1] To make up for SBS's weak self-production capabilities, the 1990 Broadcasting Act set up a new "independent production quota system (*oeju-jejak uimu pyeonseong jedo*)" requiring the three terrestrial stations to air a certain proportion of content produced outside the broadcasting firms.[2] The new regulation was designed to check the monopolistic power of broadcasters, diversify content producers, foster the broadcasting content market, and enhance services for the audience. Broadcasters assigned the bulk of the mandatory quota of externally produced material to television dramas because they believed that independent producers would be more flexible and better able to attract funding from various sources, such as investment and sponsorship. Therefore, the new quota system had the effect of gradually shifting drama production from broadcasting stations to independent production companies.

Independent drama producers, then, for the purposes of this book and in view of the circumstances in which they came into being, are production companies that have no access to broadcasting channels of their own on which they can release their products. What matters in defining independent drama producers is their independent status vis-à-vis broadcasters, so they need to secure a contract with a broadcaster to gain access to a channel. The company's size and the attributes of the products it creates are not what determines its status as an independent drama producer. During the earlier stages (1991–1994), independent producers were often subsidiary companies of broadcasters such as MBC Production and Korea Broadcasting Entertainment System and Technology. Independent production was outsourced from broadcasters, but their in-house management and in-house prototyping virtually controlled all aspects of it. It was only after the mid-1990s, when the new operations of ten regional terrestrial television stations and the introduction of digital multimedia broadcasting (DMB) and Internet-protocol television (IPTV) boosted demand for drama content, that independent producers in a real sense appeared, hoping to sell drama content to these new channel operators. Until the 1990s, however, individual firms that could independently produce drama content were almost nonexistent. Although some high-profile directors at the broadcasting stations launched their own firms, actual production was mostly carried out using the broadcasters' resources, personnel, and equipment. In addition, credibility and personal connections, not reasonable market values such as price and quality, virtually determined the market transactions in dramas between networks and independent production companies.

What really caused the proliferation of independent drama producers was the unforeseen popularity of Korean dramas during the early 2000s: the drama-driven First Korean Wave. The media liberalization of the 1990s enabled East Asian countries to move away from a defensive attitude toward importing television programming and develop a more active intraregional trade in television programs (Langdale 1997; Shim 2008; Jin 2011). The growing number of regional transactions resulted in some Korean dramas that received recognition overseas. The very first of these pioneering dramas was *What Is Love All About* (*Sarangi Mwogillae* 1991), which was broadcast and very popularly received in Taiwan, Hong Kong, and China in the late 1990s.[3] After a long period during which diplomatic relations between China and South Korea had been severed, the drama series established a new image for Korea. Indeed, it sparked a buzz about Korean popular culture among Chinese-speaking audience groups. After the success of this series, other Korean dramas such as *Star in My Heart* (*Byeoreun Nae Gaseume* 1997), *Sun-*

*flower* (*Haebaragi* 1998), and *Goodbye My Love* (*Annyeong Nae Sarang* 1999) were exported to China one after the other. Nevertheless, although the term *hanliu/hallyu*, meaning "Korean Wave," was in fact first coined during the late 1990s in the Chinese-speaking areas,[4] the impact of Hallyu during that decade remained limited to a series of temporary and local sensations.

It was the drama series *Winter Sonata* (*Gyeoul Yeonga*) that created the Korean drama fever in East Asia, exerting a phenomenal influence on and beyond the drama industry. *Winter Sonata* is a conventional melodrama that was originally aired in Korea in 2002 on KBS. In 2003, BS, a NHK (Nippon Hōsō Kyōkai; Japan Broadcasting Corporation)-owned satellite broadcasting channel, imported and aired the drama series. Completely unexpectedly, it went viral among middle-aged women.[5] BS rebroadcast the series by popular demand in early 2004; NHK rebroadcast it on a terrestrial channel later that same year. The actors who appeared in the drama became extraordinarily famous in Japan, and the male lead, Bae Yong-jun, earned the title "Yon-sama" (*sama* being an honorific suffix). Beyond mere television watching, *Winter Sonata* became a social phenomenon, causing enormous changes in cultural, economic, and political arenas in both Korea and Japan. NHK reported that the network earned more than ¥9 billion from airing the drama series. Sales of the DVD of the series amounted to more than 450,000 copies in Japan, while more than 60,000 copies were sold of the *Winter Sonata Tourism* DVDs that covered the locations used in filming the drama. More than 900,000 albums of *Winter Sonata Original Soundtrack* (OST) were sold, taking top place in the Oricon chart in 2003. Earnings from the drama series in Korea exceeded $5 billion, mainly generated by drama-driven tourism to the filming sites. More than 200 tourism and merchandising products theming *Winter Sonata* have been developed and sold both in Japan and Korea (KOFICE 2008).

The drama series that has had the greatest impact on the predominantly ethnic-Chinese locations in East Asia is *Jewel in the Palace* (*Dae Jang Geum*). This series, which originally aired in 2003 on MBC, is about the first female imperial physician at the time of the Chosun dynasty in the sixteenth century. GTV (Gala Television Corporation) in Taiwan imported and showed the series in 2004, achieving peak ratings of 62.2 percent and second place in the all-time ratings. Backed by this extraordinary popularity, *Dae Jang Geum* was rerun in 2005. The *Dae Jang Geum* craze in Taiwan even revitalized the Seoul–Taipei flights that had been stopped following the establishment of relations between China and South Korea in 1992. The series was also screened on TVB (Television Broadcasts Limited) in Hong Kong in 2004 and recorded an average of 47 percent in viewer ratings, putting it in third place in the all-time ratings; the total viewership exceeded 3.21 million, around half of the entire Hong Kong population. Hunan Satellite Television in China aired *Dae Jang Geum* in 2005 and later broadcast it again at the national level. Since its extraordinary success in East Asia, *Dae Jang Geum* has made inroads into Southeast Asia, the Middle East, and Latin America. It has been exported to more than sixty countries, driving the Korean Wave across the globe.[6]

After the astonishing sensation created by these two dramas, more than 500 million dollars' worth of Korean drama was exported to overseas markets during the period from 2002 to 2013. The proportion of television dramas has continuously increased and now dominates Korean exports of television content. The geographical coverage is also diverse, expanding from East and Southeast Asia to Europe, the Middle East, and Latin America (see table 1.1). The fortuitous overseas visibility acquired by some pioneering dramas and the expansion of the export market has fundamentally changed the Korean drama industry since the 2000s. The emergence of export markets triggered a mushrooming of drama production companies. Some star directors left the networks and started their own production companies, such as Kim Jong Hak Production led by Kim Jong-hak, who directed two stunning dramas, *Eyes of Dawn* (*Yeomyeongui Nundongja* 1991) and *Sandglass* (*Moraesigye* 1995), and Yoon's Color launched by *Winter Sonata*'s Yoon Seok-ho. The growing markets and expectations have also attracted players from various fields into the drama industry. Some music labels entered; Pan Entertainment established itself in the drama industry, earning more than $10 million from *Winter Sonata* in Japan alone; DSP E&T produced *Three Leaf Clover* (*Seip Keullobeo* 2005), *My Girl* (*Mai Geol* 2006), and *Yeon Gae So Mun* (*Yeongaesomun* 2006). Entertainment agencies also turned into production players; Sidus HQ merged with Castle in the Sky, which had previously produced *Lovers in Paris* (*Pariui Yeonin* 2004), and went on to produce *Spring Days* (*Bomnal* 2005), *Sad Love Story* (*Seulpeun Yeonga* 2005), *Only You* (*Onri Yu* 2005), and *Princess Lulu* (*Ruru Gongju* 2007). Film production houses expanded their business areas to include television drama production; Popcorn Film,

**Table 1.1.** Exports of South Korean television content by country (%)

| | Year | | | | | | | | | |
|---|---|---|---|---|---|---|---|---|---|---|
| | 2005 | 2006 | 2007 | 2008 | 2009 | 2010 | 2011 | 2012 | 2013 | 2014 |
| Japan | 60.2 | 44.1 | 55.2 | 68.7 | 63.5 | 53.9 | 59.9 | 61.3 | 57.9 | 32.0 |
| China | 9.9 | 6.7 | 7.6 | 4.8 | 6.2 | 8.8 | 10.8 | 6.14 | 11.4 | 23.0 |
| Hong Kong | 3.3 | 3.6 | 3.3 | 3.3 | 4.0 | 3.2 | 2.4 | 0.82 | 2.8 | 20.4 |
| Singapore | 1.1 | 1.8 | 3.0 | 1.3 | 2.5 | 1.5 | 1.9 | 1.08 | 0.8 | 1.5 |
| Taiwan | 11.4 | 18.1 | 17.1 | 6.7 | 11.5 | 13.2 | 13.0 | 8.68 | 8.9 | 6.7 |
| Vietnam | 0.9 | 0.7 | 1.3 | 0.8 | 1.9 | 1.5 | 1.7 | 1.66 | 3.0 | 3.4 |
| Malaysia | 1.2 | 2.3 | 1.7 | 1.0 | 0.8 | 1.0 | 1.1 | 3.33 | 0.5 | 0.4 |
| Indonesia | 1.1 | 0.0 | 0.6 | 0.3 | 0.3 | 0.5 | 0.8 | 0.55 | 0.5 | 0.4 |
| Thailand | 2.1 | 3.4 | 2.8 | 2.6 | 3.3 | 2.3 | 1.6 | 2.43 | 3.6 | 5.3 |
| Philippines | 3.7 | 2.9 | 1.2 | 1.7 | 1.7 | 2.7 | 2.2 | 1.36 | 2.2 | 1.4 |
| United States | 2.6 | 0.5 | 3.0 | 4.8 | 0.8 | 1.3 | 1.6 | 7.78 | 4.4 | 2.6 |
| Europe | 0.08 | 0.0 | 0.0 | 0.0 | 0.9 | 0.4 | 0.85 | 1.34 | 0.7 | 0.3 |
| Australia | 0.1 | 0.0 | 0.0 | — | — | — | — | — | 0.1 | 0.0 |
| Others | 2.4 | 15.0 | 3.0 | 3.2 | 2.6 | 9.5 | 2.15 | 3.53 | 3.2 | 2.6 |

*Source:* Korea Communication Commission (2005–2015).

for instance, produced *Stranger than Paradise* (*Cheongukboda Naccseon* 2006). *Daily Sports,* a subsidiary of the media giant *JoongAng Daily,* launched A Story, which has produced more than twenty dramas, including *Air City* (*Eeo Siti* 2007) and *Cinderella's Sister* (*Sinderella Eonni* 2010) (Korea Communication Commission 2007). In sum, riding on the Hallyu wave, the number of drama production companies, as registered under the Ministry of Culture, Sports and Tourism, skyrocketed from 331 in 2000 to 1,329 in 2013, yet many of them exist on paper only.[7] The number of those that have actually sold their programs to broadcasters increased from 391 in 2008 to 628 in 2011, and 503 in 2013 (Korea Creative Content Agency 2015). The newly established independent production houses also caused big shifts in in-house labor forces. High-profile directors quit their jobs at broadcasting firms and moved to independent companies with big lump sum contract deals, and many filming and lighting crews became free-lancers, serving both the production and broadcasting firms.

## Marginal Producers

Despite their sizable numbers, the market position of independent production firms is marginal in terms of their lack of autonomy and power vis-à-vis broadcasters. Independent producers become even more marginal because most of them are small sized. What characterizes Korean independent producers is the stark divide between the few major outfits and the mostly small-sized majority. The growth of major independent producers gained momentum during the early 2000s when so-called communication capital flowed into the drama industry.[8] By establishing private equity funds and practicing backdoor listing, most of the major producers went public around the mid-2000s.[9] Public listing enabled them to find various financial sources to cover megaproduction costs on the one hand, and to generate more profits through the stock market than from content production on the other. Yet the majors that have self-sufficient production and financial capability are limited to less than ten firms among more than fifteen hundred.

Most independent production firms are small, with only small numbers of contracted writers and office staff (who take care of multiple miscellaneous jobs, such as project development, casting, and filming assistance), and sometimes a few contracted directors. Starting up their business with nothing more than connections to broadcasting companies, minor independent production firms are far short of both the human and financial capital required to kick off a production. The strategy for these seemingly name-only production firms is to circulate their drama proposals among the three broadcasting stations in hopes of attracting a channel that will broadcast their drama. Only after a channel is guaranteed do their proposals become tangible and can they start to plan a funding scheme. A network buyer of a soon-to-be-made drama, however, usually offers only around 70 percent of the total production cost,[10] and even this insufficient payment is made only after a whole series has been aired, which means four to fifteen months after the initial production stage. Since preparations for the production and funding procurement schemes are already underway, independent firms have to accept the cost settlement proposed by a network. To actually start production and cover the rest of the production costs, therefore, drama producers must attract funding in the form of investments, sponsorships from enterprises or cities, or product placements, or by borrowing that results in debt. As these financial flows show, most independent drama producers jump into the market with buyers' and investors' money rather than their own. Although this flexible way of securing a budget lowers the entry barrier to the industry, the unstable financial base contributes to the precarious positioning of most independent drama producers.

To facilitate investment and other forms of funding, producers need heavyweight names in their cast lists. Given the export-oriented nature of the industry, producers particularly prefer Hallyu stars who have already established recognition and popularity in East and Southeast Asia. Yet this star system, which independent producers opt into as a survival strategy, has actually made their situation worse. During the 2000s, the independent production system turned drama production into a market-friendly business that clearly differentiated between star actors and others with less monetary value, causing an unfettered rise in appearance fees for top talent. For example, the maximum guaranteed fee per episode for leading actors began to rise drastically during the early 2000s, breaking through the $10,000 level in 2004 and continuously increasing, reaching around $30,000 to $50,000 in the late 2000s.[11] In 2008, to curb the ever-increasing star guarantees, the drama producers' association created a rule that an actor's performance fee per episode should not exceed $15,000. Yet the ever-increasing competition for star actors easily nullified that ruling in the late 2000s. Therefore, when independent producers pay $60,000 to $100,000 per episode for actors in the two leading roles, these (two) stars' guarantees account for as much as 70 to 80 percent of the budget (generally $80,000 to $100,000 per episode) that they receive from broadcasters. Producers are supposed to use the remaining 20 to 30 percent of their budget to pay for other supporting roles, crew, equipment, and on-location shooting. Unless a drama hits the jackpot in terms of audience ratings and attracts more sponsorship during the course of its airings, independent producers end up having to cover the deficits.[12]

The lack of self-sufficient production capabilities also speaks to the marginality of independent producers. As stated above, only after securing a channel do producers' proposals become tangible and a substantial production team is established. Most small-sized production firms, however, do not have independent production capabilities. Once a channel is fixed, production firms "rent" personnel (mostly film directors) and equipment from the broadcasting firm. Undertaking a so-called combined production (between a producer and a broadcaster) is also a way of gaining a channel in the intense competition among miscellaneous producers. The actual filming of a drama series is centered on the "leased" director; thus, the voices of independent producers, that is, those who initially proposed the project, become diminished over the course of the actual production process. Moreover, the director provided by the broadcasting firm holds the exclusive right to edit the film, controlling the eventual direction of a drama series and the final product. Under the established precontract and postproduction system, there is extremely limited room for independent producers to exercise their discretion over production matters. For these reasons, significant numbers of independent drama producers in Korea lack, and rarely develop, independent production capabilities.

Independent producers' marginality is also reinforced by the industry's structure, in which terrestrial channels are limited to only three networks that, naturally, have monopolistic power. Taking advantage of their monopoly on television channels, the three big terrestrial networks usually, with only a few exceptions, force independent producers, by contract, to surrender the copyright to their dramas. Components of the copyright include broadcasting rights in various countries; the right to sell the dramas to second-round channels such as cable and Internet stations; copy and distribution rights over DVDs, VODs (video on demand), and CD-ROMs in Korea and overseas; transmission rights; information use rights; rights over secondary property products; performance rights; and music copy rights (see table 1.2). While the areas covered by copyright are diverse and complex, as shown in table 1.2, networks have most of the rights; independent producers only retain the music rights (only in the case of KBS) and 50 percent of the profits generated from exports are redistributed to them but only from Asia and only for three years.[13] Some independent producers have been able to exercise full power over the distribution rights to second-round channels and overseas markets, but such cases are very rare and limited to a few major producers who do not need finance from networks (i.e., those who can self-finance by attracting investment from other sources), and in such cases, a broadcasting firm usually offers less than 50 percent of the production cost. In sum, independent drama producers are in a disadvantageous position regarding profit redistribution. The reason independent producers acquiesce in unfair contracts with the broadcasters lies, first, in their urgent need to gain channels, and second, in their dependence on receiving advance payment from a network to start filming. Winning a contract with a broadcasting firm that has channels and funding, however unfair it might be, is a top priority and profit redistribution is something to be dealt with later.

**Table 1.2. Distribution of copyrights between broadcasters and independent producers**

| Drama series | No. of episodes | Network | Independent production company | Copyright holding Broadcaster | Producer |
|---|---|---|---|---|---|
| *Cloud Stairs* | 16 | KBS | JS Pictures | 1–12 | 13 |
| *Golden Apple* | 16 | KBS | JS Pictures | 1–12 | 13 |
| *The Snow Queen* | 13 | KBS | Yoon's Color | 1 | 13 |
| *Spring Waltz* | 21 | KBS | Yoon's Color | 1 | 13 |
| *Mr. Good Bye* | 16 | KBS | Olive 9 | 1–12 | 13 |
| *Shining Inheritance* | 17 | KBS | Olive 9 | 1–12 | 13 |
| *Hwang Jin Yi* | 24 | KBS | Olive 9 | 1–12 | 13 |
| *Thank You Life* | 24 | KBS | Pan Entertainment | 1–12 | 13 |
| *Hello, God* | 16 | KBS | Kim Jong Hak Production | 1–12 | 13 |
| *Man of the Vineyard* | 16 | KBS | Kim Jong Hak Production | 1–12 | 13 |
| *The Invisible Man* | 20 | KBS | HB Entertainment | 1–12 | 13 |
| *Special of My Life* | 8 | MBC | Kim Jong Hak Production | 1, 2, 5, 6, 7 | 3, 4, 8–12 |
| *What Star Did You Come From* | 16 | MBC | Kim Jong Hak Production | 1, 2, 5, 6, 7 | 3, 4, 8–12 |

*Source:* Korea Communication Commission (2007).

*Notes:* KBS = Korean Broadcasting System; MBC = Munhwa Broadcasting Corporation.

1. Domestic broadcasting rights (terrestrial, cable, satellite channels); 2. broadcasting rights in North America (terrestrial, cable, satellite channels); 3. broadcasting rights in Asia (terrestrial, cable, satellite channels); 4. broadcasting rights in other foreign countries (terrestrial, cable, satellite channels); 5. copyrights and distribution rights over video in South Korea; 6. copyrights and distribution rights over CD-ROM, VOD (video on demand), DVD in South Korea; 7. copyrights and distribution rights over video in North America; 8. copyrights and distribution rights over video, CD-ROM, VOD, DVD in other foreign countries; 9. transmission rights over the Internet; 10. information use rights; 11. rights over secondary property products; 12. performance rights; 13. redistribution of 50% of profits generated in Asia, music rights (KBS).

## Speculative Nature

The number of independent producers increased explosively within a short period of time due to the fortuitous success of some pioneering dramas in overseas markets. Having grown out of expectation rather than actual market demand, the industrial position of independent producers is again marginal; they have to deal horizontally with enormous competition among themselves and vertically with the monopolistic power of broadcasters. Their proliferation and peripheral industrial position are jointly responsible for their speculative attributes. Drama production is always speculative, but I argue that the Korean drama industry became even more speculative during the 2000s. I focus particularly on the sudden overheating in the industry during the 2000s due to Hallyu, which eventually led to the drastic shifts in production and content. By their "speculative" nature, I mean (1) the ways Korean drama producers had collective expectations about the Korean Wave, which seemed to guarantee the unconditional success of Korean dramas in overseas markets, and (2) a tendency on the part of Korean drama producers to see uncertainty about the popularity of a drama as an opportunity for a big hit from which they would be able achieve greater turnover rates in the short term.

While the emergence of overseas markets drove the sudden mushrooming of independent producers, overseas markets can be accessed almost solely through the domestic airing of programs on terrestrial stations,[14] which means that foreign buyers tend to be interested only in those dramas whose success has already been verified in the domestic market. Given that there are only three terrestrial stations, the competition among the more than fifteen hundred producers to gain access to a channel is fierce.[15] Excessive competition aggravates the speculative nature of producers' thinking and actions, because they stake on a few dramas that they barely have the opportunity to produce. Small-sized independent production houses often fail because they do not find an on-air station and, in many cases, because the program on which everything has been staked records poor ratings. A hard-won channel does not necessarily translate into high ratings, and the commercial success of television dramas remains uncertain. Nevertheless, the number of producers has not begun to shrink. Rather, companies try to stay in the business at all costs, hoping to achieve the one hit that will compensate for all their losses. Since nobody knows whether, and to what extent, a drama will strike gold, that very uncertainty drives independent producers toward the fantasy of a jackpot.

Unpredictable nature plays both as risk and opportunity, particularly in the cultural industry. The uncertainty sometimes functions as opportunities for new figures (directors, writers, and actors) to gain fame. Yet what I point out regarding the Korean drama industry is the excessive extent to which drama producers regard uncertainty as the very chance to achieve a hit, much as a gambler views the roll of the dice as a chance to come out ahead. Both investment and speculation assume the risk of loss in return for the uncertain possibility of gain. While investment systemically calculates the potential risks and prepares reasonable measures to deal with them, speculation bets more on the uncertain possibility of gain. Edward Chancellor (1999) discusses speculation by comparing it with gambling: "While a bad investment may be a speculation, a poorly executed speculation is often described as a gamble. . . . The name given to financial uncertainty is 'risk.' Economists differentiate gambling and speculation on the grounds that gambling involves the deliberate creation of new risks for the sake of diversion while speculation involves the assumption of the inevitable risks of the capitalist process" (Chancellor 1999, xi–xii).

Given the then ever-expanding waves of Hallyu, not a few drama producers believed that once they produced a drama, popularity would automatically follow. Considering the extremely slim chance of winning a channel and the equally slim chance of making a hit, the blind expectation of popularity is nothing more than the creation of risks—that is, equivalent to the practice of gambling. Actually, the overall industrial ambiance I sensed in the field is not that different from gambler-like fantasy. One informant put it bluntly: "We only need one big hit that will compensate for past losses and guarantee future profits. The big hit will secure us a channel and casting for a while. If we keep trying, someday that one jackpot is going to come our way."[16] Although this remark is an extreme case of raising the speculative tendency to the level of gambling, it is worth noting some other interview quotes that imply the extent to which speculation dominates the industry: "The industry considers that megahits like *Winter Sonata* or *Jewel in the Palace* are not possible any more. But other ways to turn a drama into a business product have been developed and producers' positions vis-à-vis broadcasters have also strengthened during the 2000s. Two or three solid hits, if not a jackpot hit, will surely bring in enough of a fortune"; "It is not really about the production or ratings. What matters is to get a channel, and that will bring investment and sponsorship. If one is savvy enough, one will make profits even before the production, let along the airing."[17] The last quote suggests that the drama production has become an entirely profit-seeking business as far as speculative producers are concerned, one that is entirely disconnected from its presumed basis in cultural creativity.

The speculative nature can also be found in Korean drama producers' cultural practices. The film and music industries have developed measures to deal with their products' unpredictability, strategies such as the use of genres, formulaic plot devices, expensive special effects, and reliance on the star system. They also employ business organizations such as portfolio management, vertical integration, vertical disintegration, and networks of pseudoindependents (Bilton 1999). The Korean drama industry has also used some cultural methods to manage the uncertainty. Yet the solutions are more patchy than systematic: Korean broadcasters and producers tend to follow previously successful models, relying on conventional repertoires and the star system, rather than developing more systematic and creative measures, such as collective writing, investing in fresh themes, and producing more polished and sophisticated plotlines. Because the former hit makers gained success by using, for example, such Cinderella story romance, the industry as a whole tended to be convinced that repeating the same story format, rather than experimenting with new styles, would be safe, or even bring unexpected accomplishment. Although the attempt to structure drama production around similar formulas and brands was successful—at least during the 2000s—these methods now show serious limitations and are facing criticism.

I argue that the perhaps temporary overseas popularity of Korean popular culture has reconfigured the Korean drama industry into a speculative field in which the unpredictable, and thus risky, nature of cultural production is regarded as an opportunity. Unexpected overseas popularity has not only turned the drama industry into an export-oriented field but has also implanted a collective illusion about its export markets, drawing in more gambler-minded players. Its speculative nature has done more than redefine methods of finance and distribution. It has also, and more important, reconstructed production practices, forms of sponsorship, interactions between production and consumption, and storytelling. The next sections will show in more detail how speculativeness has reshaped the essential features of Korean television dramas.

## Live Production

The process of "last-minute live filming" (*saengbang chawaryeong*) is a standard practice in the Korean drama industry.[18] Apart from the first few episodes, filming is usually done only a few days in advance of (or on the same day as) the airdate. Script changes are often made last minute, while the final editing of the film is just as rushed, with little time to review the episode before it is released. The closer to the final episode, the more tense the shooting because the demands of production mount. Drawing on the conventional way of referring to last-minute production in the industry, I call these practices as a whole *live production*. Many hit dramas suffered from lamentably poor endings because of hasty scriptwriting and rushed shooting. For the last episode of *Sign* (*Ssain* 2011), shooting was completed only fifty minutes before broadcasting. It is reported that four staff members raced against time to bring the video to the editing room.[19] As a result, the protagonist's voice was lost (due to lack of sound) for twenty minutes during the broadcast. In the middle of episode 19 of *The Equator Man* (*Jeokdoui Namja* 2012), the screen suddenly reproduced scenes from the beginning and then went black. Subsequently, a caption was displayed stating that, due to unforeseen circumstances, episode 19 had ended and the final episode would be aired on the next day. News articles revealed that the edited version of film shot on the airdate was not delivered to the network's master control room in time.[20] In *Athena: Goddess of War* (*Atena Jeonjaengui Yeosin* 2010) and *Painter of the Wind* (*Baramui Hwawon* 2008), injuries to the leading actors led to one episode of each series being canceled. Both incidents were due to the tight shooting schedules.

What and who are driving these "crazy," but constantly repeated, practices? Three factors are responsible: first, uncertainty about channels; second, the emphasis on raising viewer ratings; and third, attempts to cut production costs.

Independent producers cannot shoot more than two or three episodes before broadcasting without the guarantee of a channel. Yet the more usual practice for independent firms is not to produce any filmed episodes, or even a trailer, before the confirmation of a channel. There are more than fifteen hundred independent production firms in Korea, as has already been mentioned, and only three terrestrial broadcasting stations. The disparity in numbers indicates the fierceness of the competition among producers to win a channel and has led to the establishment of a precontract and postproduction system. Again, as discussed above, independent producers circulate drama proposals (usually consisting of a show synopsis and a script of the first episode) among the three broadcasting stations to win a channel that will broadcast their drama. Only after a channel has been confirmed do their proposals become reality and a substantial production team is established. Broadcasters usually narrow down the possibilities to a short list of two or three dramas before choosing a winner only a few months before the actual airdate. Under these circumstances, the preproduction of a whole drama series is extremely risky. The series *Dance in the Sky* (*Bichunmu*) was filmed in its entirety in 2004, but aired only in 2008 on SBS because it took the producer four years to find a distribution channel. The martial arts genre was booming at the time the film was made, but had become passé by the time of airing. Consequently, *Dance in the Sky* did not go over well with viewers. In fact, the series was ridiculed for its out-of-date computer graphics technology. Its failure educated other producers about the risk of preproduction within the uncertain landscape of the Korean drama industry. Even for risk-taking speculative producers, the risks surrounding the public airwaves pose a more serious problem than popularity in the abstract.

Last-minute filming is a business practice intended to realize high viewer ratings. Broadcasting firms and drama producers share an interest in viewer ratings. Higher ratings not only generate more sales of commercials but also raise their unit price. In addition, ratings are the basis not only for whether a drama will be sold in overseas and additional markets but also for its price in those markets. This critical commercial logic has created a system of what is called *jjokdaebon* (a slice of script), or "hasty script," in the Korean drama industry. In this system, extremely short sections of the script arrive on set, barely meeting the live-shoot schedule. Without having the whole plot of an episode or time to study the script, actors shoot the short scene contained in the one-page script. Later, multiple short scenes are patched together during the editing process, leaving questions about the controlling plotline and message. The business rationale for last-minute script writing and revisions is to allow the audience's voices to be listened to. After airing the first few episodes and observing the viewers' response, directors and writers collaboratively rework the direction of a drama by changing plotlines, introducing new figures, or adding some provocative scenes. If a particular character attracts the audience's attention, stories are reconfigured around that character. A drama producer remarked: "Television series have to change in accordance with the audience's reaction; thus, the script must be carefully polished and a lot of time has to be invested in it. Dramas that are shot in advance cannot gauge the viewers' reaction, so they are often not accepted by them."[21] Some 100 percent preproduced series did in fact fail to achieve either commercial or critical success. The preproduced series *I Love You* (*Saranghae* 2008), *Road No. 1* (*Rodeu Neombeowon* 2010), *Tarma, the Island* (*Tamnaneundoda* 2009), and *Paradise Ranch* (*Paradaiseu Mokjang* 2011) all received poor ratings and the industry insiders agreed that this was due to inflexibility and an unwillingness to modify story lines. The drama plots are being adjusted all the time, and the translation of scripts into actual film is a last-minute occurrence.

To cut production costs, the filming process is made as short as possible, which also contributes to last-minute shooting. Production costs are two-tiered: costs for creative workers and actual production costs. Above the line, money is invested in star actors, ace writers, and sometimes high-profile directors who are paid on a per-episode basis. Below-the-line expenses, usually less than half the budget, are for supporting and extra cast members, on-the-spot crew members, camera work, sets and special equipment, visual effects, and on-location shooting. Given that crew and supporting actors are paid by the day, the best way to cut the actual production cost is to reduce the number of filming days.[22] In *On Air* (*Oneeo* 2008), a drama that depicts the situation inside the Korean drama industry, one dialogue between a producer and a staff member at an independent production firm is particularly instructive: "Once the cameras roll, the minimum cost will be no less than $20,000. . . . So we'll take a day off." To produce a drama with minimum cost and maximum efficiency, most episodes need to be shot only a few days before (or on the very day of) the airdate.

The mechanisms used to maintain eleventh-hour production have led to labor exploitation as the intensive workloads necessitated by tight deadlines are shifted onto workers. South Korea has intensive landscapes of drama airing and watching. The fierce commercial competition among broadcasters for advertisement revenues has put an extraordinary emphasis on prime-time television dramas, leading to a "drama war" among the three terrestrial networks. The drama war has been materialized in an increasing broadcasting time. Given that the amount of television commercials cannot exceed 10 percent of the show's running time, longer running times can sell more commercials. In addition, when its airtime is extended by 10 minutes, a program may attract viewers from other channels who have just finished watching an earlier show. Hence, a longer running time can also raise viewer ratings.[23] The three broadcasters gradually increased the prime-time running time from its previous 50 minutes to as much as 80 minutes, before finally agreeing to freeze their dramas' show time at 70 minutes in 2008. In addition, Korea is unique inasmuch as prime-time dramas air two episodes per week. No commercials interrupt television shows on terrestrial channels in Korea. Weekly filming, consequently, has to fill a total of 140 minutes—more than a feature-length film—which is a challenge, especially in the last-minute production environment.

To meet production requirements, live production entails intensive and often seriously excessive labor, forcing workers into a condition in which they suffer from constant sleep deprivation and alternating periods of waiting on standby and multitasking during the three- to six-month period when a drama is being aired. Excessive working hours in drama production have caused several rounds of controversial debates in the industry. In August 2011, Han Ye-seul, who played the title role in the KBS drama *Myung Wol the Spy* (*Seupai Myeongwol*), boycotted further production of the drama by running away to Los Angeles in the middle of shooting and airing, complaining about poor working conditions. But heated criticism from the media and viewers made her return to the set only forty-eight hours after her departure. Although public discourse generated during the earlier stages of the scandal criticized her, saying that a guaranteed $30,000 per episode was sufficient compensation for all the hard work, the event actually shed light on the reality of the working conditions in the drama industry. In response to this event, the Korean Actors Association released a statement saying: "We have to blame the broadcaster and producer for killer filming schedules. . . . According to Korean labor laws, normal workers are allowed to work only 12 hours overtime per week, in addition to the regular eight-hour working day. Broadcasters, however, never felt guilty even when actors worked 100 hours overtime, reasoning they were not under the legal protection of standard labor law." In fact, Park Shin-yang, who starred in the hit drama *Lovers in Paris* (*Pariui Yeonin* 2004), once said, "The poor working conditions where the cast and production team had to work 42 hours straight need to be improved," while veteran actor Lee Soon-jae even went as far as to say, "Korean actors currently work in life-or-death situations."[24]

Excessive labor is sustained by the workers' attitude to the public nature of broadcasting. A film crew member remarked: "Not sleeping is required practice in this field. We are so used to it. Nevertheless, drama should be broadcast. It is a promise made to the public."[25] Given this explicit promise to the public, there is an implicit consensus among all participants that broadcasting cancellations should be prevented. Scholarly discussions on labor in the television industry have concerned the affective nature of the work: the pleasures of acclaim, rewards, self-realization, and creativity do matter and become the basis for self-exploitation in creative work (Hardt 1999; Ursell 2000; Hesmondhalgh and Baker 2008; Hesmondhalgh 2011). Affective labor in the Korean drama industry, however, is more associated with the responsibility arising out of the public aspect of television dramas than with the pleasures of creative work (Kim 2008). Actors are not deemed free from a duty to the public. To fulfill her acting responsibilities, Hong Su-hyun, who acted in the drama *The Princess's Man* (*Gongjuui Namja* 2011), returned to the set even after a car accident in which she fractured a rib. These incidents, however, prompt media and public discourse to highlight, and even glorify, the passionate spirit of workers rather than disclose the harsh realities of the industry.

Live production and its associated labor conditions show the speculative nature of the Korean drama industry. Because producers are drawn by expectations of export opportunities without possessing actual financial and production capabilities, the production process itself ends up being last minute and haphazard. For the sake of an immediate turnover, producers show a blind obsession with ratings at the expense of creativity in a drama series. The pursuit of short-term profits turns an already commercial genre, television drama, into a medium of vulgar materialism. To reduce production costs, the cultural production is built on labor exploitation, mirroring the labor-intensive, export-oriented industrialization during the developmental era. Controversies surrounding the exhausting labor conditions are usually dealt with as individual rather than systemic problems.

Live production, however, embodies intriguing twists. The improvised production environment has nurtured an atmosphere in which producers actively listen to the views of the audience and actually accept and apply them in the ongoing production. Benefiting from the practices of live filming, drama producers can immediately reflect audience responses and alter the story lines. Plot change is a direct form of interaction through which audience opinion can be adopted in the drama production. Plot changes mainly fall into two categories. The first kind involves modifying the planned endings of dramas. More than a few dramas have revised their proposed endings as a result of viewers' requests. The scriptwriters of *Love Story in Harvard* (*Reobeuseutori in Habeodeu* 2004) originally intended to include the death of a female protagonist. In response to frantic viewer requests, however, the drama concluded with a happy ending. Audience groups also changed the direction of the drama *Wonderful Life* (*Wondeopul Raipeu* 2005), which initially intended to feature the death of a girl, Shin-bi, who failed to get a bone marrow transplant. Meddling viewers reacted to the original story line, saying, "How could the drama be about a 'wonderful life' if it ends with the death of Shin-bi?" Writers gave in to viewer demands and, eventually, the conclusion of the drama was converted into a happy ending. Recently, passionate viewers overwhelmed the website of the drama *Secret Garden* (*Ssikeurit Gadeun* 2010), calling for a happy ending without anybody dying. Responding to the flood of viewer requests that paralyzed the drama website, a writer working on the drama posted a message on her Twitter account, assuring adoring fans that both couples in the drama would have happy endings.

The second kind of plot change is about adjusting how and how often particular characters appear. Korean television dramas have developed stereotyped character relations in which four main characters (two male and two female) form a love rectangle. The top male and female protagonists make up the lead couple and the other pair acts as the subcouple. But "sometimes totally unexpected character couples emerge into the spotlight. In such cases, we have to modify the love lines."[26] In *Giant* (*Jaieonteu* 2010), the Min-woo and Mi-joo couple garnered widespread support from viewers who called for them to make more frequent appearances. Later episodes of the drama *How to Meet a Good Neighbor* (*Wanbyeokhan Iuseul Mannaneun Beop* 2007) allowed more appearances of I-man, who originally had a supporting role, because of the character's popularity. Sometimes groups of fans have heated online discussions about the quantity of screen time their favored actors are allowed. In *Dream High* (*Deurim Hai* 2011), fans of Sam-dong and Jin-kuk competitively requested writers to give their stars as high a profile as possible and to allocate more screen time to them. Plot change indicates the flexible, adjustable, and improvised aspects of Korean television dramas, whose writers are always ready to make modifications to cater to sensitive audience groups.

Interactive production[27] capitalizes on the nature of the serial, defined by Robert Allen as "a form of narrative organized around institutionally-imposed gaps in the text. . . . These gaps leave plenty of time for viewers to discuss with each other both the possible meanings of what has happened thus far as well as what might happen next" (Allen 1995, 17). Taking advantage of live filming, the gaps between texts not only allow viewers to reflect on what they have seen and discuss it among themselves but also provide producers with time to listen to viewers and take action. Although John Fiske (1989) claims that meanings and entertainment value derived from consumers' interventions are not made use of in exchange for material profits, Korean drama producers capitalize on discursive consumption by drawing on audience groups as free labor providing feedback and suggestions. Riding on the practices of last-minute filming and the benefits of social media, the commercial utilization of the audience's discursive consumption takes place every week, almost in real time. On the other hand, the audience is rewarded by flexible texts that favor them more and serve them better.

The practices of live production have actually facilitated the drama–city and culture–place association. As chapter 2 will discuss in detail, city sponsorship, that is, the practice of municipalities delivering cash grants to productions in exchange for revealing their location in a drama, is sometimes secured even during the middle of airing a drama series. In such cases, the shooting locations should be flexibly shifted to feature the sponsoring cities. A live production system makes such unplanned interventions possible and easier by promptly adjusting story lines and thereby the spatial background of a drama. Such location promotions via television drama are not prearranged; they can be contracted even during the course of airing a series and the target places can be inserted in the drama even when the drama story has already begun to unfold.

## Product Placement

The finale for *Elegant Revenge* is airing tonight, but filming is not finished yet and the scenes in the last ten minutes have to be filmed and edited within less than ten hours. Moreover, a managing director has been trying to insert a ten-second orange juice PPL (product placement) scene (worth roughly $300,000), while the scriptwriter is refusing to change the script; the writer has explained in rather coarse terms to the director that there is no place for orange juice when the main character is supposed to be dying "elegantly" after completing his revenge. The director has therefore moved to plan B and has let an assistant writer edit the script and put the orange juice scene in it, appealing to the assistant writer's dreams of stardom (i.e., debuting as a main writer). Filming with the revised scripts is done less than an hour before airing time and a motorcycle rider is hired to rush the tape to the broadcasting station that is located more than one hundred miles away from the filming site.

This is a summary of the first episode of *The King of Dramas* (*Deuramaui Jewang* 2012), whose director publicly asserted that the series dared to depict the "100% actual" features of the industry.[28] The first episode tells how the plots of Korean dramas are modified even at the very last minute to take advantage of product placement.

Product placement entails "incorporating brands in movies in return for money or for some promotional or other consideration" (Gupta and Gould 1997, 37). The Korean drama industry only began to use PPL, even in limited ways, in 2000. The Integrated Broadcasting Act that became effective in 2000 stipulates that "any broadcasting business operator may *announce* a commercial sponsor, who provides costs, gifts, a location, costumes, vignettes, information, etc." (emphasis added). The announcement of sponsorship is mostly carried out through textual displays of sponsors' names at the end of each episode. Although the actual publicity effects of an acknowledgment of corporate names in the titles, displayed for only a few seconds, are in question, independent producers use sponsorship as one of the main channels for funding. Beside the brief textual notification, since direct displays of brand names or corporate logos in the middle of a show were totally prohibited, most dramas tried to suggest the sponsored brand or products through characters mentioning their particular functions through displays of similar logos or of the distinctive interiors of, for example, a coffee franchise. The frequency and level of placements of the sponsored products until this phase, however, remained moderate and did not hamper dramatic storytelling in general.

A sea change came about in January 2010 when the Korea Communications Commission, the nation's broadcasting regulator, eased regulations concerning product placement in television programs on national networks. Under the new law, all television programs except news, documentaries, and editorial and debate shows are allowed to display brand names and corporate logos. The new regulation has brought about a fundamental transformation in the channels of production funding and, more important, in storytelling in Korean television dramas. The financially unstable independent producers began to use product placement excessively as the main means of covering their production costs. To increase the number of sponsors, and thus the number of PPLs, Korean dramas now insert unnecessary or out-of-context anecdotes and dialogue to display brands and products. This signifies a fundamental change in the commodification of popular culture. By appealing to the tastes of a mass audience, popular cultural products are sold to advertisers (Allen 1985). The conventional method of securing better advertising deals is to present more intriguing and substantial stories to attract more viewers. Product placement, however, turns the story itself into a host of advertising slots. Now Korean television dramas do not really tell a story; instead, they display brands and products. Narrative is a supplementary tool to exhibit the sponsored commodities. Next, I analyze in detail the ways Korean television dramas insert product placement, using the case of *Secret Garden* (2010) as a classic example of how to attract and insert PPLs.[29]

*Secret Garden* features a love story across classes involving Gil Ra-im (played by Ha Ji-won), a poor but proud stuntwoman, and Kim Ju-won (played by Hyun Bin), an arrogant and eccentric CEO who maintains an image of seeming perfection. The apparently conventional Cinderella theme unfolds through several cases of body swapping between the two characters, which enables them to understand one another's class conditions. Recording up to 35.2 percent of audience share, *Secret Garden* was a phenomenally successful drama series that went on to be exported to more than thirteen countries. I was doing industrial ethnography as the drama series was about to end. When I interviewed people in the industry, *Secret Garden* was on everyone's lips not because of its high ratings and explosive popularity, but because of its savvy integration of product placement into its stories. The production company, Hwa and Dam Pictures, publicly admitted that its story lines had been carefully designed from the synopsis stage to take product placement into account; the firm cooperated with a marketing firm to strategically build characters and set their occupations and residential spaces with reference to the products that were being promoted.[30] In addition, one of my interviewees informed me that the writer of the drama maintained a close relationship with the drama production company and was extremely cooperative in including product placements in her scripts; given writers' customary tendency to avoid advertisements that will hamper the narrative logic of their story, this is an unusual case of a writer sacrificing her creativity to commercial considerations.

*Secret Garden* made extensive use of product placements intertwined with the storytelling. Even its cases of *simple placement*[31] (which refers to the ways products are either shown in the background or actually used) are well blended with character building. The female protagonist, Ra-im, often wears outdoor gear, in keeping with her occupation as a stuntwoman. Behind this particular piece of character depiction lay the sponsorship of Mont-bell, an outdoor apparel manufacturer, which paid $300,000 to support the drama series, an exceptional amount for a clothing firm. There is one particular scene in which Ra-im's stunt colleagues go to a Mont-bell store to pick up winter jackets and the store's logo is prominently displayed right behind the actors. In another scene, Oscar, one of the leading male characters who is depicted as a Hallyu star, holds a meeting with his fans at a Mont-bell store, which enables the brand's logo and store displays to be directly presented. The sponsoring brand enjoyed huge publicity by being showcased by characters and in backgrounds, selling out of the products that the characters wore.

The series' protagonist (Ju-won) and his cousin (Oscar) live in a luxurious suburban house whose spaciousness and high ceilings effectively symbolize Ju-won's claustrophobia and loneliness. Evoking the drama's title, *Secret Garden*, the house's broad and exotic garden with a lake in it features as a critical site in which the two lead characters' emotional lives are represented through dialogues, flashbacks, and imagined events. The residential space and garden are actually Maiim Vision Village, a human resources training site belonging to the Maiim Corporation (a company that sells cosmetics and health food products). Although not a single Maiim product was placed in the drama series, rendering the corporation's headquarters publicly recognizable successfully planted Maiim's brand images in viewers' minds. When public interest had been aroused in the actual location where filming had taken place, the Maiim Corporation issued a press release introducing Maiim Vision Village.

Yet what *Secret Garden* truly showcased was its art of *integrated placement*, that is, the ways product placement became a key feature of the show's plotline, and thus part of the script (Wenner 2004). A 2009 model BMW Z4, a luxurious sports convertible, appeared throughout the series as the protagonist's car. The convertible played a critical role in building the character of the protagonist (Ju-won), who drives an open car even in winter because he suffers from claustrophobia. More critically, the drama's climax highlighted the Z4. When Ra-im is seriously injured in an accident during a stunt and suffers brain death, Ju-won wants to swap bodies with her so that she can continue her life in his body while he takes her place in her brain-dead one. Knowing that their bodies can be switched in the rain, Ju-won takes Ra-im from her hospital bed and drives off in his convertible to await the coming storm. As he sits in the car, he tells her: "I'm going to miss you a lot. I love you"; then he drives the Z4 into the storm. This climactic scene in which the convertible is vital to the plotline produces a far greater effect than conventional advertising, which simply provides consumers with information about the product, because it generates powerful affective values around the BMW. The symbolic process creates more powerful advertising effects, which is why sponsors always prefer integrated placement despite the huge price difference.

The "cappuccino foam kiss" scene is one of the most parodied product placements. In *Secret Garden*, all the characters are regular patrons of one café: Café Bene. Sponsored by the then newly emerging local coffeehouse chain, the drama series used the café as the venue for the characters' daily conversations. One day, Ju-won and Ra-im meet at the café and Ra-im drinks a cappuccino. Noticing foam left on her upper lip, Ju-won kisses her to wipe it off. This kiss scene turned out to be sensational and many celebrities parodied the scene by posting photos of themselves with foam on their lips. Photos showing people sitting in a café with a cup of cappuccino also became a phenomenon among bloggers. One blogger wrote: "After watching *Secret Garden*, I have become a fan of doing sit-ups and drinking cappuccino. . . . I hope a Prince Charming will approach me and leave a sweet kiss." Merging product placement into an interesting incident in the drama, the "cappuccino kiss scene" is indicative of a well-designed integrated placement strategy.

After the huge success of *Secret Garden* in terms of PPLs, there was a fundamental change in the methods of storytelling. Not only did scenes with product placement become a necessity in Korean television series but the invasion of commercial sponsorship narrowed the genre, characters, and story lines of modern dramas down to those that would enable product placements to be easily inserted. Trendy dramas based on the Cinderella theme seem to be the most attractive material for producers, broadcasters, and commercial sponsors, because they are so well suited to a display of lifestyle-oriented consumer goods catering to a young female audience.[32] The presence of upperclass characters (known as *chaebol* in Korean) is required to attract large-scale sponsorship for the display of luxury cars and designer brands, as in *Secret Garden*. Both producers and broadcasters avoid particular genres such as thrillers, police procedurals, and dramas dealing with serious social issues, because they do not offer enough spaces for the exhibition of commodities targeting viewers' vanity.[33] Thanks to live production, the stories of Korean dramas are extremely flexible, so producers are always able to add scenes with product placement even in the middle of a series. Because late-coming sponsors merely tend to ride on the ongoing popularity of a series, their sponsorship has nothing to do with preplanning characters or plots; producers consequently need to insert awkward offbeat scenes simply to be able to accept the sponsorship. Hence, heightened commercialism not only diminishes the diversity and creativity of the stories in Korean dramas but can also render them a collage of commercial advertisements without a solid narrative.

In response to this heightened commercialism, audience complaints and media criticism have mounted. Blatant product placements have caused some viewers to grumble that this can ruin the experience of watching a show. One viewer complained: "*Secret Garden* has strong production values with a creative story and mighty performances, but frequent product placements detract from its overall quality. . . . I'm sick and tired of these advertisements."[34] The drama *Style* (*Seutail* 2009) was also criticized for its extensive product placements and suggestive stretches of dialogue that constituted indirect advertisements, leading one viewer to comment, "I feel like I'm watching one long commercial."[35] Given the financial predicament of independent drama producers, however, such criticism has been unable to stop them from relying heavily on product placement as a major funding source. Instead, even historical dramas have recently begun to attract product placement by using the technique of *time slip*, in which characters travel through different time periods. Due to the restrictions imposed by premodern settings, time-slip historical dramas intersperse some episodes set in the contemporary world, which have scenes featuring product placements. *Dr. Jin* (*Dakteo Jin* 2012), *Faith* (*Sinui* 2012), and *Rooftop Prince* (*Oktapbang Wangseja* 2012) are examples of shows featuring the narrative technique of time slip.

The excessive dependence of Korean prime-time serials on product placement reflects the speculative approach and weak financial conditions of independent drama producers. To put it another way, the speculative nature has redefined the genres, characters, scenes, and narrative methods of

K-dramas. The practice of product placement is particularly significant because it defines other forms of sponsorship, and thereby storytelling. In chapter 2, I will discuss how cities are placed in dramas through the practice of city sponsorship. In the same way that drama stories become a patchwork of commercial advertisements regardless of their actual relevance to the plot, urban places and landscapes are simply inserted into the story lines. Product placement was originally aimed at domestic audiences only. With the growing influence of Hallyu and easier travel between Asian countries, the transregional audience has become a target, too. As chapters 2 and 5 will show, drama-inspired transnational tourists now actively consume the food, products, and places that they have seen on the screen.

## Catering to the Overseas Markets

Another way in which the industry's speculative nature determines storytelling in drama is by its catering to potential importers. Just as an expectation of export opportunities triggered the sudden speculative growth in the number of independent producers, the lucrative nature of overseas markets made it imperative for the industry to tailor productions to serve them. Throughout the 2000s up until 2013, Japan was the biggest overseas buyer of Korean television dramas, with its robust markets in broadcasting and secondary products such as DVDs, drama-themed tourism, and celebrity merchandise. More than 60 percent of Korean drama exports went to the Japanese market until 2013 and the unit price of television dramas remains particularly high in Japan (see table 1.1). My informant on the marketing team of a broadcasting station remarked: "Even if you add up all the other Asian markets, profits from exports to them remain far short of the share from Japan. It is the Japanese market that absorbs the oversupply of television drama content in South Korea, instigating the numerous small-sized independent producers to steadily proliferate."[36] This profitable export market acts like a sponsor, leading Korean drama producers to engage in a variety of often desperate tactics to fabricate story lines to serve the audience in Japan.

The most obvious way for Korean drama producers to appeal to Japanese buyers is by exploiting star power, that is, by casting so-called Hallyu stars, actors and actresses who are already popular in Japan. Following the mega-popularity of Bae Yong-jun in *Winter Sonata*, several Korean stars have won celebrity status in Japan: Lee Byung-hun in *All In* (*Orin* 2003) and *IRIS* (*Airiseu* 2009); Song Seung-heon in *Autumn in My Heart* (*Gaeul Donghwa* 2000), *Summer Scent* (*Yeoreum Hyanggi* 2003), *East of Eden* (*Edenui Dongjjok* 2008), *My Princess* (*Mai Peurinsese* 2011), and *Dr. Jin*; Kwon Sang-woo in *Stairway to Heaven* (*Cheongugui Gyedan* 2003), *Sad Love Story*, *Cruel Love* (*Mosdoen Sarang* 2007), *Cinderella Man* (*Sinderella Maen* 2009), and *Big Thing* (*Daemul* 2010); Jang Keun-suk in *Hwang Jin Yi* (*Hwangjini* 2006), *You're Beautiful* (*Minamisineyo* 2008), *Marry Me, Mary!* (*Maerineun Oebakjung* 2010), and *Love Rain* (*Sarangbi* 2012); Park Yoo-chun from the idol band JYJ in *Sungkyunkwan Scandal* (*Seonggyungwan Seukaendeul* 2010), *Miss Ripley* (*Miseu Ripeulli* 2011), *Rooftop Prince*, and *I Miss You* (*Bogosipda* 2012); and Lee Min-ho in *Boys over Flowers* (*Kkoccboda Namja* 2009), *Personal Taste* (*Gaeinui Chwihyang* 2010), *City Hunter* (*Ssiti Heonteo* 2011), and *Faith*. Because the Japanese audience tends to show long-term loyalty to their favorite stars, a critical success factor in exports has been who appears in a drama. This is much more important than what the drama is about. A chief producer at a broadcasting station stated: "In most cases, if not always, the casting of Hallyu stars works, I mean works, in Japan. So when channel lineups are being decided, independent firms who cast a Hallyu star are highly likely to win a channel—mostly regardless of the story synopsis of their proposed drama."[37] The interviewee implies that the lucrative export market virtually determines what kind of stories domestic viewers get to watch. The appearance of particular celebrities trumps ratings in the competition for export contracts to Japan. The drama *Marry Me, Mary!* was sold on favorable terms to Japan despite its low domestic viewing figures merely because of the exceptional popularity of its leading man, Jang Keun-suk, in Japan. Due to market conditions in which star power controls export potential, Hallyu stars have commanded extraordinary appearance fees during the 2000s, leaving the industry with an even greater financial struggle.

With the rise of K-pop music in Japan, one recent phenomenon has been to cast K-pop idols in Korean dramas. Although the primary channel for K-pop idols to debut is as members of idol bands, idols are an intertextual commodity whose promotion is carried out through the ubiquitous creation and circulation of images via a variety of media (see chapter 3). A synergetic transaction underlies the idols' appearance in television dramas; idol producers can promote their talents to wider audiences and the drama producers can exploit idols' popularity. Successful idol acting stars include Park Yoo-chun, previously in TVXQ and now in JYJ, who starred in *Sungkyunkwan Scandal, Miss Ripley, Rooftop Prince,* and *I Miss You*; Jung Yong-hwa from CNBLUE, who appeared in *You're Beautiful* and *Heartstrings* (*Neon Naege Banhaesseo* 2011); Girls' Generation's Yoona, who starred in *Cinderella Man* and *Love Rain*; Suzy from Miss A, who acted in *Big* (*Bik* 2012) and *Gu Family Book* (*Gugaui Seo* 2013); and EXO's D.O., who appeared in *It's Okay, That's Love* (*Gwaenchanha Sarangiya* 2014). The casting of a K-pop idol as a lead character brings huge publicity not only in Korea but also in various other foreign countries. Once idols mention the drama in which they will be appearing on social networking services (SNS), postings can be circulated everywhere within a very short time thanks to their global fandom. Fan-driven distribution is a bigger deal than media and press attention thanks to its explosive and affective nature: passionate fans volunteer to raise publicity. Besides, the loyalty of passionate fan groups tends to raise viewer ratings as well.

Employing idol singers, however, has raised a number of issues. Celebrity idols are trained as singers and dancers; acting is not their primary area of expertise. The lack of acting ability on the part of some singers diminishes the overall quality of a drama. Not a few veteran actors have raised issues about the singer-actors. For example, an actor who has more than twenty years of experience remarked: "Acting requires emotions. Idols are only technically trained for acting, and even that is totally inadequate due to their crazy schedules (for performing as singers in various venues). Casting an idol is advantageous in terms of attracting investment and product placements. However, their poor acting turns a drama into vulgar commercial content."[38] Viewers also pointed out idols' lack of acting skills, saying: "I cannot concentrate on the drama because of their awkward acting. Why don't producers cast new actors who have been properly trained to act?"[39] Drama producers' responses to such comments are usually based on the idea of reducing risk. Producers (if not directors) tend to avoid the risk of employing newcomers who have not had any exposure to the public. One producer commented: "In reality, there are few new actors who are good enough to be cast. Idol singers are at least familiar with the camera. Some new actors even fall far short of being adjusted to appearing on camera."[40] In addition, it is said that idol singers' appearance fees are quite low relative to their name values. Since paying the top four lead actors comprises more than 60 percent of the total production cost of a television drama, having an actor who is both popular and inexpensive is always preferable for producers.

A more fundamental reason for casting K-pop idols in dramas, despite the pervasive criticism, lies in the fact that idol stars have repaved the way for exports to Japan. Particularly since the K-pop–driven Second Korean Wave, the celebrity qualities of individual idols have developed into something that cannot be neglected even in the drama industry. Given that 30 to 50 percent of profits come from drama copyrights sold in the Japanese market, the casting of idol singers has become standard practice, rather than a one-time publicity event. When a particular drama production company cast a super-idol star who was big in Japan as a leading character, it accepted unfavorable terms from a broadcaster, receiving less than half the normal production costs in the hope of gaining the export rights to sell the show in Japan. This case indicates the significance of casting that targets the Japanese market. In another case, a writer whom I interviewed revealed that when one particular idol singer was cast in a drama, the production company pressed for his appearances in the drama to be expanded, despite his having only a minor supporting role, to facilitate exporting the program to Japan. In any case, acting matters less overseas because most dramas are dubbed into local languages; the mere appearance of K-pop idols and their good looks tend to mean more to foreign viewers. The separation between casting and acting is an indication of how Korean prime-time dramas have tended to "display" people and products more than deliver stories.

Second, Korean television dramas have adjusted their content with a view to lowering transnational barriers to penetrate the Japanese market. In *Bread, Love, and Dreams* (*Jeppangwang Kimtakgu*, 2010), as an interview with a staff member at the production firm of the drama revealed: "The name of the title role, Kim Tak-goo, was intentionally created to target export to Japan. Kim Tak-goo (*Kimu Tagoo* in Japanese) is one of the easiest Korean names for Japanese to identify and pronounce. The pronunciation is also very similar to that of the Japanese superstar, Kimura Takuya. An easy name significantly lowers the cultural barriers in the overseas market."[41] Recently, more and more dramas have also featured incidents that take place in Japan. *IRIS*, a spy drama involving North and South Korea, includes several episodes set in Japan (sponsored by Akita Prefecture). *The Innocent Man* (*Chakan Namja* 2012) shows events happening in Aomori Prefecture in Japan and features the exotic landscapes of the area. In *Miss Reply*, one of the main male characters grew up in Japan and went to Korea. Since he travels back and forth between Korea and Japan, Japan plays an important role in the story.[42] Such an intentionally orchestrated role for Japan in a Korean drama serves to facilitate its appreciation by Japanese audiences.

A third way of catering to the Japanese market is by assimilating Japanese culture. There are an increasing number of cases in which Korean television dramas have adapted Japanese manga, plays, or novels, including *Behind the White Tower* (*Hayan Geotap* 2007), *Naughty Kiss* (*Jangnanseureon Kiseu* 2010), *Royal Family* (*Royal Paemilli* 2011), *Dr. Jin, That Winter the Wind Blows* (*Geu Gyeoul Barami Bunda* 2013), *The Queen of the Office* (*Jikjangui Sin* 2013), and *The Queen's Classroom* (*Yeowangui Gyosil* 2013). The remaking of Japanese originals boomed because it guaranteed distribution stability both in Korea and Japan. In Korea, of the hundreds of drama proposals they receive in a year, broadcasters tend to favor remade dramas when granting a channel because the public has already proved the quality of originals. Industrial insiders comment: "Remade dramas at least get us our money back. With already proven fresh and solid stories, they always guarantee stable, if not very high, ratings"; "The strong points of Japanese dramas are innovative characters and themes, while most Korean dramas develop stories around class relations and secrets of birth."[43] The potential of Japanese dramas to communicate with Korean audiences also buttresses ratings: "It is hard to guarantee success by remaking U.S., U.K., or Chinese dramas because of the different systems and topics involved. When a solo writer creates a whole drama series, it is impossible to capture the deeper levels of U.S. and U.K. dramas. But Japan is different. Japan and South Korea have similar social issues, such as those concerning irregular workers (addressed in *The Queen of the Office*; a remake of *Haken No Hinkaku*, 2007) and education (as in *The Queen's Classroom*; a remake of *Jyoou no Kyoushitsu*, 2005). Shared experiences and sensibilities ease the transnational barrier."[44]

From the independent producers' perspective, a more fundamental reason to favor the remaking of Japanese originals is to get the upper hand in negotiations with broadcasters. Having acquired the rights to the original, independent firms do not need to deliver all the rights in a drama to a broadcaster under contract. Remaking also curtails the fees paid to writers, as adaptations do not require producers to hire a star writer as is the case with an original teleplay. Such economic factors lie behind the boom in Korean adaptations of Japanese originals within the industry.[45] What is most notable is that Japanese dramas and films are often remade as Korean television dramas and reexported to Japan. Their acceptance in Japan is facilitated by the Japanese audience's enhanced familiarity with the material; the adaptation of Japanese serials is a means of overcoming the double barrier between the Korean and Japanese markets.

The appropriation of Japanese styles is not limited to stories. Japanese fashions, music, and food are actively represented in television dramas through scenes and characters. The history of Japanese colonial rule in Korea prevented cultural exchanges between the two countries until 1998, when the then president of South Korea agreed to phase in Japanese cultural products. Despite the official opening up of cultural markets, South Korea continued to be hesitant to accept Japanese cultural content. Whereas Japan is proactive in airing Korean television dramas, Korean terrestrial broadcasting stations do not show the Japanese equivalents.[46] Nevertheless, despite South Korean cultural protectionism, Japanese styles are overtly and heavily represented in Korean television dramas as facilitators of exports to the Japanese market. Discussing the global popularity of Japanese pop culture, Koichi Iwabuchi (2002) suggests that "culturally odorless" products in which "a country's bodily, racial, and ethnic characteristics are erased or softened" have been critical in making inroads into international markets; for example, "the characters of Japanese animation and computer games . . . do not look 'Japanese'" (Iwabuchi 2002, 28). Cultural odorlessness helps the comfortable acceptance of the content by international consumers. Since the Korean Wave in the early 2000s, the "cultural odor" of Korean dramas has certainly been suppressed. Rather, scenes in Korean serials have been increasingly "Japanized" to tailor them to the Japanese market.

After a decade-long Japanese domination of the export market, however, China is newly emerging as the biggest export destination for Korean dramas (see table 1.1). Local policy and industrial dynamics in China are very dissimilar to those in Japan, causing substantial changes in Korean industrial practices. China has retained a defensive attitude to importing foreign content. Airing overseas films and television dramas cannot exceed 25 percent of daily broadcasting time and is completely prohibited during prime time (19:00–22:00). The Chinese government also bans the import of foreign dramas consisting of more than fifty episodes. Against the background of these strict regulations, one of the popular ways of exporting Korean content has been to sell a format or the originals from which Chinese producers can create a remake version. *Temptation of Wife* (*Anaeui Yuhok* 2008) was broadcast on Hunan TV as the Chinese remake drama *Hui Jia De You Huo* in 2011 and got to number 1 in the national ratings. Zhejiang Satellite TV aired and achieved great success with *Fall in Love with Anchor Beauty* (*Ai Shang Nu Zhu Bo*), based on the Korean drama *All About Eve* (*Ibeuui Modeun Geot* 2000). *Fall in Love* (*Yī Bùxiǎo Xīn Ài Shàng Nǐ*), a Chinese adaptation of the Korean original *Autumn in My Heart* brought in a huge profit for Hunan Satellite TV in 2010. Two Korean television dramas, *I'm Sorry, I Love You* (*Mianhada Saranghanda* 2004) and *Secret Garden*, were reproduced as films in China, *Sorry, I Love You* (*Wo De Ling Jie Nan You* 2014) and *The Secret Garden* (*Mi Mi Hua Yuan* 2012). Other successful cases of format export include such entertainment shows as *Where Are We Going, Dad?* (*Appa Eodiga*) and *I Am a Singer* (*Naneun Gasuda*), both originally produced by MBC. Hunan Satellite TV bought the formats for both and achieved great ratings, producing and airing multiple seasons of the same format.

Nevertheless, the Chinese audience has a much broader experience of Korean dramas via informal routes. Online video sites such Youku, Tudou, and Sohu have functioned as platforms through which Korean television dramas have been widely and freely circulated in ethnic Chinese regions. In the early stages, individual users informally recorded and uploaded K-dramas. Having observed how popular and profitable they are, site operators have recently begun to buy the transmission rights of Korean dramas officially and release the dramas free to consumers, as the sites' revenues are based on advertising sales. The distribution of Korean dramas via online streaming sites in China has narrowed the time lag between the two countries, enabling almost real-time viewing of episodes in China immediately after their airing in Korea. The accessibility of content via mobile units also enhances online drama watching, since it frees consumers from spatial and temporal constraints. In addition, online platforms operate under relatively relaxed regulations regarding content. These features of the platform and of state policies have found good fits with Korean television dramas, causing more Chinese movie site operators to be interested in importing them. Released on Youku, the biggest online streaming site in China operated by Youku-Tudou, *The Heirs* (*Sangsokjadeul* 2013) attracted more than one million viewers. The movie streaming site, iQiyi, which is operated by Baidu (the largest Chinese search engine) bought the VOD rights for *My Love from the Star* (*Byeoreseo On Geudae* 2013) and distributed it via eight streaming sites including iQiyi, PPTV, LeTV, and Xunrei. Online distribution of the drama recorded more than 3.7 million viewings within a period of just four months, igniting the Second Korean Wave in China.

A new censorship rule, however, brought about a decisive change in the situation. The State Administration of Radio, Film, and Television, China's official broadcasting regulation bureau, announced in September 2014 that all foreign shows must be approved before they could be posted on video-streaming sites, starting April 1, 2015. The prior screening and approval regulation implies that streaming content will be treated the same as regular television programming. Existing television rules dictate that the censor must review the whole season of a show before any episodes can be aired. The necessity of prior screening an entire series effectively barred the direct export of K-dramas given the live production practices in Korea. Those who faced the most daunting task as a result of the new Chinese regulation were not Chinese video site operators, but, surprisingly, Korean drama producers. To deal with Chinese censorship and hold on to the Chinese market, Korean producers began to launch completely preproduced dramas, including *Descendants of the Sun* (*Taeyangui Huye* 2016), *Saimdang, Memoir of Colors* (*Saimdang Biccui Ilgi* 2017), *Cheese in the Trap* (*Chijeu In Deo Teuraep* 2016), and *Uncontrollably Fond* (*Hamburo Aeteushage* 2016).[47] Korean drama producers seem to have ended their long-standing practice of live production, due to concern about exporting to China. As discussed above, live production, despite its chronic deficiencies, was practiced basically for the sake of viewer ratings, since it enabled audience responses to be checked and the script to be altered on the basis of audience feedback. The new preproduction format indicates precisely what the industry is targeting to attract investment and improve turnover rates: the export market.

This chapter has explored how the Korean Wave created the speculative turn in the Korean drama industry. The fortuitously acquired overseas popularity of some Korean television dramas planted collective expectations about export markets and jackpot-like profit making. While these speculative anticipations attracted numerous independent producers to the drama industry, their industrial position remained marginal with respect to financial conditions, production environment, and profit redistribution. Such disparity led to the industrial players becoming even more speculative, reshaping production practices, forms of sponsorship, and ways of storytelling. The live production system is widely practiced to reduce labor costs, listen to audience voices, and stay afloat in the industry. Ironically, the exploitation of flexible labor and passion-induced intensive working practices caused by the live production system have acted as sources of market competitiveness in a cultural industry in which abstract values such as creativity and innovation are conventionally thought to rule. At the same time, the financial predicaments of independent drama producers have forced them to rely heavily on commercial sponsorship. As a result of the concerns of potential importers and commercial sponsors, Korean prime-time serials have often tended to become a collage of scenes for sponsorship, also reversing the conventional mechanism to attract more advertisers from the creativity of the narrative to the narrative itself. As cities emerged as one of the major sponsors of drama production, the speculative nature and rampant practices of sponsor seeking brought about an interesting twist, opening up a space for the coconstruction of story and place.

Chapter 2

# SPECTACULAR PLACES

## Drama-Filming Sites

**Moment 1:**

"Cut the ropes!"

As the ropes are severed, the wooden fences that functioned as floodgates fall away, releasing an enormous volume of water that rushes down toward where the Sui troops are halfway across the river.

"What is that noise? It sounds like a great flood of water!"

"It is a water attack! A water attack!"

A dumbfounded and desperate army general screams. The screen freezes at the scream on a close-up of the general's frightened face. Against grandiose background music, huge texts appear one by one in time to pounding drum beats; the first two read "Munkyung City" and "Danyang County."

This is episode 45 of the prime-time television series *Yeon Gae So Mun*, which features the life of Yeon Gaesomun (603–666), a powerful general in the waning days of Goguryeo (37 BC–668 AD), one of the Three Kingdoms of ancient Korea. The episode depicts the climax of the Battle of Salsu, a major battle that took place in 612 during the second Goguryeo–Sui war. When the Sui army reached Salsu (thought to be the present-day Chongchon River), the water level was shallow as Eulji Mundoek (a Goguryeo general) had previously cut off the flow with a dam. When the Sui army arrived in the middle of the river, Eulji opened the dam and the onslaught of water drowned thousands of Sui soldiers. As happens in most conventional Korean serials, that episode ends with a cliff-hanger. While the tension continues for a while, the audience is presented with a series of texts that name the sponsors of the drama series. The appearance of Munkyung City and Danyang County at the top of the list informs viewers that they are the production's biggest sponsors and actually provided the gigantic historical sets on which most of the series was filmed.

**Moment 2:**

A young woman wearing a blue dress is running along a rocking bridge made of ropes and planks that overlooks the sea. A young man in a dark blue shirt is following her. The girl is almost at the other end of the bridge when the boy yells: "*Stop right there!*" She turns back to face him. As he strides purposefully forward, his face is grim. "What do those things have to do with anything? I trust you. I like you. And I want you." He crosses the bridge toward her and as soon as she is in his arms, the planks stop shaking. Everything is still. They kiss! As dawn is breaking, the overall color of the screen becomes blue and lyrical background music is heard.

This scene comes from episode 21 of *Shining Inheritance* (also known as *Brilliant Legacy*, [*Challanhan Yusan*], 2009), a megahit series that recorded peak ratings of 47 percent. A kiss scene on a swaying bridge, which conveys the kissing couple's beating hearts and makes the audience feel exhilarated, is a clear demonstration of the talents of the writer and the director. It may perhaps disappoint some people to learn, however, that the kiss scene actually emerged out of a financial contract between the producers of the series and one of its sponsors, Donghae City. According to the contract, particular places in Donghae had to be featured in and blended with the story, and the suspension bridge, *Chullungdari*, was one of those places. That episode ends with the close-up kiss scene; while the screen freezes in still frame, the credits start to run, accompanied by background music, revealing the sponsors' names, including Donghae City. As the sponsoring city intended, not long after the episode aired press reports and blog posts started appearing that spoke of a romantic weekend trip to the rocking bridge and other attractions in Dong-hae. A seemingly dangerous suspension bridge located somewhere in Korea was about to become *the* romantic place.

The moments I have described show the degree of exposure given to the names of municipalities associated with television dramas in the form of sponsorship. This chapter[1] deciphers the process by which cities have become one of the major sponsors of Korean drama production since the 2000s. As discussed in the introduction, one reason for the emergence of regional cities as supporters of television drama production lies in their desire for publicity, stimulated by uneven development and decentralization. Aspiring regional cities and financially desperate drama producers found they could offer each other a solution to their particular needs. The other reason derives from the spatiality of television dramas;[2] drama production requires physical spaces that can be used as filming venues or backgrounds. When producers wanted to both diversify film locations and receive financial sponsorship, Korean cities came forward as space and funding providers. Cities thus became directly involved in the production of television dramas through their provision of space, place, and funding. I call this practice "drama sponsorship by cities." It comprises two types of practice: first, cities construct megasize drama sets to be used as major filming venues and then further developed as tourist attractions; second, drama producers strategically display locations from the cities featured in television dramas in return for cash support. This chapter examines how urban spaces are inserted into television dramas in a manner similar to product placement; how media representation creates new meanings for these places; how drama-driven tourists reshape those meanings; and how municipalities capitalize on their representation in drama, on media spectacles, and on users' engagement in their promotion.

## Constructing Drama Sets

The construction of settings for dramas is an original type of sponsorship by municipalities. Called an "open set" (*opeun seteu*) because it is built outdoors, this type of set is a complex in which architecture in the styles of particular (mostly premodern) historical periods is constructed. The emergence of outdoor sets was mainly driven by a change in the subject matter and production practices of historical dramas[3] in the 2000s. Unlike previous authentic historical dramas (*jeongtong sageuk*) that mainly depicted the kingdom's indoor politics and ruling male aristocracy,[4] the fusion historical dramas that became popular in the 2000s were based more on writers' imaginations than historical facts. Recent fusion historical dramas have diversified their themes as well, exploring the lives of underrepresented classes such as women, scholars and scientists, and peasants and slaves. Breaking away from the monotonous concentration on the Chosun dynasty (1392–1910) in previous dramas, fusion historical dramas have broadened the historical frame of reference, taking in several other dynasties that preceded Chosun. The new subject matter and the diversity of historical periods required new settings that could be used as backgrounds and filming venues. In addition, the lengthy production and broadcasting schedules of historical dramas necessitated construction of a separate set dedicated exclusively to filming a particular drama.[5] Taken as a whole, these changes in production practice brought about the emergence and proliferation of drama sets. Forty-two outdoor sets whose size is over 3.3 hectares were built across South Korea during the 2000s; over ninety when smaller-sized sets are included. The sets represent palaces, towns, institutional districts, markets, and streets. Because they are mainly used for shooting outdoor scenes, detailed and accurate representation of building facades and the vivid streetscapes of a particular historical period matters. Although each area is portrayed as a separate and distinct space within the drama, different areas and buildings are usually built together within the same location.

The construction of settings for historical dramas presents producers with two challenges: space and money. First, outdoor sets require sizable empty spaces where modern elements are nonexistent or can be totally eliminated. Mountainous areas or large open fields are usually the preferred sites. This requirement drives drama producers away from Seoul, where all the broadcasting firms and production houses are located but which is already densely developed, out to underdeveloped or less urban cities. In finding sites for sets, therefore, what matters is the availability and topography of land, not specific localities. With the exception of a few historical heritage sites that can be utilized as backgrounds,[6] the actual historical settings of the events depicted in dramas and the physical locations of the sets where these events are reenacted are totally separate. Television dramas never seek out the original localities and the artificially created historical settings are represented as the virtual urban. Second, set construction generally costs more than $5 million. This expense is far beyond the capabilities of financially struggling series producers. As mentioned in chapter 1, disbursement of funding from a broadcaster to an independent producer takes place after the airing of a whole series, that is, at least one year after the initial outlay for the production of a long-term historical drama. In the itemized accounts, art production has a separate budget appropriated from the production costs. This budget, however, mostly covers costumes and props. The responsibility for preparing the budget for a critical portion of art production, that is the construction of sets, usually falls on producers, thereby driving them to find sponsors.[7]

Due to the spatiality of drama production, particularly its need for nonurban physical space, regional cities have emerged as perfect sponsors. Although the planning, editing, and broadcasting processes for television dramas are centered in Seoul due to the place-specific agglomeration of the broadcasting and entertainment industries, the physical production process of television drama involves a broader geography; indeed, the actual filming of television dramas requires vast spatial resources for sets and the use of recognizable places and landscapes as backgrounds. Thus, the shooting locations of television dramas are scattered among various locales. Cities that can provide land for a set are also expected to pay the construction costs and deliver tax incentives. In return, the city names are displayed at the end of every episode as sponsors. Although the sets used for dramas rarely depict the places where they are actually built, the textual reference to financial sponsorship informs viewers of the physical locations of the sets.

Despite the mutually synergetic nature of the transactions, however, the party that is more desperate is the drama producers. In seeking space and funding, their approach to local cities and counties is very strategic. A project coordinator remarked: "We usually define three to four potential candidate cities (counties) and conduct brief research about them. We then arrange meetings with local leaders via local contacts—by the way, it has to be a mayor or a county governor; we don't consider high-ranking officials at all, we present possible 'local development plans' in association with the drama set construction. Sometimes we capitalize on the 'star names' of directors or actors, but the presentation should be more about 'local development' than about the drama itself. If our presentation grabs local leaders' interest, it does smooth the way for a city's drama sponsorship."[8] This interview suggests the placelessness of drama sets; they could be located anywhere that offers space and money. More important, the interview clearly indicates the mixture of the regional cities' underdeveloped status and desire to promote themselves on the one hand, and the aspirations and pressures of elected local leaders on the other. As discussed in the introduction, elected leaders equate local development with creating publicity that can put the municipality's name on everybody's lips and attract visitors. Drama producers woo regional cities with the power of the media to do both.

Drama set–driven local development became trendy after the showcasing of Munkyung, a small former mining town in North Gyeongsang Province. In 2000, Munkyung City gave $300,000 for the construction of a set for the drama *Taejo Wang Geon* (2000), the story of a progenitor of the Goryeo dynasty (918–1392). Thanks to the drama's extraordinary popularity (its highest viewer rate was 60.2 percent),[9] the number of inward tourists increased from 420,000 in 1999 to 2.06 million in 2000, and more than 2.4 million in 2001.[10] The city government renovated the aged set in 2008 and made it into a Chosun dynasty milieu by extending its size and adding grandiosity to its architecture. The remodeling gave the city prominence as a popular drama-filming site: more than thirty television dramas and twelve films were shot in Munkyung as of 2012. No longer a neglected mining town, one of its major revenue sources is now a media-related one. Its success has demonstrated the promise of drama sponsorship and drama set–oriented tourism. Ownership of a drama set remains with the city rather than the producer. When well-managed and advertised, a set can be a potential tourist attraction and give a boost to the local economy.

Another successful model is Wando County, a small and remote fishing village that invested $8 million[11] in 2004 to build a set for the drama *Emperor of the Sea* (*Haeshin* 2004). *Emperor of the Sea* tells the story of a historical figure, Jang Bogo, who virtually dominated the sea trade from Tang China to Japan during the ninth century. As the drama's viewer ratings exceeded 30 percent on average, the so-called *Haeshin set* hit the jackpot. Wando enjoyed an increase in tourist numbers of 20 million and earned around $10 million from admission fees to the set in 2005 alone. According to data Wando County released in 2008, the total number of tourists reached 50 million and the direct and indirect economic impacts of the drama sets exceeded $160 million.[12] The county governor, first elected in 2002, was easily reelected in 2006 and 2010 thanks to the tourism boom brought about by drama sponsorship. A local official said in an interview, "In Wando, it is said that no election is needed since the governor is virtually fixed."[13] The political assets the county governor achieved through drama sponsorship have been extended to the intercounty level where Wando County received several "local autonomy awards" (*hanguk jibangjachi gyeongyeong daesang*), which symbolize the extent to which the county has risen to be a prominent player among many other local municipalities.

How exactly have drama sets become a tourism booster? Their power lies in their association with spectacle. Historical dramas not only utilize drama sets as filming venues but also give context to them in spectacular ways with historical costumes, props, ceremonies and rituals, and battle scenes. *The Legends of Four Gods* (*Taewangsasingi* 2007), *Jumong* (*Jumong* 2006), and *King Sejong the Great* (*Daewang Sejong* 2008) illustrate the spectacular nature of the built environment of ancient dynasties; in their imaginative reconstruction of the period, they not only show its architectural style but also the ways the ruling kingdom consolidated its power through physical entities. The splendors of the imperial palaces are visual representations of nation-building processes and political dynamics. The physical drama sets evince the spectacular events depicted in its stories, evoking memories from dramas in the visitors, thereby acting as spice to attract tourists. To remind people of scenes from the drama, giant-sized panels showing stills from the show are placed at multiple points, together with props and costumes. Thus, visitors can extend the experience of watching the drama at a physical site. A drama set is an experimental theme park based on the spectacles conveyed by historical drama.

Sets also satisfy people's curiosity about television production. Although they are not open to the public during the actual shooting period, their operators make various efforts to recreate the process of filming for visitors. Photos taken on location during the actual shooting of the film are displayed, with notices informing people what types of scenes were shot at which points and from what perspectives. Candid pictures of actors waiting their turn to go on set are shown, too. For drama and celebrity fans, as the consumption section will indicate, a set is not only a space in which filming is done but also a place where their special memories are developed. Like religious monuments, the drama sets attract pilgrims. Putting premodern architectural styles, fashions, and clothing on show in vivid ways, they also serve as history lessons. Although they are artificially created, the way they function similarly to perfectly restored historical heritage sites appeals to certain tourists, including students.

## City Placement

A growing area of drama sponsorship is *destination placement*, that is, the strategic exposure of real places and landscapes from sponsoring cities in movies or television shows in exchange for funding.[14] Destination placement has increasingly been seen in recent years as an attractive marketing vehicle that raises awareness of the destination, enhances its image, and results in a significant increase in tourist numbers. As Korean television dramas are eager to use city places and landscapes for story development, destination placement is heavily practiced by Korean and East Asian cities. I call these practices *city placement* because not only do their places and landscapes appear in dramas but the name of the sponsored city is specifically stated in the credits at the end of each episode.

The history of city placement in Korean television dramas follows two lines of development inside and outside the Korean drama industry. First, Korean television dramas began to use places and landscapes not merely as backgrounds but as driving forces of narrative development. Prime-time television dramas in the 2000s became distinguished from daily and weekly dramas (that mainly dealt with relationships and conflicts within families, and thus were mostly filmed in indoor sets representing people's homes) by actively displaying domestic and overseas cities. In 2004, the drama *Lovers in Paris* popularized the phenomenon of the spatial development of stories. In this drama, the two main characters meet in Paris during the early episodes and later develop a friendship and love back in Seoul. The drama's skillful exploitation of the romantic and exotic places and landscapes of Paris, which were blended with the events and characters, generated a national sensation. The "Paris stories," however, are confined to the first few episodes; the remaining ones are based in Seoul. The spatial movement of characters and story lines from Paris to Seoul was inevitable due to funding constraints and the filming schedule. Despite the limited display of Paris, however, the series confirmed that "showing" matters as much as "telling," and like commodities, places (cities) could be a subject of conspicuous consumption placed in dramas. After the great success of *Lovers in Paris*, spatially oriented story development, particularly stories with elements of back-and-forth between Seoul and other places, became a trend in prime-time Korean television drama, as featured in, among many others *Only You* in Vicenza, Italy; *Lovers in Prague* (*Peurahaui Yeonin* 2005) in Prague; *HIT* (*Hiteu* 2007) in Hong Kong; *Que Sera, Sera* (*Keserasera* 2007) in Singapore; *On Air* in Taipei; *IRIS* in Budapest and in Akita, Japan. Given the practice of live filming (see chapter 1), however, overseas cities have limited spontaneous accessibility; Korean drama producers have therefore turned to domestic cities that are close to home but boast distinctive scenery that Seoul can never offer.

Second, Korean cities have experienced *creation of place* driven by television dramas. In the aftermath of the unexpected popularity of the drama *Winter Sonata*, which ignited the Korean Wave in Japan, the city of Chuncheon, a major filming site for the drama, became a tourist destination for both domestic and overseas viewers. The successful dissemination of *Winter Sonata* throughout East Asia brought 267,691 foreign tourists to the city in 2004; 295,673 in 2005; and 228,869 in 2006 (Korea Tourism Organization 2006). Compared to 28,500 in 2002 and 70,809 in 2003, these numbers indicate an approximately ninefold increase. The drama generated a great ripple effect in Chuncheon, with a revitalized local economy and heightened recognition status. The case of *Winter Sonata*, however, was not one of city placement; the drama's director intentionally chose the lyrical landscapes of winter in Chuncheon as the drama's controlling image. The accidental popularity of the drama and the city, however, taught both drama producers and Korean cities about the benefits of preplanned and refined marketing strategies of city placement.

The combination of these two types of development—place as a driver of narrative and the drama-induced creation of place—triggered the rampant practice of city placement, whereby municipalities deliver cash grants to drama producers in return for opportunities to display their attractions and scenery on television. During the period from 2003 to 2013, more than thirty Korean cities and counties practiced city placement. Of these, seven did it more than twice, a measure of how desperate local authorities are to promote themselves. Because cash sponsorship (usually less than $1 million) is less expensive than the construction of huge outdoor sets (which can easily cost more than $5 million), and because the showing of actual (rather than virtual) places within localities is a more advantageous way of promoting them, the practice of city placement has flourished. Recently, other East Asian local governments have engaged in promoting their own areas through Korean television dramas, aggressively recruiting Korean drama producers and supporting drama filming in their region. In return for local scenery and landmark sites being shown in several episodes, Akita Prefecture in Japan sponsored the production of the Korean drama *IRIS* and Tottori Prefecture supported *Athena: Goddess of War*. Like Korean regional cities, Akita and Tottori Prefectures have suffered underdevelopment and economic hardship.[15] Thanks to drama-channeled place marketing, they each enjoyed an immediate surge in their number of visitors, both from Japan and other parts of East Asia, their names became well known, and their local economies were boosted. Having witnessed the effects of showcasing these pioneers, other Japanese cities followed suit: Okinawa was featured in *Scent of Women* (*Yeoinui Hyanggi* 2011), *Shark* (*Sangeo* 2013), and *It's Okay, That's Love*; Osaka in *The Fugitive: Plan B* (*Domangja Peullaen Bi* 2010); Hokkaido in *Love Rain*; Amori in *The Innocent Man*; and Onimichi (Hiroshima Prefecture) in *Sign*. Tochigi Prefecture sponsored the drama *City Conquest* (*Dosi Jeongbeol*), which was partially filmed in 2013, but the production was canceled because it was unable to win a network channel in Korea.

City placement indicates the shift in direction from place seeking to (spatial) sponsor seeking, that is, from searching for places that harmonize with drama stories to searching for sponsor cities that can cover part of the production cost in exchange for using their sights as backgrounds in the drama. The terms of the contracts between producers and cities define the ways a city or area is depicted in dramas. For instance, when the city of Boryeong sponsored the drama *War of Money* (*Jjeonui Jeonjaeng* 2007), the specific contract terms included showing textual notices of Boryeong's production sponsorship in all sixteen episodes of the drama; the creation of a minimum of three episodes specifically relating to Boryeong; the shooting of scenes involving the main characters in Boryeong; a statement of Boryeong's sponsorship on the official website, drama posters, and recordings of the original sound track; introduction of Boryeong's filming locations in the promotional materials for the series; and highlighting Boryeong's local specialties and heritage in the drama.[16] In some cases, characters directly mention the urban sponsors in scenes from the drama. For example, *Rooftop Princess* includes a scene in which characters working at a home-shopping company discuss launching a tourism product and, in the process, characters actually speak about Jian County, one of the sponsors. In the story, characters make a field investigation to develop detailed product schemes and their movements follow the conventional tour routes of the area, including Mai Mountain specifically.[17] Moreover, the relationship between the main characters develops substantially during the pilot site survey, rendering the places featured not merely backgrounds but meaningful and memorable settings.

The contract-based insertion of urban (or rural) spaces in television dramas is very reminiscent of product placement. As in PPL, city sponsorship is not necessarily predetermined but can be organized even in the middle of a series airing. The critical question is how to match up the places that have abruptly decided to buy themselves some promotion with the story lines that are already underway. Advertising places through television dramas is facilitated by flexible and spatially organized narrative development. Dialogues, incidents, and even story lines are adjustable—and indeed need to be adjusted to show particular places to viewers. Here it is worth returning to the example of *Shining Inheritance* that was briefly mentioned in the beginning of this chapter. The primary background of the drama is Seoul; thus, most scenes unfold and were filmed in Seoul.[18] Yet in episode 21, the four main characters suddenly go off on a business trip to Donghae. *Donghae* is a homonym; it can mean both the east coast and an urban area located on the east coast, Donghae City. In the story, the restaurant company for which three of the four main characters work puts in a bid to provide catering for an East Sea cruise. But these sudden and temporary spatial movements by characters and the corresponding shifts in background were designed to accommodate a late-joining sponsor, Donghae City, within the plot.[19] Under the sponsorship contract, some episodes had to be devoted to strategically displaying the city's key attractions. Episodes 21 and 22 are the ones in question. The cruise ship featured in episode 21 is actually operated by the city; the catering bid is supposed to take place on the cruise and therefore multiple venues on board the cruise ship are naturally featured in the drama. Other parts of the action are intentionally tailored to highlight other key sites in the city. Eun-sung (played by Han Hyo-ju) and Hwan (played by Lee Seung-ki) already have a crush on one another when episode 21 begins, but they are not in a relationship yet. They have prepared the documents for the catering bid together and are going on the business trip to Donghae. By good fortune, they arrive at their destination early. With plenty of time to spare, they explore the beach; the radiantly happy scenes in which the two take off their shoes, run along the sand, and have an animated conversation are inserted to show off Donghae's beautiful shoreline.

Later on, a third character, Seung-mi, a stepsister of Eun-sung who also loves Hwan, suddenly appears. Although a company manager has sent her to deliver revised documents for the bid, she is mainly concerned that Eun-sung and Hwan are spending time together. A fourth character, Jun-se, who is fond of Eun-sung, also joins the group, ostensibly to work on the catering bid with them. The peculiar emotional tensions generated by the foursome are the means by which the drama incorporates city sponsorship into the basic plot. Jun-se has booked campervans for the four of them, so they happen to spend one night at a campsite. The unexpected stay in campervans and the equally abruptly arranged seafood barbeque at dinnertime (during which the four emotionally push and pull one another) were designed to feature Mangsang Auto Camping Resort in Donghae City. The next morning, Eun-sung gets up early, just as dawn is breaking. She leaves the campervan, and walks away from the campsite. Standing at the lookout post near a lighthouse (Mukho Lighthouse in Donghae), she gazes at the scenery below. She then puts on a heart necklace that Hwan had left in her house when he stumbled in completely drunk. At that moment, Hwan appears from below. Seeing him, Eun-sung runs toward the rolling bridge described in the chapter introduction. The suspension bridge on which they kiss is actually Cullungdari near the Mukho Lighthouse in Donghae.

Here, I should provide some explanation of kiss scenes. A kiss scene in Korean drama is *the* most critical moment as far as both story development and audience expectations are concerned. Modern Korean dramas, particularly those produced in the 2000s, focus on the emotional vicissitudes of four leading characters (two male and two female) who form a love rectangle. One of the formulas is that the top lead couple go through ups and downs (throughout many episodes) caused by such things as class barriers, family opposition, continuous interruption by the two subleads, crossing one another, or mutual misunderstanding, until they finally recognize each other's love at the end of the series. A kiss scene is the culmination of this type of roller coaster storytelling, the dramatic climax that settles the fluctuations in the love plot for the time being.[20] It is important to note that a kiss scene in Korean drama demonstrates much more than physical affection; rather, it is a peak romantic moment set against a beautiful background, with lyrical music, the couple staring into each other's eyes, and a passionate confession of love. Since Korean dramas rarely contain obvious sex scenes, the role of a kiss scene is not to show desire in action, but to make the audience feel an echo of the characters' emotions.

By setting such a critical moment close to Mukho Lighthouse and Chullungdari, *Shining Inheritance* did a more than wonderful job for its sponsor, Donghae City. How many people even knew about Chullungdari before this drama was screened? As for Donghae residents who recognized the places, had they ever attached any meaning to them before the kiss scene? The thrill and exhilaration of the kiss scene filmed around these two locations not only made a swift and dramatic impression on viewers but also invested the places with special meaning. They were forever after associated with the romantic kiss and pounding hearts. After the airing, these newly created associations began to be circulated through the media, the Internet (e.g., blog posts, online communities, and news postings on portal sites), and tourism products. Now people call Cullungdari "the place where Han Hyo-ju and Lee Seung-ki kissed," and the area around Chullungdari and Mukho Lighthouse has emerged as an iconic destination for romantic trips. This case demonstrates how affective representation of space in television dramas generates, adds to, or modifies the meanings and images connected with the space, and communicates these newly created meanings to viewers. I argue that affective values generated by drama elements (plots, characters, and their emotional flows) "create" a place charged with particular emotions and meanings.

Affective representation and place making are not always successful in city placement, however. In many cases, the sponsors (municipalities) and producers (mostly writers) experience conflicts and struggles. The conflicts come from different perspectives on landscape. Vanessa Mathews (2010) discusses the distinction between "landscape as space," which relates to nonspecific settings, and "landscape as place," which relates to site-specific settings. In the former, emphasis is on the interaction between characters; in the latter, the film's narrative determines the filming locations. Sponsor cities always expect "landscape as place": they want their landmarks strategically displayed. Korean television dramas that value characters' emotional flows tend to focus on interactions between them. In the case of *Dream High*, sponsored by the city of Goyang, the sponsor explicitly complained that the episodes based in the city focused more on the characters than on the places that were supposed to be highlighted.[21] That is to say, *Dream High* did not do for Goyang the job that *Shining Inheritance* did for Donghae.

To minimize such conflicts, city placement became more strategic in the late 2000s; locations are now prearranged with a view to anticipated tourism product development. The producer of the hit drama *Bread, Love, and Dreams* worked closely with its sponsor, Northern Chungchung Province, and a tourism agency in Osaka to strategically develop drama-derived tourism products. During the planning stage of the drama, the producer, the sponsor, and the tourism agency invited a group of Japanese women to Northern Chungchung Province, showed them several locations, and asked them to identify the places they preferred. Based on this pilot survey, the producer and sponsor city carefully selected places and landscapes in advance, and strategically showed them off in the drama. Needless to say, the production firm and the Osaka-based tourism agency cooperated again to launch drama tourism products featuring *Bread, Love, and Dreams* after its airing.

## Drama Tourism and Affective Place

Drama locations attract a wide range of people. Given the mass appeal of television dramas, the number of drama-inspired tourists is extraordinary, and the recent period since 2004 has witnessed drama tourism emerging as a new and critical mode of exploring Korea. One notable aspect of this phenomenon is the rise of regional areas previously overshadowed, except for some traditional tourist sites, by the glitzy attractions of Seoul. Korean television dramas have enabled both domestic and overseas tourists to discover hidden corners of Korea. This section examines how exactly people consume drama locations. Consumption needs to be analyzed first because, as I will later show, it is the critical element in the promotion of drama sites. What interested me ethnographically at the sites where dramas were filmed was the hierarchy among tourists. Different groups of people have different levels of motivation and engagement with the drama locations. I will use this tourist hierarchy as an analytical tool to examine consumption practices.

The first level, the so-called group tourists, consists of those whose visits are arranged by tourism agencies. An array of buses carrying from thirty to two hundred group tourists to drama locations was the most common sight I witnessed during my fieldwork. This category includes both domestic and overseas, and both male and female, tourists—the majority are members of Japanese informal social groups or village-unit Chinese travelers. Most of them are aware that the places they are visiting are associated with television dramas, but their interests remain vague. For instance, in reply to my question as to why they were traveling to drama locations, one Chinese informant at the Jeju location for *All In* remarked: "Korean dramas have raised my general interest in South Korea. But my visit to this place is organized by an agency like many others."[22] Although television dramas advertise Korean cities to a broad range of viewers both inside and outside the country, in practice, local players such as travel agencies and bus operators play a vital role in actually bringing tourists to the places they know from the drama series.

Group tourists' movements are highly regulated by travel agencies and travel guides, so their visits are characterized as "disciplined rituals" (Edensor 2000, 334). At the drama sets, they stick to the designated routes and present a collective spectatorial gaze. Tour guides provide incessant explanations about the sets—what scenes from the drama were filmed at which points, for example. Letting tourists know about the familiar scenes in dramas is, thus, one of the main tasks of on-site guides. The tour leaders also designate certain key picture points, and the tourists practice the disciplined ritual of taking photographs with specified backgrounds. The photograph taking lasts for a short time, during which each visitor (individually or in groups of two or three) repeats the same rituals. In such collective practices, there is little room for moments of immersion in the place. After the formal activity of picture taking, most tour participants lose interest. Yet there is some room for agency. On some sets for historical dramas, traditional Korean costumes and life-size cardboard photos of the main characters are provided. Wearing the costumes, some of the tourists have their photos taken with the character cutouts, assuming unconventional, dramatic poses. A few of them even engage in reenactment of the relevant scenes from the show, taking their cue from the still pictures displayed around. Albeit brief and limited, these moments with the costumes certainly transcend regimented rituals, generating some drama-associated feelings. Overall, however, group tourists' more directed consumption of drama sites is evidence of their lower degree of fandom as far as the dramas are concerned.

Disappointment is also a significant part of drama tourism, particularly among group tourists. Many of those who visited the set for *The Legends of Four Gods* expressed complaints: "The set does not look as spectacular as in the drama. I was a bit disillusioned by the much smaller size and the crude back view. We found that the elaborate facade is merely a wooden wall with nothing at all behind it."[23] The tour guides were busy explaining why the set looks small (it is 70 percent of actual size, because the screen enlarges objects). Without the characters, computer graphics, and audio, the physical sets are stripped of most of their aura. Similar levels of disenchantment are also felt with city placements. On a day in 2011 marred by severe sandstorms, I met a couple of young female tourists who were visiting Cheongju to explore the film locations of *Bread, Love, and Dreams* and *Cain and Abel* (*Kaingwa Abel* 2009). Both talked about being disappointed by the undramatic landscape they actually encountered there: "Without this sign (that notifies people that it was used as a film location), we wouldn't even be able to recognize this building (which featured as the bakery, the main backdrop for the drama). . . . It certainly isn't all because of the weather. . . . And the neighborhood is very different from what we saw in the dramas."[24] The site is decontextualized from the surrounding localities. It only functions as "produced" background; that is, it takes on a particular meaning only within the context of the drama. When the stories and characters are not present, the drama location is merely part of the ordinary view.

The second category comprises drama-inspired tourists (both domestic and from overseas), in large and small groups. The drama enthusiasts are mostly repetitive watchers of particular dramas and returning visitors to their shooting locations. The intensiveness and frequency of drama location tours mean that most of them have in-depth information about the particular scenes that were shot in particular locations and about the locations themselves. As their decisions about places they want to visit are largely motivated by the dramas they find so compelling, their behaviors differ from conventional tourists' spectatorial sightseeing. Reconstruction of scenes from the drama is one. *The 1st Shop of Coffee Prince* (aka *Coffee Prince*, [*Keopipeurinseu Ilhojeom*], 2007) is a drama series depicting a romance between a tomboyish woman (Eun-chan), who dresses like a man to get work, and a young food empire mogul (Han-kyul). Since the drama's astonishing success in Korea and overseas, the coffee shop that was used as the main background for the drama has become a tourist hot spot. Still operating as a coffee shop and with the same name as the title of the series, the film location keeps much of the setting of the drama, including the waffle vendor, the picture that Eun-chan drew on the glass wall, and the original soundtrack. I met a small group of Japanese tourists, one of whom informed me: "I have watched *Coffee Prince* more than twenty times and have visited Seoul eight times. Watching the drama, I really miss my younger days. And visiting here (the café) makes me feel young. I appreciate this place still looks just as it did in the drama. Looking at the old couple making coffee (the current store owners), I feel that is what Eun-chan and Han-kyul would be like if they had aged in the drama."[25] To drama fans, the café is not a just a commercial space; it is a place where the drama is still going on, evoking memories of particular moments and emotions. The way the informant described the current storeowners as embodying the distant future of the couple in the drama suggests that audience-tourists do not simply receive an image of a place that figured in the drama; rather, they reconstruct it through personalized interpretation and their imaginations. Their consumption of the location is, therefore, subjective and emotional.

Reenactment is a critical practice among drama-driven tourists. *My Love from the Star* garnered phenomenal attention in China in 2015 (see ch.1 for details) and the popularity of the series sparked an unexpected craze for chicken and beer in China, as the lead characters often had *chimek* (a combination of *chi*, short for chicken, and *mek* for *mekju*, meaning beer) in the drama.[26] Things that are done or seen on screen get played out in real life—this applies not only to food but also to tourist sites. Incheon, whose locations were used as backgrounds for the television show, has become a must-see place for Chinese tourists. One of the most memorable moments in the series is the scene in which Do Min-joon (the male lead acted by Kim Soo-hyun) uses his supernatural powers to stop Song-yi's car from falling over the cliff.

Someone puts Song-yi (the female lead performed by Jun Ji-hyun) in danger, placing her in a car whose brakes have been cut. Awakening in the moving car as it races toward a cliff, Song-yi yells for Min-joon to save her. He sharpens his hearing and listens intently; figuring out her location, he materializes out of thin air and drops in front of the car, slamming his hands down on its hood and bracing all his weight against it to stop it from going any further. The car tilts up on its front wheels, then crashes back down in a dead halt. Snow falls, a storm brews, and both Song-yi and Min-joon gather their breaths. Song-yi raises her head slowly, and sees him there in front of her.[27]

This scene mirrors the moment when Min-joon first landed on Earth four hundred years previously (during the Chosun dynasty) and saved Ihwa. As the story suggests that Song-yi might be the reincarnation of Ihwa, the cliff is where Min-joon has saved Song-yi's life twice. The two scenes were filmed in Seoksan, an abandoned rocky mountain site, once a quarry, located in Songdo, Incheon. Grasping the fact that the useless site had now been turned into a valuable commodity as a result of their sponsorship of the drama, the municipality installed the same red car near the cliff, so that drama tourists can reenact the car-stopping scene. Renaming the site "Love Cliff," the city of Incheon also arranged an activity around Song-yi's *binyeo*, a traditional Korean hairpin that Ihwa passed to Min-joon at the moment she was killed. Tourists are supposed to hang a mass-produced *binyeo* on a fence erected for the purpose after writing their wishes on a red star. This so-called storytelling tourism product, designed by the sponsor city, has actually attracted thousands of Chinese tourists. Despite the embarrassingly undramatic present condition of the stony mountain, drama tourists become involved with the location, because what they want is neither the authentic experience nor the actual local context. Posing in the same posture that Min-joon adopted to stop the car, the drama tourists imitate his supernatural power. Since it is used as a critical storytelling tool in the drama, the *binyeo* also helps drama fans to materialize their personalized reconstructions. "Hanging up the 'love binyeo,' I could feel the sympathetic love of Ihwa, who died in Min-joon's place."[28] The drama enthusiasts want a personal embodiment of the drama's scenes, practicing rituals of reenactment that are subjective and motivational rather than disciplined. The practice of reenactment connects the fans, the memorable scenes from the drama, and the shooting location. Through bodily enactment, consumption of the drama site becomes haptic and corporeal, and the bleak stony cliff turns into an affective site filled with special emotion.

The last category of visitors, celebrity fans, consists mainly of Japanese women who are members of Hallyu star fandom.[29] Celebrity fans go to any place associated with their beloved stars and tend not to focus on particular drama locations. Yet holding celebrity fan meetings at sites where dramas were filmed or that are scheduled to be used for filming was once a surefire means of publicizing both dramas and municipalities. Star agencies, production firms, municipalities, and Japanese travel agencies worked together to bring in those who wanted to attend the meetings and who would pay for the privilege.[30] Song Seung-heon, who starred in *East of Eden*, had a fan meeting in 2008 at the Hapcheon Movie Theme Park, a major filming venue

for the drama. Before the meeting, a press conference about the drama series also took place on the set, before an audience of hundreds of Japanese
fans. The translator was able to evoke the atmosphere of the convention:
"The fans wanted to get 'the scent of the star.' Most of them sat on the stairs
where Song had been in the drama, posing in the same posture as he did.
Some of them even smelled the scent of the stair railings. They hoped to
have 'their own special secrets' by getting to know what the star did while
on the set."[31] Bae Yong-iun, a star who achieved honored status in Japan and
was called "Yon-sama," had his fan meeting before the shooting of *The Legends of Four Gods* on a site in Jeju that was planned to be used as a set. The
account of a provincial civil servant who observed the event is remarkable:
"The site on which set construction was planned was just somewhere on
the middle of the mountain with no sign of the scheduled drama. But the
Japanese fans seemed to be already acquainted with the place. According to
the translator, many of them remarked, 'I am just happy to be in the same
place where Yonsama will work. Inhaling the same air as Bae will refresh
me enough.'"[32]

"Celebrity involvement," defined as the tendency to develop a heightened
affection and attachment to a celebrity (Lee, Scott and Kim 2008, 809), is
the critical reason members of the fan community of Hallyu stars decide to
visit particular places. As celebrity involvement is often tantamount to worship, visiting a destination associated with the adored star can be perceived
as a pilgrimage. That is to say that any places associated with the star are
meaningful to fans and visiting them is a way for fans to build stronger empathy with him or her. Yet what differentiates tours undertaken by fans of
Hallyu stars from conventional pilgrimages is that they are not only about
following in the footsteps of their favorite performers but also about appreciating the characters that the stars played in a particular drama. The
filming sites of *Winter Sonata* and *All In* have life-size cardboard stand-ups
of the two main characters in each drama, but with the female characters'
faces cut out. Female fan-tourists are usually eager to poke their faces through
the cutout hole, thus momentarily becoming the female character. Taking the
female role in this way is both a form of reenactment of scenes from the
drama and a way of appreciating its characters. The celebrity fans take on
their personalities and try to conjure up what they must have felt and experienced in particular scenes. In drama-driven Hallyu, star empathy is pretty

much equated with character empathy, and gatherings of fans materialize this character appreciation in locations where the drama took place.

Although they do it to different degrees and in a variety of forms, drama location visitors all engage in the affective consumption of the places shown in dramas. By "affective consumption" of place, I mean the ways drama fans develop emotional and empathetic involvement with sites above and beyond their superficial consumption of them as spectacle or scenery. Television dramas mediate places and visitors, thus the place is not an entirely strange space as far as the tourist is concerned. A site featured in a drama is at least "somewhere I watched on TV" or an affective place to which the audience-tourist is personally bonded (Kim 2012). The ways visitors develop this emotional involvement with drama locations include giving them personal meanings, reenacting drama scenes, reconstructing the presentation of the drama, and developing empathy with the character through the place—even disappointment can create emotional involvement, too.

## Publicizing Drama Locations

Although being featured in television dramas is the primary way of advertising urban and rural places, sponsor cities also carry out their own various promotional efforts. In the secondary circuit of promotion, the most critical factor in publicity for places associated with dramas is, ironically, the presence of early-coming tourists. The conventional tactic when releasing press promotion of a drama site is to mention the number of drama tourists who have already visited and how they behaved while they were there. Some of the titles of press releases by Incheon advertising the drama locations for *My Love from the Star* have included "'We Missed the Locations of *My Love from the Star*,' 6,000 Chinese Tourists Visited Incheon,"[33] "You from China Who Follow *My Love from the Star*,"[34] "6,000 Chinese Landed in Incheon to Visit the Places in *My Love from the Star* and Enjoy a *Chimek* Party,"[35] and "Like the Heroes of *My Love from the Star*, 4,500 *Youkers* (Chinese Tourists) Enjoyed a *Chimek* Party in Incheon."[36] The content of each release reports in detail the ways the Chinese tourists reenacted the red car–stopping scene and enjoyed *chimek*. Both the presence and number of foreign tourists grab media attention and advertise the locality. Most civil officials I interviewed agreed: "The simple fact that thousands (or even just hundreds) of Japanese or Chinese tourists visit the drama location *does* work to enhance the municipalities' public profile. Even if we cannot calculate the exact economic impacts, letting people know about our (local) municipalities via television dramas or press reports is worth the sponsorship."[37]

Yet drama-driven tourists do not always wait until after the airing of a series to pay a visit. It can happen even before the production is conducted as a result of one-off activities such as film premiers and festivals. Since 2000, Korean drama producers have customarily held a production press conference as a promotional effort to advertise their dramas to the public and media. Production press conferences often proceed with a roughly fifteen-minute trailer for a drama and interviews with the producers, directors, and actors. Some cities host this critical media event in the hope that the name of the sponsor city will be revealed in media reports. A comment from an interview I had with a provincial official is particularly notable: "When we planned to build a drama set, there was enormous opposition from environmental and civic groups because constructing the set would damage the ecologically valuable assets in the planned site. Promoting drama sponsorship was a daunting task against such local opposition. But a media event in the shape of a production report conference held on the planned site reversed the situation overnight. Thousands of media reports poured in not only introducing the drama but also highlighting our province and our sponsorship. The one-day media event not only publicized our province but enhanced local patriotism to mute the opposing voices."[38]

Due to the snowball effect whereby the initial publicity attracts more visitors, all three categories of drama tourists matter to the sponsor cities. To attract group tourists, cities rely heavily on local travel agencies, lobbying them to include places depicted in dramas on major tour routes. As the on-site manager of a drama set said in an interview: "Our major job is lobbying the tour bus and tour taxi companies that virtually dominate the tourism industry in this area. Because the tourists that these tour companies carry daily outnumber independent visitors, our interests lie in forging connections with these agencies."[39] Although television dramas advertise Korean cities to a broad stratum of viewers both inside and outside of Korea, in practice, local players do matter in actually bringing them to the places seen on the screen. Small groups of viewers, organized mainly by individuals sharing their drama-watching experiences through online fan sites, compose the majority of drama tourists. After visits to filming sites, some of the passionate ones go back to the Web and post detailed information about the sites (photos, directions, and tips), furthering discussions about the drama and the site-visiting experience.[40] Recognizing these groups of active fans, or scattered pioneers, and the marketability of drama tourism (Korea Tourism Organization 2011), both Japanese and Korean tourism agencies have developed more organized trips to drama sites in association with "star fan meetings." In 2006 alone, Japan boasted two hundred fifty organized tours to the filming sites of Korean dramas.[41] Most of those were three- or four-day intensive trips to sites connected with one particular Korean drama. One of the most common ways to draw loyal celebrity fans is, as discussed above, to host a fan meeting with a Hallyu star in association with Korean entertainment agencies and Japanese tourism agencies. Hallyu star fan meetings often draw particular media attention because the celebrities are likely to create a sensation.

Publicity methods reveal the mechanism for selling televised places. To a superficial understanding, the primary marker of place is a television drama that creates emotional connections between viewers, the drama, and the location. The drama's power lies in turning a merely physical space into a place filled with emotion, imagination, and fantasy through the representation of stories, characters, and cinematic scenes. This emotion-laden place attracts prospective tourists by evoking interest, enchantment, and yearning. At a deeper level, however, the essential advertiser of a place associated with a drama is the audience that has reacted to the affective values that a drama generated there. This is evidenced by the fact that the municipalities' primary promotional asset is the presence of drama tourists itself. The affective resonance that commercial entertainment confers on space dramatically advertises cities on the one hand; on the other hand, the actual selling process capitalizes on the audience-tourists' consumption of the drama locations, harnessing their emotional engagement with the place.

## When the Tale Fades Away

Cases that involve either drama set construction or city placement have demonstrated that the production and consumption of popular culture are closely connected to the production, marketing, and consumption of place. The production of television dramas is associated with the production of

place, while, at the same time, the consumption of television dramas facilitates the consumption of the televised space. In such cases, the relations
between culture and space go far beyond the mere depiction of space in culture or the adoption of cultural images in spatial (re)organization. Culture
and space intersect to produce each other and promote each other's consumption. In terms of the economic effects of advertising, the synergistic
association between television dramas and cities is obvious inasmuch as each
capitalizes on the other's attributes. The production of television dramas
taps the space, place, and funding that the cities provide, so that drama production and urban production take place together; television dramas, likewise,
extend, expedite, and dramatize the marketing of cities. By these means,
culture and cities can promote each other's consumption in the short term.

The marriage, however, does not always go smoothly. Conflicts arise
because of the differences in the nature of operation and management between popular culture and urban space. Drama-mediated city promotion
seeks to capitalize on the broad and fast reach of popular culture. As discussed in chapter 1, however, nobody knows whether a drama series will be
a hit or not. Sponsorship from cities comes before or during the airing of a
drama series; the outcomes of the investment, and thus the fortunes of cities, rely on the unpredictable popularity of television dramas. City promotion via television drama can, therefore, have only limited stability. If the
viewer ratings of a drama remain low, the promotional efforts of a sponsor
city are muted. Youngyang County spent $300,000 on sponsorship for the
drama *The Return of Iljimae* (*Doraon Iljimae* 2008), but the drama finished
earlier than scheduled due to low viewer ratings and the county never enjoyed the publicity it had paid for.[42] Pocheon City and Goyang City invested
$100,000 and $1 million, respectively, but did not gain the amount of publicity they expected. Not a few local officials have remarked: "Sponsoring drama
is like gambling. Although drama producers stake their fate on promising
directors, writers, and star actors, these big names do not guarantee publicity for us. It is a risky venture."[43] This unpredictability, however, appears to
boost speculative expectations among sponsor cities, in the same ways that
drama producers gamble on the uncertainty of a drama series. The growing
number of cases of drama sponsorship by cities proves that municipalities are
by no means averse to speculative ventures.

Even successful dramas offer limited sustainability to sponsoring cities.
Television dramas move swiftly through fads and fashions, so the consump-

tion of television dramas is inherently short-lived. The immediacy of television drama has, nevertheless, a lingering effect on physical spaces, that is, on drama sets and sponsoring cities. Apart from a few sets that are continuously reused in the production of several dramas, most witness a few years of boom followed by a dramatic drop in tourist numbers and effects on the local economy. The *Seodongyo set*, in which Buyeo County invested $6 million for the drama *Seodongyo* (2005), received 200,000 visitors in 2006, its first year of opening, but had only 87,0000 in 2007, 49,000 in 2008, and 27,000 in 2009. Within just three years, the number of tourists had fallen by 90 percent. On the brink of demolition after five years of deficit, the run-down set only survived thanks to massive renovation in 2012 and 2015.[44] Naju City's Samhanji Theme Park, in which the megahit drama *Jumong* was filmed, likewise boasted 510,000 tourists in 2006, but confronted dramatically dropping numbers of tourists and continuously rising management costs. After years of deficit operation, the municipality resigned the operation of the set to a private entity.

The most striking example is Jeju's gigantic set for *The Legends of Four Gods*. In 2005, every municipality's eyes were on Jeju because it was officially chosen as a major filming venue for *The Legends*. Combining the best talent in the industry—director Kim Jong-hak, writer Song Ji-na, and then top Hallyu star Bae Yong-jun—the series was nicknamed "Lotto in the drama industry" even before its airing. Jeju Province allocated 51.46 acres of publicly owned land for set construction and spent a total of $50 million on the series.[45] This astonishing investment was part of a bigger plan to create a media theme park consisting of the set, condos, and museums, which would attract 2 million tourists a year to Jeju. Obviously, it was the drama production company that came up with the idea for the construction of a theme park under the local development plan. With the full support of the provincial government, the production firm was able to buy the land at a reduced price[46] and was designated as a codeveloper of the media theme park. The administrative procedures that any developer was supposed to go through, including an environmental impact evaluation, were waived thanks to the provincial government's cooperation. After six years of operation after 2007, the set was demolished in 2012. Local people say that the set in which such an enormous amount had been invested was forcibly removed because the drama producer "dined and dashed." During the sponsor-seeking period, the production firm was determined to paint a rosy picture, but it never took any action after the filming was finished and simply packed up and left Jeju. The provincial government did not even receive back the $250,000 that it lent the producer to assist with habitat preservation and mountain restoration costs incurred during the construction process.[47] Some locals who sold their land with the intention of opening a restaurant and snack bar within the set also ended up not receiving their deposit back from the production firm.

Television dramas enjoy the benefits of instant popularity, which sells advertisements well. Drama producers and broadcasters try to extract maximum profit from their popularity at its short-term peak. Conflicts arise, however, when the instant features of popular culture are transmitted into physical space, because the urban environment and local communities do not work in the same way as volatile television dramas. Drama producers have little concern about the impact of drama-driven tourism; once they have completed their on-location filming, they simply leave. As discussed earlier, since the producers' initial selection of locations has a lot to do with seeking sponsorship, an early-stage decision about a filming site is not based on any consideration of the long-term impacts on the community. While drama producers insist that sponsorship comes as a result of municipalities' own decisions, sponsoring cities have to deal with long-term management and utilization issues when the popularity of a drama fades away.

Drama sponsorship is the very state's projects as local governments dominate decision-making processes without listening to residents' views.[48] As shown earlier, there is a perfect match between the financial needs of drama producers and the political ambitions of elected local leaders. Although local councils are supposed to pass budgets, the city mayor and county governors, as the local budget's primary executors, have absolute power to promote drama sponsorship. This exclusive process often results in a situation in which the authorities confront the opposition of local residents. Suamgol is a disenfranchised neighborhood in Cheongju City. Originally a place for refugees from the Korean War, the neighborhood was transformed into a mural village as local artists began painting on the walls of buildings and alleyways as a means of postponing or canceling upcoming redevelopment schemes. Yet the shantytown unexpectedly won national fame when the drama *Cain and Abel* used it as one of the shooting locations for episodes 9 and 10. While the drama represented the village romantically by featuring it as a background for the sad but sweet love story of the main characters, the actual residents were rather embarrassed by the unwelcome attention they received.

In contrast to the nostalgic images presented in the drama, displacement and poverty were the actual realities of life for the residents, and they felt uncomfortable about the exposure of their shantytown in the mass media. Witnessing the power of the media, and regardless of the local people's willingness or otherwise, the city government promoted Suamgol again by sponsoring another drama, *Bread, Love, and Dreams.* Thanks to the drama's being a megahit, the inflow of tourists increased even further. But the residents' sense of deprivation deepened as a bakery that was used as a set for the series turned out to be the only local actor that made a lot of money. Finally, the residents' complaints surfaced again when the city began building a set for yet another drama series, *Glory Jane (Yeonggwangui Jaein* 2011). Suffering from the constant noise, lighting, parking problems, and the incessant tourists, the residents' collective action expressed their rejection of filming that never brought any tangible economic or social benefit to the neighborhood.

The above story reveals not only the distance between the state and local residents but also the distinction between representation and reality. Representation involves a broad set of meanings that go beyond designation. As a representational medium, television drama is not a neutral space that merely mirrors the "real" but a communication practice through which meanings and power are mediated (Aitken and Zonn 1994; Hopkins 1994; Bollhöfer 2007; Fletchall, Lukinbeal, and McHugh 2012). Representation in drama creates new local images/histories/identities, which are often detached from the actual ones. One striking example showing the distinction between fantasy and reality can be found among the drama-inspired tourists visiting Chuncheon, where *Winter Sonata* was filmed. As drama and celebrity fans with a high degree of emotional attachment to the city enjoy its tranquil landscapes, some of them are moved to wonder about the presence of a U.S. military base in the area, raising questions such as "why are there U.S. military bases in Korea?" and commenting on "how much of a contrast there is between the peaceful landscapes of the drama locations and the military site."[49] Problems arise when such pseudoimages/histories/identities narrow, distort, and erase the actual realities of an area, flattening the richness and complexity of a community. The Suamgol case shows how local residents may be forced to deal with a distorted media representation, the state's arbitrary decisions, and the unwelcome gaze of tourists. Local reality is veiled when places are represented in television dramas, but drama tourism highlights the discrepancy between fantasy and reality, ironically accentuating local problems. In Suamgol, drama tourism turned out to be a conflictual and contradictory process that simultaneously disempowered localities and created new pressures for local autonomy and resistance (Gotham 2005).

Given such challenges that cities might bear after their association with popular culture, it is noteworthy to observe what has happened to those so-called failed cases. If the drama sponsorship does not yield enough of a tax base through the tourism boom, the municipal account might continue to have a deficit. Some politicians failed to be reelected, while some other mayors and governors survived even after the unsuccessful efforts at place selling. Local councils that approved the budget assignment for drama sponsorship seem to remain unaffected and sometimes indifferent. Who had taken and should take responsibility for such "budget-wasting" cases? All the city and county officials I interviewed stated that their municipalities achieved enough publicity through their sponsorship of television drama, "While the media may criticize the fact that our drama set has become useless, we reaped more in publicity effects than we invested. Even short-term publicity is better than nothing."[50] Despite the politicians' insistent claims, how to measure the intangible publicity effects remains questionable. There is a critical gap between the municipal governments' rosy expectations about the possible outcomes of the drama sponsorship and the lack of systemic mechanism to check local governments' use of taxpayers' money. Criticism from residents and the media is often reduced to the individual level, causing local politicians to loose reelection at best.

*Learning effect* is the measure both the local government and society have developed to prevent potential budget wasting through drama sponsorship. Given the cheap, quick, and potentially sensational outcome of drama sponsorship, local states are always tempted to practice it, especially small-sized cities and counties. Recently, one small county I will call county A received a suggestion from a drama production firm to shoot a drama in the area and the producers asked $700,000 in exchange for the potential advertisement effects. After intense discussion about the drama sponsorship among the county government, the local council, and local residents, county A decided not to do it. More exactly, the county budget was not large enough to venture into the sensational project. Surprisingly, county A blamed county B, which had recently sponsored $1 million for a drama series, for its extravagant spending on the drama sponsorship. A county official remarked, "County B's overspending has raised the bar, which has the effect of increasing the overall amount of sponsorship, affecting other municipalities."[51] Learning from other cases not only leads to blind pursuit of the same practice but also provides an opportunity to reflect on their actual financial situation.

Local societies also learn about the failure cases, preventing their own municipalities' attempts to engage in the same practice. Anseong City once actively tried a drama sponsorship with a plan according to which the city delivered $9 million to a drama production firm that would produce a television series featuring Baudeogi, a celebrated artist of the Chosun dynasty and Korea's first official entertainer. Born in Anseong, Baudeogi led the development of Namsadang, a renowned troupe that combines regional traditional arts, such as acrobatics, singing, dancing, and circus performances. Thus, the drama sponsorship was part of the mythification and commodification of Baudeogi in promoting the city and the then–city mayor. While opinions were divided, most local residents and the local council opposed the drama sponsorship, eventually nullifying the government's attempt. Claiming that the spending of taxpayers' money should be cautious, the local council, in particular, asked for a formal process to collect citizens' extensive opinions. One local media criticized the city's effort with the following remark: "The city is trying to raise the supplementary budget of $9 million not for the free school lunch program, not for the unemployed, not for the economically struggling farmers, but for a drama production firm."[52] Local politicians were also critical of the then-mayor's entrepreneurship, stating, "Observing other municipalities that wasted their resources and are left only with deteriorated drama sets, we should have a comprehensive feasibility study by inviting investment experts, cultural experts and residents."[53] Learning from other cases, people in Anseong successfully prevented the possible budget misuse case.

The above two examples in which the attempts to carry out the drama-featured place promotion failed, however, are the only cases, as far as my collected data indicate, to halt the state's project. Despite multiple limitations and controversies, many municipalities still practice drama sponsorship, and the number of cases has actually grown in recent years. Why do Korean cities continue the practice even after witnessing several cases of failure? We have to go back to the instant and speculative nature of television drama to answer this question. As mentioned earlier, the limited capabilities of small regional cities, in addition to the legal restrictions imposed on them, drive them to build the virtual urban rather than to initiate real urban projects. The underlying political reality is that drama sponsorship costs less than building infrastructure. Moreover, when the sponsored drama is a hit, the gains on investment become exponential. Such cheap, quick, and potentially profitable ventures cannot be unattractive to elected local leaders who long to be reelected. It is definitely worth a try so long as local criticism of their spending taxpayers' money is endurable. Regional cities' very marginality leads to such speculative ventures, putting them in an ironic situation in which such speculativeness accentuates or deepens their peripheral status.

The speculative nature of drama production opens a window onto the co-production of story and place. Drama-channeled place marketing is equally speculative. Anticipating both the tangible benefits of boosting the local economy and the intangible benefits of raising awareness and accumulating political capital, many municipalities wager on the slim chance of achieving successful place promotion through the medium of drama. The marketing of place via television dramas tells us a great deal about gambling on something that has limited stability and sustainability. Essentially, drama-featured place marketing entails the commodification of urban or rural space through fabricated representation, artificial images, and pseudohistories. Creating a fantasy costs significantly less than improving reality, but it reduces the public's role in actual reality and drives it toward a superficial level. Korean television dramas insert urban spaces like products, trifling with their material realities and carelessly presuming to redirect urban or rural fortunes. Ironically, superficial representation has the power to draw deep audience engagement by generating affective value in the places featured in the dramas. The commodification of drama-featured urban space capitalizes to the maximum on such consumers' emotional and empathetic spatial attachment. The sponsor cities may neither intend nor expect such an accelerated and sophisticated commodification process, but by attracting consumers' emotional investment in the televised places they certainly try to extract maximum publicity from minimum investment.

# PART II

# The Affective Consumption
# of K-Pop Idols and Places

Part 2 focuses on the K-pop–driven Second Korean Wave (after 2011) and cases of K-pop–mediated urban place promotion. Like part 1, part 2 explores industrial and urban practices combined: chapter 3 examines the production and consumption of K-pop idols; chapters 4 and 5 discuss cases of place branding associated with K-pop. The chapters are linked by an endeavor to show how K-pop–themed urban place branding harnesses the same image-oriented and consumer-driven mechanisms that characterize the ways K-pop is produced and consumed. K-pop idols are a metacommodity created to sell secondary products, including celebrity merchandise and K-pop places. Through their visual allure and intimacy-building skills, idols forge affective relations with their fans/audiences, prompting the latter to consume products and visit places that feature them. Korean municipalities wish to use this affective power to turn sites associated with idols into memorable experiences for fans. There is no reciprocal production of K-pop and place of the kind discussed in part 1, but municipalities employ the established images of idols to brand their areas, capitalizing on the idols' seductive power to attract K-pop tourists. For K-pop agencies, the ambassador role for municipalities is one of the revenue sources driven by the created idol images.

During my undergraduate course Globalizing East Asian Popular Culture, the students and I have had meaningful discussions about the definition of K-pop. The students' keen interest in, and in-depth knowledge of, K-pop surprised me, because most of them do not have an East Asian background. This was a situation in which I was actually able to see the broad penetration of K-pop beyond Asia. One of the questions we tackled was, Can K-pop be equated with idol music? For foreign audiences who have encountered Korean music only recently and do not know its past history,[1] K-pop is usually represented by recent idol-focused music—what is usually defined as "strategically produced and commercially tailored music" (Shin and Kim 2013, 256). From the late 1990s, music performed by pop idols began to dominate the popular market in Korea; in the age of the globalization of K-pop, the idol-focused music reigns supreme. As chapter 3 will show, K-pop production is primarily concerned with cultivating desirable images for idols that will assist in selling secondary products, the critical part of revenue streaming. Admiring and worshipping idols is the predominant feature of the consumption of K-pop by both domestic and international fans. Since both production and consumption revolve around idols, in dealing with K-pop, this book will focus more on K-pop idols than music content.

Part 1 highlighted the association between marginal drama producers and marginal regional cities in the production and consumption of television dramas and drama sites. Part 2 shifts the geographical focus to two affluent districts in Seoul: Gangnam and Myeong-dong. Regional cities were peripheralized as a result of the country's uneven development, so their underdeveloped environments were adopted by television dramas as exotic landscapes. The two powerful districts in Seoul, on the other hand, were beneficiaries of the same uneven distribution of national resources. Chapter 4 discusses how the promotion of Gangnam has been sustained through the suppression of other areas since the 1980s, so that eventually the area built up a rich cultural infrastructure, including a cluster of entertainment agencies. Chapter 5 examines how Myeong-dong has maintained its status as a symbolic place throughout its history, enabling its current reconfiguration as a destination for global tourists.

The privileged status of Gangnam and Myeong-dong, reflected in their economic, cultural, and symbolic prowess, contrasts with regional cities' economic stagnancy and low visibility. Both parties, however, have a strong desire to promote themselves, so they engage in the same place marketing practices associated with popular culture. Even so, the different conditions in regional cities, on the one hand, and high-end districts of Seoul, on the other, push them to employ different promotional media. The fiscally weak regional cities resort to inexpensive, one-off sponsorship of drama productions in hopes of achieving a short-term boost; Gangnam and Myeong-dong simply make use the rich cultural and commercial infrastructure already established within their municipal boundaries. Gangnam and Myeong-dong capitalize on the clustering of entertainment agencies and retail stores in their areas, and conviniently promote K-pop images to bring in global K-pop fans. Thanks to the already established abundant cultural and symbolic capital, they have lesser danger to risk the uncertain popularity of a single program. Because Gangnam and Myeong-dong have the status of fantasy places for international fans, where the chances of encountering their adored idols are far higher than elsewhere, then so long as the global hype surrounding K-pop continues, those districts are likely to thrive on K-pop tourism. Nevertheless, they are as speculative as regional cities in simply harnessing K-pop images and capitalizing on fans' affective attachment to the images in place promotion without significant place marketers' investment. Despite the disparity in mobilizable resources, both regional cities and districts in Seoul rely on speculative practices in seeking immediate returns without long-term investment.

The data presented in part 2 come from a both virtual and physical ethnography of K-pop fan communities and K-pop places. Although I do not belong to any specific fan clubs, I have accumulated K-pop knowledge through long-term observation of fans' activities in various online communities such as Bestiz (www.bestiz.net) and DC Inside (www.dcinside.com).[2] These two websites operate on an anonymity-based system and are open and accessible to anybody. Anonymity plays a critical role in enabling the affective consumption of K-pop idols: if it is guaranteed, people do not hesitate to reveal their very private emotions publicly and share them with others. Reading or listening to narratives and discourses relating to people's affective engagement with K-pop idols helped me to identify not only the consumption practices but also the operational logic of the K-pop industry. Chapter 3 will show how fans emotionally engage with the visual qualities of K-pop idols; chapters 4 and 5 will discuss how such affective commitment by fans is eventually utilized in place marketing. I collected data relating to international K-pop fans and their consumption patterns by reading numerous postings on Allkpop.com, YouTube, Tumblr, and many other websites. The virtual ethnography method is closely interrelated to my argument: chapter 3 will examine how the very functionality of social media sites—its graphic-oriented nature, virality, and spreadability—interplays with the visually focused operation of K-pop.

The physical ethnography took place in multiple venues. During May through July 2014 and June through July 2016, I visited several K-pop sites in Gangnam, including K-Star Road, the Gangnam Tourism Information Center, SM Artium, the Cube Café, and Klive (which is actually in Dongdaemun). The majority of my field research consisted of observation of fantourists' behaviors and on-site interviews with them, inquiring about why they were motivated to consume places associated with K-pop. Thanks to my broad knowledge of K-pop idols, the short on-site interviews with K-pop fans went well. I conducted field research in Myeong-dong in March 2011 and May and June 2014. Staying in Myeong-dong almost every day from early morning to late at night during the fieldwork periods, I observed what was happening on the streets and inside stores among store clerks and customers. My observations were supplemented by casual talks with store managers, assistants, and customers; I sometimes jumped into conversations between customers and store assistants. The on-site interviews contributed more to useful data collection than sedentary interviews detached from the context would have done. The dialogues with informants were mainly about cosmetics, beauty, Korean popular culture, tourism to Korea, retail rents, and Myeong-dong. I also engaged with the landscape of Myeong-dong, analyzing streetscapes and store facades and floor layouts. Archival sources, including existing scholarly works, news articles, magazines, government statistics, and reports by the Korean Tourism Organization complemented the ethnographic data. My collection of information on the subject of Myeong-dong's history benefited greatly from existing scholarly work, magazines, and news articles. Similar to the ethnography of the Korean drama industry, I cumulated immense knowledge about the K-pop industry from news articles because of the difficulties in actually meeting with entertainment agency operators, particularly those in the big three agencies. Because of the news-buying and sharing traditions, as in part 1, I credit individual newspapers rather than individual reporters for news article sources.

Chapter 3

# Image Producers

## The (Re)Production of K-Pop Idols

This chapter examines how K-pop idols are produced, consumed, and utilized in profit generation. All three sections are constructed on the same plan: K-pop idols appeal to consumers by developing desirable images and building intimacy. They are not a simple media text; rather, they are both a human product and an agent intended to forge affective relationships with fans/audiences, turning the latter into devoted consumers of the secondary products that idols endorse. Korean municipalities likewise draw on the affective sensibility generated by idols to attract K-pop tourists to their areas (as will be discussed in chapters 4 and 5). This chapter delves into the means by which K-pop idols' seductive power to engage the affective commitment of their fans is constructed. I argue that the idols' alluring aura emanates primarily from their visual quality; that, in the end, is what draws fans into affective consumption of idol-associated products and places. In discussing this kind of visually oriented production and consumption, I explore a variety of topics: the cultivation of K-pop idols, the deliberate development of idol concepts, fans' voluntary and affective reproduction of idol images, and the profit-generation schemes that capitalize on these images.

## The Development of the Idol Industry

The formation of the idol system and culture in Korea was strongly influenced by the Japanese model.[1] In Japan, however, idols encompass a broader range of talent, including "highly produced and promoted singers, models, and media personalities" (Galbraith and Karlin 2012, 2), whereas in Korea the title *idol* is mainly reserved for young pop singers and performers who are strategically produced by entertainment agencies. Even though idols appear widely in television dramas, films, and various television shows, their primary point of entry into the entertainment industry is as members of bands called *idol groups*.[2] In the Korean context, therefore, the idol system and culture are inseparable from the operation of the K-pop industry.

Idols are extremely "produced" products of entertainment companies and management agencies, called *gihoeksa* in Korean. Emulating the Japanese *jimusho* system, SM Entertainment (hereafter SME) pioneered the Korean *gihoeksa* system and started producing prepackaged K-pop bands in the mid-1990s.[3] YG Entertainment and JYP Entertainment joined the move in that same decade, and these three major agencies have driven the organizational dynamics of the K-pop industry ever since. They developed a "concentrated and domineering musical production system" (Shin and Kim 2013, 259) by vertically integrating the in-house processes of artist selection, training, image making, song writing, management, contracting, and album production.[4] As the market has expanded, smaller agencies such as Cube, DSP, Loen, FNC, Starship, and Pledis, among many others, have also entered it. As *gihoek* means planning or designing, the *gihoeksa* creates performers from scratch through its "in-house" production system. In addition, the *gihoeksa* controls every aspect of the idols' public image and career, including the coordination of artistic and media content, macro- and microscheduling (i.e., deciding when to release a new album, stream a concert, or announce a television show lineup), and long-term market planning.

Idol production begins with finding a hidden talent. The way agencies often put it is to say that they "try to find a 'gemstone' and 'process' it." Expressions such as these, used in the field, imply that the aura of idols is strategically produced through the *gihoeksa* system, and individual idols' artistic ability matters less. In earlier days, trainee recruitment was channeled mainly through connections or head-hunting. There is a famous story that Lee Sooman, the founder of SME, visited several performing arts schools to find a voice and scouted Bada, who later became a member of S.E.S. Street casting was also prevalent: staff at management companies simply went out into the streets and found attractive faces. As the industry has grown, the ways of scouting trainees have diversified to include open auditions (would-be group members visit *gihoeksa* to get a test), global auditions (management companies hold international auditions at major cities across the globe), online auditions, and televised audition programs. Although the agencies went searching for trainee candidates when the industry was launched, now that K-pop is thriving, wannabes come knocking at the doors of *gihoeksa* to get a much sought-after chance to audition.[5] Since the end product of the idol-manufacturing process is someone who is to be admired for their attractiveness, musical talent is not necessarily the best quality to have for someone wanting to be selected as a trainee. In the earlier stages, *gihoeksa* tried to find youngsters who could sing and dance in order to speed up production, but talent spotting has now developed in the direction of discovering beautiful faces. The emphasis on appearance is growing even greater because musical talent can be improved through long-term training.

Management agencies offer binding contracts to those young people (starting from kids in their early teens) who pass the primary screening. Under the "in-house training system," the contracted trainees get many years of instruction in singing, dancing, acting, foreign languages, and communication techniques.[6] Management companies usually divide their trainees into four categories (Lee 2011). The first comprises soon-to-be released groups that have a fixed team name, a finalized membership, an allotted role for each member of the team, and even a debut song. The second consists of those who have belonged to a fixed team and practiced as a team for more than two years. Management agencies officially provide room and board and a stipend to those who belong to the first two categories. The third group is made up of those who have dropped out of a team and thus are available as candidates for other teams, while those who have just passed the *gihoeksa* audition and require four to five years of training comprise the last category. The hierarchical categorization of trainees points to the dropout mechanism in the training process: if someone is not able to level up within a given period of time, he or she is forced to quit. Quite a few trainees cannot endure the intensive process and voluntarily give up in the middle of it.[7] Even if one goes right through the whole tough process, one's debut as an idol is never guaranteed. Only an extremely small proportion of trainees (less than 10 percent) actually debut. The abundant reserves of candidates who can step in as substitutes make the chances of success even lower and incite endless competition among trainees. As they strive to get that hard-to-win chance, intensive labor and self-exploitation are pervasive among them. Through the mechanism of infinite competition, management companies get more work out of their trainees than they have actually contracted for. A staff member at a management firm remarked, "The intensity of competition has resulted in better quality, bringing about the current high standards in K-pop."[8]

Uncertainty rules the K-pop industry. Only a few produced idols actually survive in the industry. Eighty-two girl groups made their debuts between 2013 and 2015, but fewer than ten achieved substantial public recognition. Even though a new group often attracts public interest, long-term popularity can never be relied on. The *gihoeksa*, therefore, is spending money to cover development costs without either any immediate return or any secured future return on their investment. It is said that the *gihoeksa* usually spends $100,000 to 200,000 to produce a group. SME invested $300,000 to launch Girls' Generation. It is a huge investment for a product with such unpredictable earning potential. The risk factor in idol production, on the other hand, is inherent in all human capital. As Chris Bilton (1999) contends, the process of cultural production depends on human relations that remain volatile and unpredictable. The products of the idol production process do not always function as they are designed to do because they are basically human beings. For example, SME had to deal with the departure of three members of TVXQ, originally a five-boy group.[9]

To deal with their unpredictable human capital, management companies have adopted various disciplinary measures to control trainees. One agency has come up with a ten-point "code of conduct" that trainees should observe: (1) punctuality at rehearsals, (2) no smoking, (3) a ninety-degree bow, (4) no cell phone use except during dinner, (5) no dating, (6) politeness during class, (7) no drinking, (8) no lateness or absence, (9) no food, and (10) staff members only in practice rooms.[10] Other agencies have similar rules to discipline trainees. The strict surveillance and disciplinary control of trainees is often covered over with the rhetoric of dreams. The tough training process is not intensive labor, but a prerequisite for trainees to pursue their dreams. Idol wannabes, therefore, voluntarily participate in forced overwork. To exploit trainees' dreams to a maximum, the hallways and practice rooms of *gihoeksa* are filled with huge photos of already famous idols.[11] The idea is that trainees identify themselves with these established idols and endure their current hardships in order to achieve similar success. The family metaphor is another means of controlling trainees and idols. The three major agencies use similar rhetoric, referring to themselves as the "SM Town," "JYP Nation," and "YG Family," respectively. Despite their different scales, all three place emphasis on a sense of community that veils the capital–labor relations between *gihoeksa* and trainees. Under this positive fantasy of familyhood, trainees persist in exploiting themselves and their dreams. Disciplined by the family rhetoric, K-pop idols frequently express their thanks to the company chairman and staffers when they win first place on a television music show.

After going through the tough training process, some trainees have the good fortune to debut as members of newly formed idol groups. The launch of a new idol group is strategized by putting together the "best combination" of members, each of whom shows a particular talent for singing, dancing, rapping, foreign-language speaking, or looking good. Because idols are not deemed to be serious artists, the division of labor within a group is done in such a way as to make the group as a whole competitive. Simply being good-looking functions as a critical talent within a group; those with pleasant faces are called the "visual" members. A "visual" will normally take the center spot in the dance choreography or on the album cover. As the debut of a new idol group is a new product rollout, determining the composition of the group is conceived to be the same as packaging different product lines to carve out a wider niche. Beyond the mere functional logic, the rationale behind diversity in the lineup of the band lies in exploiting the broadest possible market. Each individual member develops and plays a specific personality type (character) so that the group as a whole can serve multiple audience segments. In Girls' Generation, for example, Yuri acts as the sexy character, while Sunny does *aegyo* (a calculated cuteness). Yoona is the "visual" of the group; Jessica played the chic role, leaving Sooyoung responsible for articulate speaking and a sense of humor.[12] Promoting a diversified attractiveness, Girls' Generation as a whole was able to maximize its consumption potential.

One industrial standard was to form a five-member group, composed of a main vocal, a subvocal, a rapper, a dancer, and a visual member. The first- and second-generation idols such as H.O.T., TVXQ, Big Bang, SHINee, and Wonder Girls fall into this category. A recent trend among K-pop groups is having too many members: Super Junior alternates twelve or thirteen members; Girls' Generation, Nine Muses, and TWICE have nine; although three members have withdrawn from the group, EXO is made up of twelve, including EXO-K and EXO-M; SEVENTEEN has a crew of thirteen. The practice began with Super Junior, once called a collection of left-over trainees at SME, where it was a means of disposing of the oversized and aging trainees. Yet the multimember group has been developed into a savvy industrial strategy. As fans' tastes are diverse, the more members in a group, the wider the spectrum of preferences it can serve. The multimember groups produced by SME, such as Super Junior, Girls' Generation, and EXO, are often labeled by fans as "assorted gift sets."[13] Large groups reduce the risks associated with fans' unpredictable choice of favorites. They can also repackage themselves into smaller groups, so-called units, or even spin off a soloist, contributing to profit-diversification schemes. Super Junior has operated five subunits: Super Junior-K.R.Y, Super Junior-T, Super Junior-M, Super Junior-H, and Super Junior-D&E, each made up of different members. G-Dragon, a lead member of Big Bang, runs two subunits (GD × Taeyang and GD & T.O.P) and also performs as a soloist. Girls' Generation's subunit TTS and its soloist, Taeyeon, likewise have achieved substantial commercial success.

When releasing a new idol group, the *gihoeksa* invests a significant amount of effort in crafting unique and marketable images for it.[14] *Concept* is a word widely used in the K-pop industry. To develop its own brand, each group tries to sell its unique qualities against competition from the floods of other idol bands. While most girl groups, for instance, place themselves somewhere between innocent girls and sexy femmes fatales, 2NE1 established an exclusive image of themselves as independent and empowered women calling for female solidarity. The multinational group f(x) has experimented with unusual concepts based on its electropop style. Although f(x)'s queering concepts do not appeal to broader audience groups, the band has attracted some extremely devoted fans who admire their uniqueness.

The art of storytelling is often used to impress the concept of a newly debuted group in the public mind in a strong and rapid way. For their debut song "Mama," members of EXO were promoted as beings from Exoplanet who had supernatural powers such as healing, teleportation, time control, and telepathy. EXO's twin units, EXO-K and EXO-M, who sing the same songs in Korean and Mandarin, originated from the "Tree of Life" on Exoplanet. This birth narrative has been actively reflected in the group's lyrics, choreography, and concert themes. Similarly, under the concept of the school trilogy series, Bangtan Boys (BTS) released three albums titled "2 COOL 4 SKOOL," "O! RUL8, 2?," and "SKOOL LUV AFFAIR," each presenting songs dealing with dreams, happiness, and love. With lyrics tackling issues such as school bullying, the pursuit of happiness, and the rejection of social norms, BTS's storytelling of school lives won enormous support from teenagers.

Concepts are also used in the diachronic development of a group. Every time a K-pop group releases a new song, album, or single, it is produced and marketized along with a specific theme. The design concept rules everything from musical elements such as catch phrases and choreography to fashions, including clothes and hairstyles. A concept also functions as a site in which K-pop groups practice multiple masculinities and femininities. Girls' Generation made its debut in 2007 with the song "Into the New World" in which the girls' untainted purity was highlighted. The group's megahit song "Gee" (2009) changed its members into lovely young ladies with skinny jeans, T-shirts, and long hair. In "Tell Me Your Wish (Genie)" (2009), the girls were given a navy concept and dressed in tight military jackets and hot pants. They were transformed into cheerleaders in "Oh" (2010) and medieval knights in "The Boys" (2011), while for a more recent song, "Lion Heart" (2015), they played in a 1960s retro style. While maintaining a wholesome image as "sexy yet innocent girls" (Epstein and Turnbull 2014), Girls' Generation has performed and sold different types of femininity over time, going through a transformational journey from girlhood to sexy womanhood.[15] Similarly, boy bands display growth through a metamorphosis in body and character from innocent boys into masculine adults. This diachronic transfiguration is a market survival strategy: there is always something fresh on offer to appeal to fans and sustain their interest.

From recruiting trainees to team composition and concept crafting, the production of K-pop music centers on the creation of images of idols. K-pop is a package that is not confined to music. With few exceptions,[16] idols do not produce their own music and only perform music that they are given to perform and is designed to highlight the images created for them. These images are intended to cover both synchronic distinctions that make one K-pop group stand out among many others and diachronic versatilities that enable a particular group's image to be refreshed. Strategic image making is imperative, since the images produced for the idols are directly associated with revenues insofar as they ensure wide popular appeal. They also render idols fantasized subjects, thus obscuring the harsh labor conditions and disciplinary regulations they undergo in the industry.

## Idols and Affective Sensibilities

As outlined in the previous section, K-pop idols are strategically produced commodities, and the process that produces them, from searching them out as trainees to devising concepts for them, is mainly concerned with their visual qualities. Nevertheless, the production process itself does not automatically lead to idols functioning as commodities in the market. Idols are human products, rather than mere media texts, that their ongoing performances constantly redefine their market competitiveness. Their ability to captivate consumers' minds is the key to their successful operation because idols are produced and marketed as attractive people. What exactly is it, then, that makes a K-pop idol a seductive commodity? This point is critical because, as the following section will show, idols are essentially metacommodities, designed to sell other products, including celebrity merchandise and K-pop places. I argue that the felicitous interplay between K-pop idols' iconic status and their intimacy is the resource that enables them to build up their fandom. Idols have to be objects of desire and familiar subjects at one and the same time.

The appeal of idols emanates from the very nature of their iconic status (Herwitz 2008; Nagaike 2012). It is in the nature of an idol to establish and sustain the iconic quality that enables him or her to exist as an object of worship. The aura of K-pop idols springs from the visual spectacle that they present to the world. Given the image-based idol production system, potential K-pop idols are basically blessed with extraordinary good looks. Such natural beauty, however, is a mere resource to be processed further. The *gihoeksa* makes use of various production skills to develop the appearance of each idol through fashion, hairstyle, makeup, and accessories under the umbrella of a group concept. Sometimes, both idol candidates and those who have already made their debuts undergo plastic surgery to enhance their physical qualities. Some international fans claim that the perfect faces of K-pop idols are entirely due to plastic surgery. Cosmetic surgery, however, does not play a large part in creating the K-pop image because agencies search out young people who are "already pretty enough" for the stock of idol candidates. The visual qualities of the trainees that each agency has on its books testify to the fact that cosmetic surgery is not an urgent necessity. Visual perfection is achieved through strict body control rather than clinical assistance. It is common knowledge that measuring their weight is a weekly routine for trainees. In episode 9 of Mnet's *SIXTEEN*, a survival reality show where 16 JYPE female trainees compete for the seven spots in a new girl group, Park Jin-young (JYP) says to one trainee: "Have I ever criticized you for your dancing or singing? What do you think is your problem?" and the trainee replies, "Taking care of myself." JYP then says critically: "Your dance looks slow. If you gain weight, of course you'll look like that. The first thing that I do when I get up in the morning is getting on the scale. While the other girls practice their singing, you have to lose weight."[17] K-pop entertainers are forced to engage in constant management of their bodies during training and even after their official debuts.

The corporate regulatory system, however, is only partial; self-management of the body is required for the perfect visual quality that bolsters the entertainers' iconic status. It is well known that both male and female K-pop idols put enormous effort into keep their bodies in ideal condition. When Eunji in Apink was asked which member had changed most since the group's debut on a television show, she picked herself, saying: "I have lost 15 kg since the debut. I've been working hard with a personal trainer and have been boxing because I thought I should improve the shape of my body."[18] The so-called girl group diet menus that are supposed to not exceed eight hundred calories a day have sparked lots of media and online discussion. Male idols are not free from strict self-regulation of their bodies either. In a scene from *Naver StarCast*, aired on August 20, 2013, and featuring EXO members, one of them, Lay, asked another, Xiumin: "Why do you try so hard to lose weight? . . . I know you work hard. So please rest, don't be stressed, and eat something." In reply, Xiumin confessed, "I was disappointed to see myself on TV when I put on weight." Key, a member of SHINee, has also mentioned that he does not eat carbohydrates at all to keep fit.

Embodied in the production of the idols' iconic status is a process of neoliberal human capital creation that valorizes individuals' self-regulation, self-development, and branding.[19] K-pop idols consider their body as a developable asset and engage in its continuous improvement and management. It is vital for them to achieve a flawless outward appearance through their own bodily discipline. Beauty acts as an oppressive regime for both established idols and aspiring trainees; they are under an obligation to constantly screen and control their bodies and appearances. This very oppressive structure rewards K-pop idols with the iconic status that markedly differentiates them from their main consumers, Korean teenagers, who are likewise oppressed, but only by the strict regulations governing uniforms and hairstyles at school. What turns K-pop idols into objects of desire among ordinary teenagers is precisely their idealized quality, the contrast between their looks and those of real-life people. That is why even "girl groups" have more female fans than male. As the section on consumption will show, appreciation of the stars' spectacular appearance is the dominant element in idol worship. The iconic aura of K-pop stars radiates from their impeccable physical qualities.

K-pop stars' affective power, however, comes from their familiarity. The K-pop industry is highly dependent on idol fandom. Fandom wields its power over sales of music albums, the digital music chart, and publicity for idol groups. For fandom to come into being and be maintained, idols should not exist in some entirely distant and unreachable sphere. Intimacy building is required to entice audiences and eventually turn them into fans. The primary channel for K-pop idols to become familiar to their public is reality shows. Produced by and aired on cable channels, idol reality shows intensively feature one particular group and trace the members' real lives off stage. Following from pioneering shows such as 2NE1's *2NE1 TV* (2009), 2PM's *Wild Bunny* (2009), and Infinite's *You're My Oppa* (2010), more than forty idol reality programs had been broadcast by 2015. The same group may appear on several different shows (Block B, for instance, has appeared on *Signal B*, *Match Up*, and *5 Minutes before Chaos*), or the same program may feature multiple groups in a series (e.g., MBC Every 1 produced six seasons of *Showtime*: *EXO's Showtime*, *Showtime: Burning the Beast*, *Apink's Showtime*, *Sistar's Showtime*, *EXID's Showtime*, and *Mamamoo x GFriend Showtime*).

Idol reality shows sell the "real" lives of K-pop idols. Using several observation cameras, the programs allow the audience to watch as K-pop idols go about their daily lives. For example, idol dorms where members live together are shown to the public, which also gets to see idol entertainers' "bare faces."

Idols are also seen in recording studios and in dance practice rooms particularly late at night or early in the morning. Idols are also encountered in various real-life contexts in which they go shopping for groceries, cook, eat in restaurants, play in a water park, or travel overseas. Crying scenes are common in which idols reaffirm the love and friendship that exists among group members and staff. Despite the artificially created settings, reality shows become a site in which idols' real-life personalities are revealed, rather than the entirely calculated personas that they present on stage. At a press conference during *Apink's Showtime*, Apink members shared their thoughts about the reality program. Nam-joo said: "We think we're going to put in a lot of ourselves as is. I think people will be able to feel like they're doing things with us rather than watching a program." Na-eun added, "Not too long ago, we filmed at a water park, and I got so excited playing there that I didn't even notice the cameras."[20] Viewers enjoy watching idols' humane and friendly aspects. Indeed, they forge close ties with them based on their ordinary qualities, as if they were boys and girls whom they might easily come across in their own neighborhoods. Idols become special subjects, but close ones.

By disclosing idols' real-life personalities, reality programs also provide the general audience with frequent opportunities to accumulate greater knowledge of them. According to Mark Duffett (2013), stars and fans are in an asymmetrical relationship in which the stars have power and the fans have knowledge.[21] Fans try to balance the power relations by collecting information; as they get to know more about the stars, the distance between the two is bridged. Acquiring knowledge gives fans immense pleasure because they feel that they are getting closer to their idols. For example, Lukács (2010a) suggests the notion of a "culture of intimate televisuality" in which Japanese viewers take pleasure in accumulating knowledge about *tarento* (media personalities). Once a fondness for an idol is formed, knowledge accumulation on the part of audiences/fans surpasses the passive and private arena and enters wider public circulation. Fan community members engage in collective, discursive consumption of the aspects of idols shown in the reality shows;[22] the anonymous public "talks together" about the personality, beauty, and everyday lives of idols, taking personal pleasure from this kind of group discussion. This collaborative and discursive consumption process produces secondary content such as captured images, short movies, GIF images, and SWF images that are then further distributed on various media, particularly online social media due to their virality and spreadability. Through fans' active reproduction, images shown in reality shows become a resource that can be further utilized by other media, including television commercials and entertainment shows. The fans' knowledge-gathering process serves to constitute idols' intertextuality, endlessly cross-referenced between newspapers, magazines, online social media, and television (Galbraith and Karlin 2012). While management agencies and some advertisers capitalize on fans' "labor of love" that spreads idol images across diverse media, fans themselves gain great pleasure from their voluntary transmedia circulation of idol images. Because fan-audiences directly participate in the process as critical agents, intertextuality creates a deeper and more affective relationship with them.

## The Mechanism of Profit Generation

As shown in the above discussions, both the production and operation of K-pop idols have a great deal to do with the construction of desirable images for them. K-pop is all about achieving that "right look" that is prized by the audience. Behind this image-focused production process are profit-generation channels that are not necessarily associated with music. The recent development of the Korean popular music industry reveals a fundamental shift in the way profits are made. Until the 1990s, sales of music—on LP, cassette tape, or CD—were a primary source of revenue for production houses. The first decade of the twenty-first century, however, witnessed a drastic decline in CD sales. Between 2000 and 2005, South Korea lost a whopping two-thirds of its album sales, while the global market shrunk by a more modest 18 percent.[23] The decline of the physical record market ushered in a digital crossover. As early as 2006, South Korea became the first major music market to become more than 50 percent digital (the 2012 global rate was just 38 percent).[24] As of 2012, total revenues from digital sales had reached $670 million out of a total of $750 million. The soaring digital music market reorganized the profit-distribution system in a manner unfavorable to production houses, despite the fact that the size of the pop music market had expanded over time. While more than half of the profits now go to the distribution platforms and wireless carriers, record labels and entertainment companies, which actually produce the music, earn lower profit margins.[25] A chief director of KMP Holdings (KMP is an abbreviation for Korean

Music Power), a music distribution company established as a joint venture among seven entertainment companies, including the major three, remarked, "Few production houses, except the major three, can expect actual profits from the sale of music."[26] Yet the situation is not bright even for the big three. For example, SME recorded a total of $287 million of sales revenue in 2014. Yet revenues from digital music and CD sales remained at $45.5 million, less than one-sixth of the total, at a time when physical CD does not function beyond an idol merchandise. These figures reveal that the traditional exchange system organized around physical and digital music no longer functions as effectively as it once did.[27] Against the backdrop of the crash in the music market, the profit-generation schemes within the K-pop industry have fundamentally changed. Music is only one dimension of idols' popularity and is responsible for only part of the revenue they generate. The principal sources of revenue for *giheoksa* are endorsement deals and performances at events, both of which depend on the attractiveness of idols' images.

Signing endorsement deals is the ultimate way of making money in the entertainment industry. Corporate or product sponsorship brings pure profit at no cost, because it utilizes established (idol) images. The Korean advertising industry is well known for its heavy reliance on celebrities. Of the 2000 commercial advertisements released in Korea in 2010, for example, 65 percent featured them. By comparison, the same figure for the United States, the United Kingdom, and France was less than 10 percent. Bruce Haines, a Briton who currently heads the largest advertising agency in South Korea, Cheil Communication, revealed that the biggest difference between U.K. and Korean advertising lies in the fact that Korean advertisers are hugely dependent on celebrity endorsement. As Carruth (2009) puts it: "Of course, it's not uncommon in the west for stars to endorse a product, but generally the ad has a core idea and makes use of the celebrity endorsement to enhance the original concept. Not so in Korea. In its crudest form, Korean advertising degenerates to beautiful people holding a bottle." Recently, K-pop idols have risen to be a valued currency in the advertising market given their favorable images and the size of their fandom. Commercials capitalize on particular idol images built on their appearances on various media. Miss A's Suzy was once called the "$10 million girl" due to the twenty-two endorsement deals she signed during the period from February 2012 to April 2013 alone.[28] The number of modeling contracts she landed increased even further thereafter. Although Miss A did not set about vigorously releasing new songs, Suzy's successful movie debut in the film *Architecture 101* (*Geonchukhak Gaeron* 2012) earned her the nickname "the nation's first love." Thanks to her pure image combined with her extraordinary physical appearance, she became the most sought-after female celebrity in the advertising industry. In August 2014, Hyeri from Girls' Day appeared in *Real Men* (*Jinjja Sanai*), a variety show about celebrities' experiences in the military. After only a four-day experience in the military on the show, a brief clip in which Hyeri showed *aegyo* (carefully crafted cuteness of expression) went viral. Thanks to her cute but energetic image, Hyeri landed seventeen endorsement deals. Cheerful images from her performance in the television series *Reply 1988* (*Eungdaphara Ilgupalpal* 2015) brought more deals for product sponsorship. Once a favorable image has been created, its commercial value is heightened through its constant circulation via different media. Thus, the most urgent task for idol producers is to get an opportunity for their idol to appear on television shows where remarkable images can be built. Releasing an album is simply a means of generating publicity and obtaining an entry into other media.[29]

Idols have risen to become a desirable commercial model because of their sizable fandoms as well, which have been growing even greater with the globalization of K-pop. Fans—those who forge affective relations with idols—consume the products that their idols endorse in affective ways, that is, as a means of being connected with them. Product reviews, therefore, are likely to be favorable and fans' collective supportive comments, when circulated online, can bring a rapid promotional effect. Advertisers frequently hold fan meetings at which only those who buy promotional products are allowed to meet idols in the flesh, in the same way that a *giheoksa* runs fan-signing events for which attendees are picked by lottery, with each album purchased entitling the purchaser to one ticket in the lottery. Marketing with K-pop stars is a direct commercialization of fans' desire to get closer to their idols. EXO starred in multiple commercials and publicity campaigns across Asia thanks solely to the incredible size of its global fandom. Maintaining its long-term top position against competition from floods of other girl groups, members of Girls' Generation appeared in 18 commercials in 2008, 17 in 2009, 18 in 2010, and 18 in 2011, endorsing a wide variety of products from cell phones and theme parks to roast chicken.

Event performances contribute substantially to the revenue streams for idol producers as well. The performances in question, called *haengsa* in Korean, are occasions during which singers and entertainers perform live at a concert organized by sponsors. *Haengsa* include local festivals, college festivals, and corporate events. As local events, *haengsa* are not publicly broadcast and the size of the audience depends on the sponsor. An event performance appears similar to a concert inasmuch as the audience watches a show, yet its exchange value system is much more like that of a commercial advertisement. While the audience buys tickets to attend a concert, *haengsa* are open to the public free of charge. Companies and local governments put on such events and pay for them for much the same reasons that they pay for commercials featuring the groups. Idol group images and brands are bought to sell other tangible and intangible commodities, such as corporate or city images. Popular music once had a first-order commodity relationship with consumers. Now, the primary mechanism for generating profits operates via idols' images that are sold to advertisers. The selling of cultural text (music) through idols has now turned into a process in which the idols themselves become a commodity to be sold to sponsors, thus forming a second-order commodity relationship.

It is not only advertisers who capitalize on idol images, however. Entertainment agencies are the foremost exploiters of crafted idol images for their profit-diversification schemes. Idol merchandise consists of commodities that directly commercialize idol images. Originating from the Japanese "goods culture" ("goods"/*gutjeu* is a term taken from English to refer to commodities), celebrity merchandise covers literally all products related to stars (particularly idol groups) from photos, accessories, clothing, and stationery products to home goods and snacks. As they serve as a unique means of identifying oneself as a fan, star goods have gained greater significance in the recent history of K-pop. The first-generation celebrity merchandise in the 1990s was mainly limited to star photos of different sizes, usually bundled with a music album (cassette tape or CD), different colored balloons and raincoats (each color representing a particular idol group), star name badges, and star T-shirts and hats. The fan clubs of second-generation idol groups in the early 2000s voluntarily produced and circulated various types of star merchandise among fan club members such as stationery, sticker photos, and wristbands with group names on them. Recognizing the market potential, since around 2005 entertainment agencies have aggressively produced celebrity merchandise as a means of widening the channels to profit. As K-pop fandom has grown, the goods market has also thrived. Since fandom is about desiring the same lifestyle as idols, celebrity goods now go beyond cheering tools (such as balloons and light sticks) and have diversified into everyday products such as sticker books, accessories, cell phone cases, art toys, candles, necklaces, cushions, pillows, cups, pouches, and eco-bags. Each product is designed with an idol image or idol group logo, only having affective values to assert fandom with significantly less use values.

Idol merchandise stands at the summit of the idol industry. "It is the tail that wags the dog" (as in the Korean proverb, *baeboda baekkop jangsaga heunghaetda*), an appropriate metaphor to refer to a situation in which more revenues come from idol goods than from musical content. Major management companies have opened online and off-line retail outlets to sell idol goods. YG Entertainment has launched the online shop YGeshop to sell products themed with YG artists. In January 2013, SME opened a "pop-up store" inside a Lotte Department Store to sell new SM artist merchandise. A pop-up store is a short-term sales space, and this one was originally supposed to operate for just one month. As the sales revenue reached around $600,000 within twelve days, however, Lotte offered more space, and now the SM Town pop-up store is one of the department store's most profitable shops, recording a billion dollars' worth of sales every month. SM Entertainment has added more diverse product options, including flip-flops, travel packs, oil-absorbing blotting paper, nail stickers, and Blue Marble board games. Despite their relatively high price (e.g., EXO earphones cost more than $1,200 and an EXO rabbit toy sells for $560), fans' desire to wear and use items associated with their favorite stars all day long keeps them buying, however expensive the goods. One particular feature at the SM pop-up store is a "lucky bag" containing a variety of anonymous wrapped-up goods. Although no one knew what products were inside, more than one hundred lucky bags were sold on the day the shop opened. The company also carried out one-off marketing exercises; for example, rather than offering tickets for the EXO concert in 2015 at conventional online booking sites, issuing tickets to those who spent over a particular amount on goods at the SM Town pop-up store, with the amount spent determining where the seat was as well. Since 2013, 1,500 to 2,500 people have visited the pop-up store daily, and around 50 percent of these visitors have been Chinese and Japanese tourists. K-pop retail outlets have become a must-go destination for international K-pop fans. To cater to their growing numbers, SM Entertainment has opened further pop-up stores at Incheon International Airport and Dongdaemum Design Plaza. YG Entertainment has also launched an off-line pop-up at a Lotte Department

Store and Cube Entertainment is now operating the ground floor of its agency building as a souvenir shop.

Amazed by the profitability of K-pop spin-off products, SME has also marketized the act of "performing K-pop" by opening a karaoke place named EverySing. In addition to providing spaces to sing and dance to SM artists' songs, EverySing also features a comprehensive gift shop selling the SM-branded merchandise. Visitors can also try on costumes worn by SM idols in music videos and take photos in sticker photo booths. The agency had a media promotion day when lots of SM artists were employed to promote the place: Yoona from Girls' Generation exclaimed, "We wish you could see how we play there, relaxed and goofing off between various broadcast schedules."[30] The quotation from the interview lures devoted fans to the karaoke place by suggesting that they might encounter SM idols there, or at least be able to take part in the same leisure activities as they do.

Combining the concepts of buying, performing, and experiencing K-pop, SME recently opened an entertainment complex, filled with a range of content based on SM stars. The SM TOWN Atrium is a multicultural complex where fans and tourists are able to undergo the ultimate SM experience. It has six floors: The first floor is a welcome zone that leads to the second floor, where SUM, a merchandise shop, offers visitors souvenirs and fashion items featuring SM artists. Given both the shop's name (SUM) and the high price of its products, fans joke that they need to bring a huge sum of money to buy anything there. Obviously targeting foreign tourists, SUM also offers gift products designed to reflect traditional Korean culture. The third floor is devoted to a studio where visitors are able to record their own music videos with the help of SM employees. The recording booths and photo studios replicate those that SM artists actually use. The studio is available on a reservation basis only, and there are always long waiting lists. Adorned with stills and albums autographed by SM artists, the fourth floor is the LIVErary Café, which offers tea, coffee, desserts, and music. Items on sale include sparkling water with a photo of Taeyeon (or another SM artist) on the wrapper, ice creams themed for every group, and cupcakes with hat-shaped icing and lettering on the hat that spells out the names of SM groups such as EXO, Girls' Generation, SHINee, and Super Junior. The fifth and sixth floors are a theater showing hologram performances and musicals. Combining cultural content with cutting-edge technology,[31] the hologram performances project three-dimensional images of singers onto the stage so that spectators feel they are watching an actual concert.[32] In sum, no idols are actually present in person at SM Artium, but their images are inscribed everywhere on cups, cupcakes, and so forth, or appear in virtual shows.

Following SM TOWN Artium's lead, multicultural spaces exploiting K-pop content are now spreading quickly. YG Entertainment has opened Klive in the Dongdaemun area. It too consists of a hologram concert hall, photo zone, exhibition hall, gift shop, and café. Klive also has digital attractions in which audience members can participate: the augmented reality (AR) elevator makes riders feel as though they are standing next to K-pop stars; a "secret window" allows visitors to watch not-yet-released videos through special 3D glasses; at the six-meter-tall Giant Tower, people can view photo albums of their favorite stars; in the Start Photo Box, people can pose for pictures with 3D images of YG artists and print the images. SM Entertainment has launched similar entertainment complexes in Osaka, Japan, and has been promoting one in China; YG Entertainment has also announced plans to open more in Myeong-dong, Jeju, Japan, and China. Integrating technology and cultural content, these hologram performance halls and multicultural spaces invite K-pop fans from across the globe into a world of fantasy. Fantasy images of K-pop stars appear in front of their eyes as if their desire to encounter their idols can be satisfied in reality.

How large, then, is the number of fascinated fans willing to spend $18 on an EXO ice cream and $1,200 on EXO earphones? Although the ever-growing idol-focused retail shops demonstrate their profitability, I personally doubted the feasibility of such fantasy-driven places and products. My hands-on visit to the place in June 2016, however, broke down my preconceptions. The place was packed with fans and visitors,[33] and I barely managed to make my way among the crowds, who do spend money in the multicultural space. Despite the expensive prices for what are intrinsically souvenirs, international fans describe the merchandise as "treasures." The music video–shooting experience is run exclusively on a reservation basis and costs $300 per person, but it was fully booked up. I particularly wondered why fans spend money on desserts that cost around $15 to $20, yet provide only brief satisfaction, as opposed to the kind of celebrity merchandise through which fans collect and accumulate memories. One fan eating an EXO ice cream priced at $18 remarked: "Fans have eighteen dollars in their hearts. They do and I do."[34] EXO cupcakes, $8 each, were sold out. "It is a place where fans can gather together to enjoy macaroons and other desserts, with each flavor corresponding to a specific SM group. It is fun to indulge that fangirl every once in a while with a few extra hundred calories dedicated to the group you love."[35] The data suggest fans' affective consumption of idol images and idol spin-off products. Idols have the affective power to captivate their fans to the extent that they consume intangible images inscribed in multiple products that are translated into tangible material profits.

The profit-generation schemes demonstrate how cultivated idol images sell other products. The visually highlighted idol images are a metacommodity to sell other products, including music, celebrity merchandise, and K-pop places as pseudoavatars of K-pop idols. Once images are cultivated, they can be endlessly reproduced in products, virtual shows, and experimental tours. The bigger argument of this book is that Korean municipalities also buy such strategically produced idol images in their place-promotion efforts to attract idol fans as tourists. As the next two chapters will show, the fan-tourists consume the idol image–attached places in the same affective ways as they spend money on the idol-featured cupcakes. For fan-tourists, affective consumption is not about money but about invaluable experiences. For place marketers, affective consumption is all about material profits and another route to raise publicity at the same time.

Yet there is a critical problem with the seemingly eternal idol images: youth does not last forever. The commercial potential of K-pop idols is built on their youth. Not just teenagers but those who miss their younger days admire the young idols' beautiful bodies. The bright energy emanated from the idols' youth is the source of their ability to forge intimate relations with fans. Traditionally, within the Confucian hierarchy, youth was not a privileged value in Korea. In rice-farming culture, youth represented labor resources. This convention continued during the Japanese colonial period, during which young Koreans were forcibly mobilized as military and sexual labor. Likewise, during the economic development process, youth meant cheap and easily replicable labor power at best; individual self-sacrifice in the form of submission to labor exploitation was taken for granted for the sake of national development. One of the few groups of young people to be celebrated was the college students who demonstrated against the military dictatorship and were praised as warriors advancing democracy during the 1980s. Since the Asian financial crisis in the late 1990s, the younger generation has lacked the abundant job opportunities that the previous generation enjoyed during the era of economic growth. Rather, young people are forced to constantly develop themselves in order to be sold as valuable human capital in the current neoliberal economy. The globalization of K-pop and nationalist praise of the phenomenon have made young women and men in their late teens and early twenties welcome and wanted in popular imagination, albeit in regulated and commodified ways, for the first time in the country's history.

Because the aging of idols is unavoidable, the crafting and commodification of idol images that basically utilize their youth is limited. While the restricted commercial availability of idols causes the intensified and accelerated commodification to extract maximum profits during the limited time, it has also opened up active collaboration between drama and K-pop producers. As mentioned in chapter 1, Korean drama producers increasingly hire well-established idols as a means to further exports. Appearing in television dramas provides idols not only greater chances to sign endorsement deals, as occurred in the cases of Suzy and Haeri, but more important, offers them stable transitions from singers to actors. Because acting is not necessarily premised on youth, K-pop idols strive to be an actor as their final destination in the entertainment industry. The K-pop music production houses have also expanded their business into the production of television dramas and films, employing their own idols as actors. JYP Entertainment coproduced the drama *Dream High* with KeyEast Entertainment. SM Entertainment produced several television dramas, such as *Heading to the Ground* (*Maenttange Heding* 2009), *Paradise Ranch*, and *Prime Minister and I* (*Chongriwa Na* 2013), although none of them turned out be successful.

## The Formation of International Fandom

K-pop producers' recent profit-diversification schemes are designed to meet demand from global K-pop fans. The formation of international fandom has opened substantial new markets for the Korean idol industry, which had fully saturated the small domestic market. The globalization of K-pop, however, did not come about entirely accidentally; planning and preparation for overseas expansion, mainly on the part of the major agencies, had been going on for over a decade. SM Entertainment has been at the forefront of this endeavor; its distinctive departure from its own Japanese models of idol production lies in exports. The member composition of each idol group reflects these outward-looking intentions: even the first-generation idol groups in the late 1990s had at least one member who was fluent in English, such as Tony in H.O.T or Eugene in S.E.S. Lee Soo-man, a founder of SME, talked about the three steps in SM's globalization process: exporting cultural products, international collaborations, and globalization. Lee stated: "The first level of *Hallyu* is the exportation of cultural products, which is exemplified by BoA and TVXQ's advancement into Japan. The collaboration between KangTa and Taiwanese singer Vanness Wu is an example of the second level."[36] Exports are conducted through indigenization, or localization, a process in which idols brush up on the language of the local market in which they will be sold. In the first case of localization, BoA set about launching herself in the Japanese market by strategically creating a nationless image: she perfected her Japanese and did not mention her nationality. Coproduction with a Japanese entertainment firm, AVEX, also helped in branding BoA as a hybrid commodity. Building on BoA's success, more SME artists, including TVXQ, Girls' Generation, SHINee, and Super Junior, were able to break into the Japanese market.

The final step in localization is completed through the direct training of local talent. Agencies scout young talents from various national backgrounds, educate them in Korea, and launch a group for the local markets by combining them with Korean members. EXO-K and EXO-M were twin groups that performed the same songs in Korean and Mandarin. Although it finally broke up after Chinese members took SME to court to be removed from the group, EXO-M originally consisted of two Koreans and four Chinese who were trained in Korea. The members of SME's f(x) include one Chinese and one Taiwanese American, and JYPE's TWICE is made up of three Japanese and one Taiwanese. Chung Wook, a chairperson of JYPE, has also suggested similar strategies for globalization: "The final goal is to export our system and product content using the local talents in local language. We try to establish a platform in which the local capital can cooperate with our system."[37]

Entertainment agencies' export and indigenization strategies have nurtured a sizable K-pop fandom in the East and Southeast Asian market. Besides producers' efforts, however, a variety of factors have contributed to the expansion of international K-pop fandom beyond East Asia, including to North America, South America, and Europe. Most credit should go to international K-pop fans themselves, that is, those who are not Korean nationals but identify themselves as fans of an individual K-pop group or solo artist. Domestic idol fans are often recognized through official fan clubs sponsored by their idol's music label. These fan clubs have official names, such as SONE for Girls' Generation and VIP for Big Bang. Their members receive special benefits such as priority concert tickets and invitations to fan meetings. Because membership is granted on the basis of an official Korean resident registration number, however, international fans cannot join. Nevertheless, overseas fans can and do organize themselves informally into fan communities through social networking platforms and fan-managed websites, and actively participate in fan culture.[38] Devoted fans have set up numerous English-language Facebook pages, Twitter accounts, YouTube channels, Tumblr accounts, blogs, and online forums solely dedicated to K-pop, K-pop groups, and individual idols. Well-known North American–based websites include www.allkpop.com, www.khype.com, www.dkpopnews.net, and www.soompi.com. A site called www.popgasa.com provides K-pop lyrics translated into English. In Southeast Asia, K-pop Kingdom (www.K-popkingdom.com) is one of the websites for those who are interested in Korean music. ViKi (www.viki.com)—a name coined by combing "video" or "visual" and "wiki"—is another site on which fans can upload, watch, and download K-pop movie clips.[39] These sites provide up-to-date information about K-pop, English translations of Korean entertainment news, and concert information. K-pop fan sites are mostly operated in a system in which small numbers of pioneer fans carry out a free service—providing information about K-pop—for a larger community, attracting more and more participants until the size of the community becomes large enough for members and visitors to become engaged in collective discussions about K-pop news and gossip. Playing a critical role in spreading K-pop worldwide, global fans have "reproduced" it. Their role is not limited to being consumers but has now extended such that they are "marketers, mediators, translators, and localizers of the globalizing culture" (Otmazgin and Lyan 2013, 70), serving as both cultural practitioners and market catalysts.

While international fans are the main agents in the global dissemination of K-pop, social media function as the platform on which visual and discursive consumption of K-pop is carried out. Defined as "a group of Internet-based applications that build on the ideological and technological foundations of Web 2.0, and that allow the creation and exchange of User Generated Content" (Kaplan and Haenlein 2010, 61), social media have facilitated the distribution of K-pop content in transformative and powerful ways. What is notable is that the functions of social media have engendered the particular ways K-pop is consumed. The discussion that follows examines fans' activities on YouTube and Tumblr, the two most critical platforms in the penetration of K-pop, and will demonstrate that the very functionality of those social media sites has configured the visual, discursive, and affective consumption of K-pop among domestic and international fans.

By providing free access to the audio and video forms of K-pop content and serving as a base for the social distribution of fan culture, YouTube has played *the* key role in K-pop's international success. While music labels in other countries tend to remove video content from YouTube (except Vevo) because of copyright issues, Korean agencies have actually utilized the free platform as a promotional tool to reach a worldwide audience, particularly outside of Asia. The year 2008 ushered in a new period in K-pop history on YouTube. In 2008, JYPE and YGE joined YouTube and started to upload idol music videos; MNET became the first broadcaster to start posting live performances on the platform; and Eat Your Kimchi uploaded their first "How to Dance K-Pop Style" video, setting the stage for the many K-pop vloggers who followed. SME joined YouTube in 2009 and KBS became the first terrestrial station to publicly display K-pop performance clips on YouTube in 2010.[40] The momentum has even accelerated since 2012 when Psy's "Gangnam Style" hit one billion views.

The video-based platform has turned out to be an ideal fit for the visual focus of K-pop. The reasons people do not just listen to K-pop but watch it lie in its music video–based promotion. Because it presents each song's general concept, stage costumes, and sophisticated dance routines, music video is a main format for launching artists and advertising new songs. Korean entertainment agencies release idol groups' music videos, performance clips, and other media materials on YouTube with free access. Because the primary access channel to K-pop is graphically oriented, the consumption of K-pop among international fans is also visual. But YouTube allows its users to comment on each video,[41] so reception can also be verbalized. Fans really discuss K-pop idols and their performances, and some fans conduct textual analysis of the performances frame by frame. International fans particularly appreciate K-pop's choreography, which flawlessly coordinates catchy tunes with synchronized dance routines acted out by multiple members of a group. As one blogger has remarked: "Their emotion was stunning and their performance was chilling. As for dancing, much K-pop choreography is jaw dropping. Sometimes the dance moves they perform might not even be difficult, but what is amazing about them is how in sync they are with the rest of the group. They can convey the message of their songs through their dance and their facial expressions when they sing."[42] The series of comments form a dialogue among fans, producing collaborative discussion of K-pop content. The collective and discursive consumption of K-pop generates additional pleasures—particularly the pleasure of sharing the same interests with fellow fans—in addition to enjoyment of the original content. YouTube, therefore, enables sequences of visual and discursive consumption of K-pop.

The visual consumption of K-pop instigates visually oriented fan activities such as producing response videos, dance covers, and parody videos. Video tagging and annotation tools of YouTube also help global K-pop fans upload, share, and tag videos for each other, not only consuming the original content but also spreading it and enhancing fan communication (Chaney 2014). Fans also create and post "moments" videos in which multiple photos of particular idols (who are not necessarily in the same group) are organized with background music, creating the same kind of delicate ambiance as if they were a real couple. YouTube's "related videos" suggestions, powered by the Google search engine, cause fan-generated movie clips to appear together with original K-pop content, so that users can see a list of videos associated with particular groups. The usual pattern for most international fans is to become K-pop–addicted only after stumbling on a K-pop video online, which catches their attention sufficiently to encourage them to find out more about the idols or music scenes involved. The "related videos" function also lists the entertainment and reality shows in which idols appear, allowing fans who search for them to encounter and study diachronic information about K-pop groups. As this quotation from an interview suggests, those who simply fall for an idol can find themselves being thrown into the sea of K-pop: "K-pop groups have their own histories. When I accidently got into Super Junior in 2013, I searched more about the group online that went back to their debut year, 2005. When I realized that there are abundant music videos, shows, and concert scenes that have accumulated over the years, I felt like I found an inexhaustible well of fun."[43] In this way, the nature of the content and the functionality of the distribution medium work together synergistically.

Management agencies use YouTube as a main channel to both listen to global fans' voices and utilize them as free, but loyal labor (Jin 2015). YG Entertainment recruited fans to visit the Big Bang page (www.youtube.com

/bigbang), watch their music videos, and leave comments. SM Entertainment bluntly urged fans to increase the view-counts for the music videos of Girls' Generation's "Mr. Mr." and EXO's "Love Me Right"; if those videos achieved ten million and twenty million views, respectively, the agency promised to release the groups' in-house dance practice videos.[44] K-pop producers draw on fans' willing and excited participation in raising publicity and generating revenues.[45] These practices bring about a convergence between cultural producers, consumers, and distributors, that is, a convergence between the ways producers create new revenue opportunities and fans negotiate their right to participate through new media tools (Jenkins 2006).

Known as *the* hub of K-pop, Tumblr is an essential social networking platform that sustains thousands of international K-pop fan communities. Originally created as a blogging site, Tumblr is now a microblogging[46] site that allows users to post multimedia content including images, links, quotes, audios, videos, and GIFs. Being very visually focused, Tumblr forms a synergetic fit with the visual consumption of K-pop not only by increasing the number of views of K-pop music videos and performance shows but also by driving the transregional movement of idol images. Tumblr-users post the digital versions of idol images in physical print: for example, those published in magazines and brochures exclusively produced in particular countries. Fan-generated images such as "airport photos"[47] are transferred to Tumblr sites; fan communities on Tumblr also post all social media updates about K-pop idols, including those from East Asia–based platforms, such as China's Weibo and Korea's Me2day. The visually specialized operation of Tumblr, therefore, drives the rapid and distant distribution of K-pop stars' images across the globe. At the same time, globally connected through Tumblr, K-pop fans build a strong affinity with one another cross-regionally by sharing and exchanging idol images. Tumblr's functionality also contributes to the quick reproduction of K-pop idol images. Much of Tumblr's content can be accessed from Dashboard, where posts from the Tumblr blogs one follows appear. Content can be reblogged with a single click on a button on the dashboard without even having to leave Dashboard (i.e., without visiting the original blog site). This extremely user-friendly and interactive platform allows speedy dissemination of content, facilitating the ability of certain content to quickly go viral (DeSouza 2013). Users can, therefore, produce high volumes of posts through regular reproduction of the original content.

Building on its graphic-based feature, Tumblr's tagging function facilitates the affective consumption of K-pop. All posts can be tagged with subject or content identifiers. Because users can follow tags and see real-time updates from any Tumblr sites that post about the tags, the tagging function makes it easy for K-pop fans to look through all the posts related to their interests. K-pop devotees are extremely fond of using the tagging function to practice OTP (original true pairing), which indicates their favorite pairings among K-pop idols. Fans pair up idols regardless of gender and group, mostly based on their interactions with each other, and post crossover moments featuring the imagined couples (similar to the "moments" videos on YouTube). OTP can be understood as a visualized form of fan fiction. Posting the photos showing the fan-generated couple together, fans develop a fictional romantic relationship between them. Fans also talk about the endless possibilities of OTPs, fascinated by the tensions and chemistry between the paired-up stars. This imaginary relationship is what keeps those who support that particular OTP hard at work, passionate, and inspired.[48] OTP practices exemplify the process by which entertainment-driven fans' visual and discursive consumption of K-pop idols leads to the affective reproduction of them. Fans are attached to K-pop idols in diverse and creative ways, and the very functionality of social media keeps such enjoyable practices possible and sustained.

I have discussed the formation and growth of the international K-pop fandom that has been intertwined with the development of social media. International fans are gaining more weight recently not only because they have now begun to feed the K-pop industry itself but also because they are potential tourists to Korea, that is, the place consumers that Korean municipalities are waiting for. The next two chapters will show the tactics of Korean municipalities to entice global K-pop fans and utilize their affective attachment in promoting the K-pop–featured places.

## The Visual Reproduction of K-Pop Idols

The previous sections have demonstrated how the production of K-pop idols focuses on cultivating idealized images and how profit-generation schemes exploit such images. Mainly focusing on international fans, I have shown that consumption practices also engage primarily with the visual aspects of

K-pop music and idols. Here, let me extend the scope to include domestic K-pop fandom and analyze how their consumption practices "reproduce" K-pop idol images. I use the terms *reproduce* and *reproduction* because fans generate idol images on their own, in a way that surpasses the ability of producers to control them. The reproduction of K-pop therefore extends the visual and affective consumption of idols; because of their appreciation of idols' visual aspects, fans want to generate the best-quality idol images through their own admiring gaze.

Korean fans aggressively promote songs by buying or streaming music, religiously attending live music shows and event performances, and sending gifts to stars. Fan activities are not limited to cultural consumption. Social engagement in the name of K-pop idols is an already established phenomenon. Fans conduct philanthropic activities such as donating rice, building schools and libraries in developing countries, or planting forests in the name of the idols they admire. The most essential part of fan activity, however, is the visual consumption of idols; fans collect idol photos, repeat-watch idols' performances and create GIF or SWF images from video clips, or produce photo books and DVDs of the beloved idols by themselves. K-pop fans literally celebrate the visual appearance of idols so that "fucking pretty" and "fucking handsome" are the most frequently used words in the appreciation of idol photos and performances. Music is a supporting element to the visual qualities of idols on the consumption side as well. Of course, fans talk extensively about idols' voices and their strong and weak points vocally; they also admire their idols' mesmerizing dance performances. Nevertheless, the visual appreciation of idols is the dominant element in K-pop consumption.

Visual consumption leads to the visual reproduction of idol images and *fansite photographers* are one of the agencies for this. Fansite photographers take photos of a particular idol or an entire group of performers in public spaces such as in airports or at concerts, or during filming. They are often called "cannon goddesses" (*daepo yeosin*) because they use professional-grade, cannon-size cameras and lenses. With superfunctional DSLR (digital single-lens reflex) cameras and superzoom telephoto lenses, the cannon goddesses take close-up photos of idols that make them look as if they were standing right in front of the viewers. These already high-quality photos undergo retouching to further enhance their quality. By taking pictures of the LCD screens of these cameras, camera fans also post low-quality "previews" of idol photos on online fansites (mostly on Twitter) to entice other fans to buy the originals. Personalized logos to identify the copyright holder are added to one corner of the photos. The original copies are produced as photo-books or DVDs that will be sold, like idol merchandise, to other fans.

Idol photos taken by cannon goddesses are fundamentally different from those taken by journalists or commercial photographers. As the currency of fandom is love and affection, fan-produced photos embody their affective gaze. Taking account of idols' features and figures, fans capture the best angles and shots—the stars' most shining moments. Shinee World (or Shawol), the fan club of SHINee, is famous for the fantastic quality of the photos produced by fans.[49] A typical comment on a photo taken by Shinee World reads: "You can only capture the true beauty of something if you're truly in love with the subject. I think this is where being a fan shines."[50] Fans' production and distribution of idol photos represents the visual and affective reproduction of K-pop. Both fan producers (photographer fans) and fan consumers (fandom in general) of idol photos enjoy the pleasures of the affective rather than commercial reproduction of idols. Despite the possibility of stars' portrait rights being violated, entertainment agencies usually tolerate fan-generated photos because of their favorable function: to expand and consolidate fandom. Exquisitely visualizing idols' lives, fan-generated photos serve to sustain fandom both domestically and internationally, and attract more fans. For international fans, the fansite photographs are channels through which they can access the everyday lives of Korean idols. Needless to say, the photos taken by cannon goddesses are circulated on Tumblr, Twitter, YouTube, and other online venues for international fans.

Fan-generated idol images go beyond private and virtual circulation and become part of everyday media and urban landscapes in the form of *idol advertisements*, a part of celebrity advertisement that is planned, sponsored, and practiced by fan clubs to celebrate stars' birthdays, promote new albums and dramas, or publicize the anniversary of a group's debut. Advertising channels are varied and include newspapers, magazines, subway ad panels, and outdoor billboards. Because of their high visibility, appeal to the anonymous public, and relatively inexpensive cost, outdoor advertisements on subway trains, subway screen doors, buses, and billboards (see figure 3.1) are preferred by idol fans. For bus ads, an entire bus is wrapped in idol images. The result (called a *bus wrap*) has an enormous publicity effect due to buses' extreme mobility and ability to travel through the broader geographies of Seoul. On the electronic signage of building billboards, a fan-produced movie

Figure 3.1. Idol advertisement at subway platform. Photo by author.

featuring a particular idol is run in areas with a high volume of pedestrian traffic such as Myeong-dong, Gangnam, and Yeoudo, capturing the public's gaze.

As K-pop fandom has grown, transcending gender, age group, and nationality, idol fan clubs have become a new source of demand in the Korean advertising market. Surprisingly, international fans (mostly Chinese, but expanding to include other nationalities) increasingly advertise K-pop idols in Korea. JungSooJungBar, a Chinese fan club for Krystal in f(x), produced dynamic advertisements in Korea to celebrate her twenty-third birthday in 2015. According to reports, more than 80 megasized digital screens at the Gangnam, Hongdae, and Sinchon subway stations showed images of Krystal 257 times a day during one month. Given that the ads cost many thousand of dollars for a single day, we can imagine the amount of money fans used for the advertisement that continued for a month.[51] If idol merchandise satisfies fans' personal desires to be with the idols they admire, advertising an idol on a voluntary basis publicly asserts their affection and loyalty.

Domestic and international fans' love and support for K-pop idols are diversifying Korean urban landscapes. The influence exerted by international K-pop fandom, however, is not limited to cultural consumption and the transformation of streetscapes. As international fans wish to visit Korea and experience idol-associated products and places in the capital of K-pop, they have the potential to change urban economies. K-pop tourism is a growing phenomenon, and in anticipation of it or in response to it, Korean municipalities have launched place marketing featuring K-pop sites, as I will show in the next two chapters.

This chapter has established that the process of production, consumption, reproduction, and profit generation involving K-pop idols is entirely visually oriented. Fans' appreciation of the visual quality of idols is directly related to their affective consumption of idol-associated products and places. Idols manifest the neoliberal enforcement of the refined body and the commodification of youth. Behind the celebration of K-pop idols lies the incessant bodily development and affective labor that commercialize their youth. As most K-pop idols' popularity is built on their youth, the industry has contrived to maximize the profits from the time-limited marketability of idols by proliferating the business arenas that capitalize on their visual images. One of the business strategies that has been devised for this purpose is the creation of

K-pop places by creating associations between abstract pop music and physical sites. The spatialization of K-pop music and idols, along with the industry's globalization, has opened a window that enables Korean cities to utilize idol images to attract global fan-tourists. The next two chapters will show that the branding of Korean cities via K-pop idols likewise involves the image-oriented and affective nature of K-pop music.

Chapter 4

# K-Star Road

## *Making Gangnam into a K-Pop–Filled Place*

This chapter examines a case of place marketing employing the aura of K-pop idols. K-Star Road in Gangnam is a government-initiated urban district branding project featuring K-pop stars. As the biggest commercial and financial district in Seoul, Gangnam is a bastion of fortified wealth, power, and status. This case, therefore, is at the opposite extreme from the regional cities' struggles to take advantage of inexpensive drama sponsorship to persuade the public to take notice of their areas. Instead, K-Star Road capitalizes on an already established cultural and commercial infrastructure to brand the area as a K-pop–filled place. The branding project is built around image- and lifestyle-based place-marketing spectacles, embodying the same mechanism used to produce and sell K-pop idols. The actual cultural "experience" of K-Star Road, however, is achieved only through the presence of audience-tourists and their emotional engagement with the strip. The fan-tourists perform and develop the place meanings that the place marketers give to it, but sometimes challenge, alter, and contest them, too. This chapter will offer detailed empirical data about the production and consumption processes at work in K-Star Road. It begins with the history of Gangnam development to reveal the social, economic, and cultural meanings of the area. The next sections demonstrate that the branding of K-Star Road is a selective process designed to create particular urban images that stand in contrast to the existing realities in an effort to turn Gangnam into a global city. I argue that the K-Star Road project, on the one hand, reduces the realities of the place to fantasized images that are entirely entertainment oriented and, on the other, exploits the presence of fans and the emotional investment that they make in the area.

## The "Creation" of Gangnam

The Chinese characters that make up the word *Gangnam* mean south of a river. The name, therefore, literally refers to the area south of the Han River in Seoul. More generally in contemporary South Korea, however, the term *Gangnam* is used to indicate three wealthy and privileged districts located on the south bank of the Han: Seocho, Gangnam, and Songpa. And above and beyond its merely administrative and geographic meanings, the term is deeply imbued with symbolic significance: it stands for wealth, power, prestige, and a fever for education. Gangnam is the center of business, finance, and commerce in South Korea, and the wealthiest Koreans live there.[1] The most competitive school districts, the most expensive imported car dealerships, and the outlets for the most prestigious high-end designers' fashion brands are all concentrated in Gangnam. Until the 1960s, however, Gangnam remained an agricultural area. It was incorporated into the city of Seoul only in 1963. But within less than three decades, it had transformed into the most affluent area in South Korea, encapsulating all of the country's vested interests. Gangnam's rapid and radical development epitomizes South Korea's developmental dictatorship, distorted capitalist growth, and compressed modernization.

As South Korea's industrialization and urbanization proceeded, the concentration of population in the capital intensified. The population of Seoul increased from 1.57 million in 1955 to 2.45 million in 1960, growing by some 180,000 per year and by 900,000 in five years (Kang 2015). This explosive population growth resulted in extreme urban density in Gangbuk (north of the Han River), requiring solutions to be found in various fields, including transportation, housing, job creation, sanitation, and public finance. Gang-nam (south of the Han River) emerged as a site to which population and urban functions could be distributed from northern Seoul. The development of Gangnam, however, transcended the merely urban and functional and was involved in more complex sociopolitical contexts.

In 1966, the Park Chung Hee regime[2] initiated the construction of the Hangang Bridge No. 3 (currently known as the Hannam Bridge). It constituted a critical section of the Gyeongbu Expressway connecting Seoul and Busan (the second largest city in Korea), whose construction began in 1968. Although both projects eventually contributed to the sudden urban development in the Gangnam area, neither was initially intended to promote urban development. The Hangang Bridge No. 3 was designed to alleviate the difficulties experienced by the military in crossing the river during the Korean War. The Seoul–Busan Expressway formed part of larger infrastructural plans to stimulate economic development. When funds for the highway construction project ran out, the Park regime promoted the Yeong-dong Land Readjustment Project. It was this project that effectively urbanized the Gangnam area.

A land readjustment program (*tojiguhoekjeongri*) is a procedure to increase the overall value of a project site by combining or subdividing lots within it along rational lines and establishing public infrastructure such as roads, schools, and parks. This method enables the public authorities to secure land for public facilities without sufficient financing, because landowners provide parts of their land in return for the anticipated increase in its value. The Park regime used the land readjustment program to obtain land free of charge for the construction of the Seoul–Busan Expressway, particularly for the 7.6 km section from the end of the Hangang Bridge No. 3 to Yangjae that contains the current Gangnam area. The first Yeongdong Readjustment Project site (*yeongdong 1 jigu*) covered 15.62 million square meters and the second (*yeongdong 2 jigu*), 12.07 million square meters (Kim 2015). In total, a massive 27,690,000 square meters of land was made available for potential urban development, caused mainly by the highway construction.

Gangnam's evolution did not remain at the level of a mere physical development project, however: land speculation began to take place for the first time in South Korea. Even under Japanese colonial rule, the propertied class had focused on profiting from the exploitation of tenant farmers rather than seeking to make money through land transactions. Likewise, during the postliberation, post–Korean War era until the 1960s, the use value of land took precedence over its exchange value. Gangnam development, however, effectively changed the ways land was appraised and used. Hwang Sok-yong's novel (2010) *Gangnammong* (Dream of Gangnam) depicts the surprised reaction of ordinary people to the process by which Gangnam development transformed land into an exchangeable and lucrative commodity.

> The bridge [the Hangang Bridge No. 3] would be finished before the opening of the Seoul–Busan Expressway. There is land where the road goes, and land makes money. That is the first principle of real estate investment. It was the period when ordinary people, including Shim Nam-soo, knew that one could earn money only through selling goods or labor. Land was merely an immobile asset that could be used for constructing a house or producing agricultural products. That was the way it was in rural areas; in Seoul, only downtown commercial buildings or fine houses in rich residential districts were worth anything. So, what did it mean that land made money? (Hwang 2010, 207)

The novel describes in vivid detail how news of the new bridge tripled the land price from 300 won (approximately 30¢) to 1,000 won ($1) within less than a month. Speculators bought land aiming to resell it quickly at a large profit. As more people participated in the speculation, the speed and frequency of the land transactions accelerated. According to the novel, in Gangnam in the mid- to late 1960s one round of land transactions raised the land value by 300 percent overnight and multiple rounds increased the value more than tenfold within a mere three months. Speed ruled the land speculation market: "One year elsewhere is equivalent to ten years here, where the speed of time is the world's fastest" (ibid., 240). Between 1963 and 1977, the value of land in Hak-dong (an area in the Gangnam-gu administrative district) soared to 1,333 times its original level, in Apkujeong-dong to 875 times, in Shinsa-dong to 1,000 times, while in Shindang-dong and Huam-dong in Gangbuk, it increased to only 25 times what it was before (Shon 2003, 158). The skyrocketing land price in Gangnam engendered a real estate middle class that made huge fortunes merely by buying up land early and reselling it at an extraordinary profit. As *Dream of Gangnam* points out, "The weird thing is that nobody lost during the period" (Hwang 2010, 221). By boosting the future value of adjacent land, construction of the expressway played a critical role in creating surplus value. That is, infrastructure construction pushed up the expected return on urban development, thereby continuously bringing speculative capital into the real estate market.

During the initial stage of any efforts in large-scale urban development, the usual practice of public authorities is to introduce measures to prevent unearned income from land speculation. The Park regime, however, was the promoter rather than suppressor of land speculation during the 1960s and 1970s. In fact, the primary beneficiary of land speculation associated with Gangnam development was the Park regime itself. For the second Yeong-dong Land Readjustment Project, the Park regime and the city of Seoul announced an ambitious plan to relocate the Ministry of Commerce and its affiliated organizations into Gangnam, and to build residential complexes to house government officials. The actual aim of the plan, however, was to boost real estate prices in Gangnam as a quick way of raising political funds. It is clear from a variety of sources that the then-chief of the Urban Planning Board in Seoul City raised $2 million in illegal political funds for the Park regime by purchasing 821,051.24 m² of land in Gangnam at an average price of 5,100 won (around $5) per square meter between February and August 1970, and selling them again at an average price of 16,000 won (around $16) before May 1971 (Hwang 2010; Jun 2012).[3] The data show that the central state exercised the art of exploiting speed and quantity in its own land speculation. The Park Chung Hee regime very much led the way in stimulating capital accumulation through the new exchange value of urban space.

The regime also promoted the construction of mega apartment complexes on the newly developed land. Each complex consisted of several multistory, high-rise residential structures and therefore required the assembly of a large tract of land for its construction. The land was still divided into numerous relatively small lots owned by private individuals, however. Using its absolute monopoly over the urban project, the city government introduced the Apartment District System (*apateujigu*), according to which only the construction of large-scale apartment complexes would be allowed on certain designated sites. Under this system, individual landowners' inability to carry out separate construction activities left them with no option but to sell their land to construction firms. Limiting individual landowners' land use and land disposal rights, therefore, the Apartment District System favored construction companies to an extraordinary degree and in various ways.[4] Builders enjoyed the benefits of easy acquisition of land, administrative and tax incentives from the state, and the hot-selling of the newly constructed apartment condos. Gangnam development, therefore, virtually nurtured the construction giants through a variety of preferential treatments and some of them later grew into *chaebol* (business conglomerates). Ji Joo-hyong describes the Apartment District System as "exceptional zoning" (Ji 2016, 321), that is, a deliberate policy of limiting individuals' property rights and exploiting private ownership to create public infrastructure free of cost and to generate a budget for further urban development. Exceptional zoning therefore typifies the sociospatial exclusivity of Gangnam, with its preferential treatment of *chaebol* and the property-owning elite.

To facilitate population distribution into Gangnam, the Park regime carried out various urban strategies: the Supreme Court, Prosecutor's Office, and Express Bus Terminal (for cross-regional buses connecting Seoul with the rest of the country) were relocated as a magnet to draw people into Gangnam; the route of the Green subway line was also altered so that it followed a circular route connecting Gangbuk and Gangnam. The most significant of these moves was the forced relocation of top-tier high schools to Gangnam: Gyeonggi High School was moved in 1976, Hwimun High School in 1977, Jungshin Girls' High School in 1978, and Seoul High School in 1979. The relocation of elite schools continued throughout the 1980s, resulting in the establishment of the "Eighth School District."[5] Those who moved to Gangnam at that time were members of the top stratum in Korean society and included high-profile civil servants, lawyers and judicial officials, doctors, and businessmen. To ensure that their class prestige was reproduced in the subsequent generation, the Gangnam elite took an immense interest in their children's education. Therefore, the Eighth School District and the class strategy complemented one another. The incoming upper-class families resettled in the sizable, brand-new apartment complexes.[6] The new residents also included the nouveaux riches who had suddenly earned fortunes from real estate speculation. The extraordinary square footage of the apartment units in Gangnam naturally set a high price bar, making the area inaccessible to the lower middle class. Through its collective consumption of modern housing and top-quality education, the upper middle class developed a spatially based class status. And as its socioeconomic status was inscribed in a particular urban space, Gangnam, it rapidly established a spatially segregated class consciousness.

The development of Gangnam created a symbiotic relationship between the state, the construction conglomerates, and the emerging upper middle class. The Park regime tried to win legitimacy through urban modernization projects and the provision of massive housing units. The construction giants, which virtually owed their existence to Gangnam development, became a good source of political funding for the state. The upper middle class, through its territorialized class identity, effectively solidified its status as a distinct social entity. Thanks to this triangular symbiosis, Gangnam development deepened the speculative use of urban space. Gangnam became synonymous with the new meaning of urban space, whose newly created exchange value was expressed in the soaring price of real estate. Thus, the creation of Gangnam became a developmental "myth" on account of the area's consistent growth in material and symbolic power.

The never-failing success experienced by real estate speculators during the development of Gangnam was, if anything, accentuated in the aftermath of the financial crisis of the late 1990s. The Korean financial crisis was a debt crisis: South Korean companies suffered from having to repay accumulated, but nonperforming loans (Chang 1998). The crisis led to the intervention by the International Monetary Fund, and as a result, bank interest rates soared (to more than 30 percent), the Korean currency depreciated, and the real estate market collapsed. The neoliberal, flexible economic restructuring in the aftermath of the crisis affected different social groups and classes unevenly. While the working class suffered from layoffs, wage decreases (or unpaid wages), high living costs due to rising prices, and snowballing household debt,[7] the upper class reinvested the abundant cash income it earned from high interest rates in then-plunging real estate stock. After a decade of economic recovery, real estate buyers witnessed an extraordinary escalation in the value of landed assets. The financial crisis therefore made a significant contribution to the further consolidation of Gangnam's power, reinforcing the myth of "invincible Gangnam."

The promotion of Gangnam, moreover, was accompanied by the simultaneous suppression of Gangbuk (north of the Han River). While Gangnam was designated a Development Promoted District (*gaebal chokjin jigu*) where various tax exemptions were allowed, construction activities in Gangbuk were strictly controlled. The city government banned the construction of a new department store, wholesale market, factory, and entertainment facility in Gangbuk in 1972. Districts in downtown Seoul were designated as

Redevelopment Districts (*jaegaebal jigu*) in 1972–1973, and the construction, reconstruction, and extension of buildings were prohibited there. The transformation of farmland and forest into land for housing was likewise forbidden in 1975. Consequently, the development of Gangnam was never a natural phenomenon; it was based on the state-controlled regulation of other areas. The intentional nurturing of Gangnam, followed by the wresting of economic power from Gangbuk, has meant that the symbolic image of Gangbuk has gradually changed from being a center of politics, commerce, and finance into a place of "backwardness" (Ahn 2010). Popular and media discourses have gradually cemented the polarized spatial identities that associate Gangnam with wealth and advancement and Gangbuk with inferiority.

The suppression of Gangbuk resulted in an extraordinary growth in the number of entertainment venues, including bars, pubs, clubs, and hotels, and other commercial facilities in Gangnam. The mushrooming of spaces dedicated to the entertainment industry caused an increase in the number of beauty salons serving upper-middle-class women during the daytime and women working in the amusement industry in the area during the evening. The agglomeration of beauty service providers, in turn, attracted related businesses such as wedding shops, photo studios, and entertainment agencies, forming the nucleus of the present-day K-pop production area. Many entertainment agencies picked the clustering of beauty shops in the area as their criterion for selecting their current locations. One entertainment agency employee remarked: "Beauty services, including hair shops and beauty clinics, are available in Gangnam. If we try to move the agency building to somewhere near the broadcasting stations, we want to make sure that there are beauty shops in the area first."[8] Some high-end fashion boutiques moved from Gangbuk to Gangnam and more overseas designers' brands opened businesses there. In the wake of the concentration of consumption and entertainment spaces in the area, media and popular discourses reinforced Gangnam's image as stylish, fashionable, and trendy. The urban areas invented by speculative capitalism have turned into a space of superficial consumerism that overtly celebrates consumption and entertainment, forming a mutually reinforcing cycle between the two.

The history of Gangnam development shows how the contemporary hegemony of Gangnam was "invented." The developmental dictatorship produced new urban space in which speculative capital was able to move freely. The exchange value of urban space far exceeded its use value, bringing sudden and enormous wealth only to the haves of society. Gangnam's development engendered a new urban upper middle class that consolidated its wealth and status through the consumption of high-priced urban space, establishing a territorially identified class power. The promotion of Gangnam was likewise concomitant with the suppression of other areas, creating uneven spatial development in Seoul and the country as a whole. Gangnam's prestige has been bolstered by a superficial consumerism that blindly glorifies conspicuous consumption, creating exclusiveness by erecting insuperable price barriers. In sum, Gangnam's hegemony has been formed by the interactions among developmental dictatorship, speculative capital movement, spatial polarization, and materialistic, consumerist urban culture. The next section will demonstrate how a local municipality in Gangnam tries to render the place a "global place" by simply overlaying K-pop images on its already established hegemony, distorting and veiling the broader socioeconomic tensions lying behind the place hegemony.

## Gangnam's Global Promotion Strategies

Until 2012, Gangnam's hegemony operated locally, that is within South Korea, but in that year Psy's song "Gangnam Style" unexpectedly became a global phenomenon and introduced Gangnam to the world. Although Gangnam in "Gangnam Style" is used in its broader meaning as explained at the beginning of the first section of this chapter, Gangnam-gu Office (*gangnam gucheong*), the local administration governing Gangnam-gu, one of twenty-five official administrative districts into which Seoul is divided, has attempted to take advantage of the congruence of the two names in its place promotion.[9] Gangnam-gu tried to transform the unexpected global attention into actual tourist inflow into the area. During the period from November 2012 to October 2015, the Tourism Promotion Department of Gangnam-gu Office issued more than forty self-produced press releases for circulation among the domestic and foreign media.[10] The consistent marketing message throughout this period proclaimed Gangnam to be a global tourist destination. Media reports constantly described the area as the "Hallyu tourism city" or a "global tourist city," reflecting Gangnam-gu's aspirations to achieve the status of an international tourist hot spot, namely, the home of the Korean Wave.

Global cities are usually defined as nodes of the global economy with a heavy presence of headquarters of transnational companies, high-level professionals, and specialized service firms (Sassen 1991). They are characterized by their integration into the world economy, in which they function as base points or nodes for the global operations of transnational corporations, financial services providers, and production companies (Brenner and Keil 2006). It is necessary to ask, therefore, whether Gangnam-gu as a mere district possesses these characteristics or wields such power. The headquarters of some major firms, financial institutions, and commerce hubs are, indeed, located mostly in Gangnam. The concentration of finance and commerce in this specific geographical area, however, is the outcome of the country's uneven development and cannot, therefore, be recognized as an asset exclusive to Gangnam. The capital city's broader financial and commercial functions cannot all be directed to and confined inside the district boundary. Gangnam-gu's global city initiative, consequently, does not correspond to the district's actual functional position in the global economy. It should rather be understood as an aspiration to be listed in the roster of global cities, joining in the on-going competition among rising cities to attract capital, investment, and people.

As interesting as Gangnam-gu's pursuit of global city status while remaining a mere district municipality is the method it has adopted to realize its global ambitions. Gangnam's strategy is to attract foreign tourists. The district office officially announced a plan to inaugurate "Gangnam's era of one million foreign tourists." This is a strange divergence from other aspiring cities' conventional tactics, which are based on the speculative construction of place by erecting signature buildings, initiating megaprojects, or holding hallmark events (Harvey 1989a; Kong 2007; Ashworth 2009; Gotham 2011).[11] Although these flagship projects are also designed to attract global tourists as well as capital, they have at least some urban content because they involve building infrastructure or places. Gangnam's strategy, on the other hand, relies on an increase in tourist numbers pure and simple without consideration of urban qualities, and rests entirely on abstract images from popular culture. Whether or not the mere attraction of vast numbers of foreign travelers could render Gangnam a global place remains questionable; a more notable point is this endeavor's obsession with the foreign. While the imaginary existence of the foreign gaze was harnessed by the developmental state to mobilize the population to accelerate industrialization in the developmental era, municipal governments can capitalize on the physical presence of foreign bodies to make their areas look more diverse, cosmopolitan, and global. Foreigners are not only visitors who would consume the urban amenities in Gangnam, but more important, are an essential component to make the area appear to be global. Whereas regional cities utilize the number of foreign tourists visiting their areas in the second-round place promotion (see chapter 2), Gangnam clearly believes that an influx of foreign visitors is what will advance it to global city status. Gangnam-gu Office has displayed giant promotional images at major entry points into Korea from other countries, specifically, Incheon, Kimpo, and Jeju airports and Korea Air City Terminal. Asserting "Traveling Korea starts in Gangnam," it has tried to build a direct connection between Gangnam and the foreign. The district office also closely works with foreign (particularly Chinese) travel agencies to direct their flows into Gangnam. If global cities are characterized by the multiplicity of flows of people, goods, services, ideas, and images (Kong 2007), the narrowed emphasis on streams of tourists only, dismissing other flows of people such as professionals, servicemen, migrants, and so forth, reveals both hastiness and exclusiveness in Gangnam's global city making.

What Gangnam can offer tourists from overseas is shopping venues, medical services (focusing on beauty), and Hallyu entertainment. The new Gangnam Tourism Information Center that opened in 2013 advertises the available experiences extensively. Although the center provides general information about tourist spots, transportation, and accommodation in multiple languages, it guides its visitors toward very specific services. The division that exclusively provides information about medical services available in Gangnam takes up the majority of the first floor of the Information Center.[12] The second floor and stairways are dedicated entirely to contemporary Korean popular culture, with exhibits consisting of photos, cardboard cutouts, and handprints of the stars and star goodies. Visitors can take photos of themselves against a replica music video background, wearing outfits worn by K-stars on stage; they can also watch digital shows with Hallyu content presented using cutting-edge technology. The particular guidance offered in the center suggests what overseas visitors should do in Gangnam. Thus, targeting an audience of "foreign tourists" not only draws a line between who is welcome and who is not but narrows down the range of desirable visitors to those who can afford the consumption-oriented experiences.

The delineation of valued visitors through an association with consumption indicates the ways *the foreign* can brand certain areas as *global*. A growing body of research has examined the politics of difference in Korea created around the ethnicity and nationality of migrant brides and workers who are mainly from China and Southeast Asia (Freeman 2011; Choo 2016). These studies demonstrate how "other Asians" suffer from severe labor exploitation, physical and social discrimination, and contested citizenship in the production and domestic arenas. When "other Asians" come to the country as tourists, however, they turn into highly valued customers, deserving special attention. The same distinction between how foreigners are treated in the production and consumption arenas applies to the perception of place. Many migrant workers reside in Garibong-dong and Daerim-dong in Seoul and Ansan City. While Garibong-dong and Ansan are known and promoted as "multicultural" areas,[13] few people perceive them as *globalized* places. Present-day Myeong-dong, on the other hand, where foreign tourists visit in huge numbers (see chapter 5), is considered to be undergoing globalization. Gangnam-gu is trying to redirect them away from Myeong-dong and toward Gangnam. Conceptualizing the globalization of place associated simply with an increase in the number of foreign visitors is problematical enough, but this particular concept is exclusively based on consumerist practices. *The global* here is something that is essentially related to the profit-generation process.

In the production and dissemination of urban images for international consumption, Gangnam is marketed as a locus of consumption and popular culture. The very notion of itself as a space of conspicuous consumption that Gangnam has exploited to achieve its current dominant position in Korea is now projected outward to global consumers. A materialistic urban culture, operating on speculative capital and superficial consumerism, is overlaid with exciting and entertaining images representing K-pop stars. The hollow space created by developmental dictatorship, speculative capital, and high-class aspirations (in the interests of consolidating their vested rights), is now filled with cosmopolitan images of the global, the stylish, and the entertaining. And the area is seeking foreigners who will consume such images.

So, how to attract the foreign tourists of the desirable kind? Gangnam-gu promoters are trying to capitalize on the global popularity of K-pop. The district office has enlisted Hallyu stars as its public relations ambassadors: Rain and Girls' Generation in 2012; Super Junior, SHINee, and EXO in

2014. Marketing through ambassadors turns the stars' global popularity to account in boosting Gangnam as a globally recognized place, linking the desirable qualities of the stars—their stylishness, trendiness, confidence, and popularity—with Gangnam (Epstein and Turnbull 2014). The opening of the Tourism Information Center was accompanied by a hand-printing ceremony involving K-pop idols such as EXO, Super Junior's Eun-hyuk, and SISTAR Hyo-rin. Gangnam-gu Office also launched K-Star Road (discussed below) in which visitors can extend their K-pop experiences and which has held several annual festivals (e.g., the C-Festival and the Gangnam Festival) to which performances by K-pop idols are central. Yet hiring stars as the *face* of Gangnam-gu ironically reveals the reality of the district. Despite the spectacular images, Gangnam as a mere district does not possess intrinsically global qualities, so the global characteristics have to be hastily constructed by employing Hallyu stars who have gathered a global fan base. If the global hype surrounding K-pop wanes, the district's global images will fade away. Image building based on K-pop is, therefore, inherently speculative and abstract, relying solely on the performativity of the cultural industry.

The speculative global ambition of image building is actually a local strategy to cement Gangnam's hegemony. Declaring itself a "city" despite its district status, Gangnam figures as a separate entity detached from the rest of Seoul and South Korea. This separate enclave is branded as a cosmopolitan and global place to reaffirm its supremacy vis-à-vis other local areas. Thus, the self-awarding of global city status dismantles the conventional dichotomy between global domination and local resistance. Playing the global card is the area's strategy for distinguishing itself, continuing the practice of "Othering" non-Gangnam areas. Gangnam's tourism promotion strategies serve to fortify local supremacy by pursuing the global, visualized through the exhibition of the foreign bodies to a local audience.

As in many other cases of local promotion, Gangnam-gu's place marketing is closely associated with the district governor's political ambition. All press materials released by the district office prominently display then district governor's name. Obviously, putting the elected leader's name on the front is a very unusual practice in place marketing. The district office's self-produced press reports, therefore, can be interpreted as being in fact targeted at local voters.[14] As discussed in previous chapters, since the introduction of the local election system in the mid-1990s, urban space has functioned as fertile ground for elected local leaders to conduct policy extravaganzas. Even hegemonic Gangnam, the biggest beneficiary of the country's uneven development, is no exception. Ironically, however, the policy spectacles targeting local voters actually do not possess any substantial content concerning the local urban conditions. Since global city making is primarily focused on welcoming foreign tourists, the area's image has to be distortedly reproduced as one of consumption and entertainment. While some capitalist venues (such as hotels, restaurants, and shops) could benefit from such spectacular and superficial images, it remains questionable how such hastily constructed images deal with local residents' actual living conditions in general, particularly for the long-term. The localness of global city making only reveals its fragile features.

## K-Pop Tourism

The growth in numbers of Gangnam's global tourism promotion is not entirely policy driven. There is genuine tourism demand from the global K-pop fans. From the middle of the first decade of the new century, die-hard K-pop fans from Japan, China, Hong Kong, Taiwan, Singapore, the Philippines, Malaysia, Thailand, and other Asian countries have traveled to Seoul specifically to attend concerts by top K-pop stars. The numbers have soared and the diversity of international fans has expanded beyond Asia to cover North America, South America, and Europe. Large numbers of fans visit Korea, as individuals or in small groups, to attend live music shows hosted by broadcasting networks or K-pop groups' own concerts. The Incheon K-Pop Concert in 2012, for example, attracted 66,000 overseas fans from 65 countries, generating an economic impact equivalent of $9 million in income to the area; the Changwon K-Pop Concert in 2012 drew in around 50,000 foreign fans (Korea Tourism Organization 2012).

Korean popular music has become an essential component of South Korean tourism revenue, and the government has promoted Hallyu tourism aggressively to monetize the international impact and influence of the Korean entertainment industry. In 2011, the Korea Tourism Organization (KTO), a state corporation affiliated with the Ministry of Culture, Sports and Tourism, paid SM Entertainment approximately $264,000 to stage a concert in France to promote K-pop and travel to Korea.[15] Hallyu stars, including Girls' Generation (2010–2012), Psy (2013–2014), and Jun Ji-hyun

(2014–2015), were employed as Honorary Ambassadors for the "Visit Korea" campaign. In 2012, the KTO also launched an Internet campaign, the "Touch Korea Tour," via the Buzz Korea website (www.ibuzzkorea.com/eng), a website dedicated to Korean tourism marketing. The campaign offered the chance for fifteen lucky fans to win an all-expenses-paid trip to Korea, during which they would meet the goodwill ambassadors (the girl band Miss A, and the boy band 2PM) and embark on a "mission" together. There were a million foreign entrants from every corner of the globe (Browne 2013).

Individual actors have also joined the campaign. To celebrate the launch of MTV Korea in 2013, the network sponsored a "Fly to the Stars Contest" in which contestants had to "like" the MTV Korea Facebook page and upload a video explaining why they deserved to meet their idols. The winner would then receive a free trip to Korea to meet his or her favorite star (Browne 2013). Television stations that hold weekly live music shows to which fans are invited as audience members usually reserve seats for foreigners; the official website for Korea Tourism (www.visitkorea.or.kr) explains how to apply to attend K-pop music shows. Branching out its business interests into tourism, in 2012 SM Entertainment took over Happy Hawaii, a travel agency specializing in Hawaii, and renamed it SMTown Travel in a bid to build up more physical outlets for foreign K-pop fans. In the same year, SM also acquired BT&I, one of the largest travel agencies in Korea in an effort to associate its cultural production with tourism. The company CEO stated, "We're looking to expand K-Pop's business model to include dining, fashion, accommodation and exhibitions by building on BT&I's original tourism, leisure and travel business" (Cha 2012).

Endeavors by the government and industry to make K-Pop more tourist-friendly are not entirely supply driven. There *are* bigger potential demands for K-pop tourism to Korea. Global fans of Korean entertainment continue to express their aspirations to visit Korea both online and off-line:

> It's the gateway drug. The more you get into the music, the more you want to know about the language, the history, the culture, the food.[16]

> I was only in high school when I first got into the K-Pop craze. . . . My ultimate dream was to go Korea and actually meet my idols, see them performing on stage or even just bump into them in the streets. Back then, it seemed like it was impossible, but I know that as I get older, I'll be able to fulfill my dream because I'll eventually have work to earn my own money.[17]

I saved up money for many years, then I fell for K-Pop, and started spending. Right now I have to plan every concert/Seoul trip in advance. . . . I am very happy with my life as it is now. I love K-pop, and I love to travel.[18]

It's no doubt every international fan's dream to visit the entertainment companies of their favorite artists, take a proof-shot signifying "I've been here" and roam the area in hope to spot some K-Pop stars. This is totally understandable considering how many of us have been behind our laptops, getting emotional and being all jealous when we read up about the many fan accounts of our *oppas* [literally, "older brothers," but meaning male idols] and *unnies* [literally, "older sisters," but meaning female stars] being nice and sweet whenever they meet fans on the streets.[19]

I have direct personal evidence of both the immediate and latent tourist demand for opportunities to visit Korea; two students in my Globalizing East Asian Popular Culture class went to Korea to visit SM Artium during the spring break in 2015, much to the envy of their classmates.

For international fans of K-pop, Korea is a place where, so they fantasize, K-pop experiences are likely to be deeper and more direct. Traveling to Korea, therefore, is an overwhelmingly pop culture–focused journey to attend concerts and television shows, to go on pilgrimage tours to entertainment agency buildings and restaurants operated by K-pop stars (or their families), and to shop for K-pop merchandise (idol goodies). Tour itineraries and activities are flexible and individually tailored, far different from the conventional guided tours that follow fixed routes around historic and heritage sites. As K-pop fan-tourists are keen to explore any place associated with their K-pop idol(s) and search out embodied experiences and entertainment, their behaviors are similar to those of the drama-inspired tourists or celebrity fans described in chapter 2. I frame K-pop fan-tourists' experiences in terms of three types of "pleasure": the pleasure of expectation, the pleasure of connection, and the pleasure of knowledge accumulation.

First, for international fans, Korea is a dream place where the chances of meeting their beloved idols in person are much higher than elsewhere. Pleasurable expectation acts like a magnet to draw more fan-tourists to Korea. The area where entertainment agencies are mainly located is a common destination for fan-tourists aspiring to encounter a star. During both my fieldwork periods in Gangnam in 2011 and 2014, I saw significant numbers of overseas fans gathered, full of expectation, mainly around SME, JYPE, and Cube Entertainment. The fan-tourists were not engaging in typical tourist activities such as sightseeing. Rather, they were waiting around, probably in hopes of spotting their idols. A small donut shop located just in front of the JYPE building was enjoying a boom in sales serving the waiting fans. The Cube Studio, a café run by Cube Entertainment that sells coffee, desserts, and star goodies, looked to be thriving thanks to those fan customers, too. Every time a car stopped outside, all heads swiveled in hopes of spotting one of the label's stars on their way to the dance rehearsal rooms or voice-training studios upstairs. One of my teenage Japanese informants said: "I'm a fan of Taecyeon in 2PM. I hope to visit the restaurants and shops frequented by him. I also want to loiter around the JYP Entertainment building. If I'm lucky enough, I might be able to spot him or other members."[20] Although fans' expectations seem overoptimistic, it is this kind of anticipation that excites fans and keeps them engaging in fan activities. Mark Duffett (2013) explains, "the primary pleasures of fandom stem from their *aim* of encountering the performer" (16, emphasis added). The pleasure of expectation is a significant element in idol worship, so it is also a critical component of K-pop tourism. Anticipation is often accompanied by disappointment: "Fans hang out here, Dunkin Donuts just in front of JYP, to wait for their favorite idols, 'cause it's just in front of JYP, you can easily see idols or their cars coming and going. But NO idols were spotted T_T [a crying emoticon]."[21] "We didn't see any stars and weren't able to get inside any of the companies, so that was a little disappointing, but it was still cool actually being able to be where the companies were."[22] Yet it is a different sort of disappointment from that felt by group tourists while touring the drama sets. Rather than shattering their fantasies, a disappointing experience fuels even more powerful ambitions among keen K-pop fans to pursue other chances to meet the stars. Fan-tourists, therefore, tend to be extremely mobile and to explore multiple venues.

Second, the pleasure of connection is generated at the moment of an encounter with a star. K-pop concerts provide fans with the opportunity for actual physical copresence with their idols. For fans from overseas, concerts are events in which the consumption of K-pop moves from the virtual, mostly via online videos, to the physical and corporeal. International fans describe how they feel at the critical moment when they finally see the idols in person: "It feels like a dream. When the idols are on stage, they look so surreal. It is like watching a video clip but they ARE ACTUALLY THERE";

"When the artists come on stage, your heart stops. 'Are they real?' Then they start moving, so you know they're real. They might as well be unicorns because you're not sure they're real but they look magical, regardless."[23] The idols' physical presence assures fans that it is not a fantasy; these are real human beings in whom they have invested emotional and material resources. Once they have felt the thrills, overseas fans say, they want more of the same and cannot stop actually visiting Korea or wishing to go there again. That is why tourists driven by K-pop music are loyal and frequent visitors, as evidenced by the following excerpts from my personal interviews with diverse generations. A Chinese teenager remarked: "This is the thirteenth time I have visited Korea. Four of them were to attend EXO and SM Town concerts." And a Japanese female in her sixties stated: "I have traveled to Korea more than twenty times with my daughter. Many of them were to attend concerts given by Rain. Standing in a concert hall is totally different from watching a drama. It gives me energy and makes me younger." Compared with drama tourism, in which one-off visitors comprise the majority, K-pop tourism is geared toward repeated visits. Although the same groups and singers perform, every single concert is a composition with different content and a different plot. In addition, K-pop groups often "come back" with a new album/single and a different concept, different outfits and hairstyles, and different dances. Enthusiastic fans keep "coming back," too, so long as their interest is maintained.

In the mecca of K-pop, international fans not only connect with stars but also with other K-pop fans (Kim, Mayasari, Oh 2013). A Singaporean fan, who had already made her name as a leading K-pop fan online, conveyed the excitement of meeting other international K-pop fans: "When I was hanging around the SM Entertainment building, I came across a couple of Japanese fans. I talked to them with the little Japanese I know and a bit of hand gestures and we soon realized that we are all EXO-Ls [fans of EXO]. We're so excited, giggling and jumping in excitement. Of course, one of the most important questions that you need to ask when meeting a Kop fan is 'WHO'S YOUR BIAS? ["bias" means favorite group or member]' . . . We chit-chatted for a bit and said our goodbyes. It was an awesome experience meeting international fans."[24] If Korean pop music functions to bond global fans, Seoul is a place where you can meet the members of this virtual and imagined community in person. Despite language barriers, physical encounters among global K-pop fans provide a sense of sharing and community.

Concert venues in Korea are places not only to meet other global fans but to experience the practices of Korean fandom. International fans explain that there *are* differences in seeing a K-pop concert live in the capital of K-pop, where they can experience entirely new fan culture presented by domestic fans.[25] Korean fans proclaim which idol group they are cheering for by displaying that group's unique color and regalia. Trinkets, glow sticks, and poster paper are also used as fan signs. For international fans, simply watching the scene or participating in the group activity is a special experience. Having the opportunity to be in the crowd and yell along with the fan chants is so thrilling for them. Bags of rice from all over the world are usually piled up in front of concert venues; fans express their support for their favorite groups by presenting rice bags that will be donated after the show in the name of their group.[26] Fans say the various countries represented in the rice donations are like a mini United Nations. While waiting for the concert to begin, fans will take pictures of themselves next to cardboard cutouts of their favorite stars. International fans can also witness how passionate fans chase their idols' cars the moment after a concert ends. Fan-informants have told me: "K-Pop concerts have a magical aura that you can only get by seeing them in the motherland of K-pop. You may have to wait a long time, but the memories, fan chants, singing, and screams stay with you for a long time. It is definitely worthwhile; the excitement before, during, and after the experience stays constant throughout."[27]

Third, visiting Korea offers global fans the pleasure of knowledge accumulation. Concerts and fan meetings are precious opportunities for fans to have face-to-face encounters, enabling them to expand their knowledge of celebrities into new areas. Knowledge accumulation by international K-pop fans, however, is not confined to learning about stars. They get to know about K-pop–associated places, the idol-branded products, and South Korea in general. Experienced K-pop tourists offer comprehensive advice on where to go, where entertainment companies are located and how to reach them, where to eat, how to get into music shows being filmed for broadcasting, how to obtain concert tickets and access concert venues, and where to buy idol goodies. Online postings pass on visual information, including transportation maps, corner-to-corner photos, and landmark displays. There are even those who have filmed their journeys in Korea and added detailed verbal explanations before uploading their material to YouTube.[28] By distributing the information they have collected to other supporters, pioneer fan-tourists can achieve a higher status within fan communities. The pioneers who first experienced K-pop in the mecca of K-pop also relate how they *felt* to be in Seoul. "Two of my bias [favorite] group's name in one post—I was screaming! Props to the designer . . . exercising our Sherlock eyes on this little designs [*sic*] just to find our favorite group's name. Lovin' the concept. NOW ENTERING MY HEAVEN."[29] Sharing affective experiences stimulates other fan-viewers to emotionally engage with the online post, provoking in them the pleasures of expectation. These sorts of personal, detailed, and affective accounts of their experiences of concerts and K-pop–associated places function as the most effective tools to advertise the places and actually attract more fans. As the next section will elaborate, place marketers both intend to or happen to utilize such fans' "labor of love" as skilled free labor to promote place well beyond the original advertisement target boundary.

## Experiences of K-Star Road

In September 2013, Gangnam-gu Office announced its plan to create a tourist attraction by designating the 1.08 km stretch of road between the Galleria Department Store and SM Entertainment and Cube Entertainment in Apgujeong-dong as "K-Star Road." The plan outlined how the street would be redesigned as an urban trekking route, along which tourists would be able to visit places telling the stories of Hallyu. The project was carried out in two different phases. In the first phase (2013–2014), the district office placed the "K Bird," a symbol of K-Star Road, on lampposts, trees lining the street, and pedestrian crossings. The K Birds draw attention to forty-eight "Storyshops," stores and businesses in the neighborhood frequented by Hallyu stars; for example, a barbeque house that members of KARA often visit, a curry place frequented by members of SHINee, a café run by So Ji-sub (an actor and Hallyu star), and shops featured in popular television dramas such as *Secret Garden* and *IRIS*. Retelling stories about various Korean pop stars, the designated shops aim to let K-pop fans have similar experiences to those their beloved stars had at those places. The district office also produced and distributed guidebooks and maps introducing the forty-eight Storyshops to foreign tourists and established photo zones in which fan-tourists could have their photos taken with life-size cardboard cutouts of their beloved idols. The second part of the project (2014–2015) included setting up three-meter-tall art toys, or so-called GangnamDols—a word coined by combining "Gang-nam-gu" and "K-pop idols" (see figure 4.1). The GangnamDol kiosks were named for the ten popular K-pop groups the district office worked with: Miss A, 2PM, 4minute, Super Junior, SHINee, FT Island, TVXQ, EXO, CNBLUE, and Girls' Generation.

K-Star Road is one part of the "K-ROAD" urban branding project that Gangnam-gu Office is promoting.[30] Urban branding originates in product branding, a marketing strategy to select some attributes of a product as its core values to facilitate the process by which consumers come to confidently recognize and appreciate those attributes (De Chernatorny and Riley 1998).[31] City branding is a development of this technique that is used to publicize a city's competitive advantages. Cities do not have single, unique identities. Where there are a number of coexisting urban identities that often compete against each other, city branding is an inherently *selective* process that distills various representations of an urban area and guides recipients to "see the city" in a particular way (Selby 2004). Urban branding is a deliberate intervention privileging certain representations of a city and embedded in certain norms and values (Jensen 2007). As Miriam Greenberg (2000, 229) defines it, the branding of the city is "the simultaneous marketing and production of a monolithic, consumer-oriented version of the urban imaginary."

Figure 4.1. GangnamDol on K-Star Road. Photo by author.

The K-Star Road project guides its audience, especially foreign tourists, to see Gangnam exclusively as the place of entertainment. As a result of this restrictive urban image making, the material reality of Gangnam—the hegemonic place created by uneven economic development, the spectacular place built on speculative capital and superficial consumerism, the place that is driving the real estate bubble that is seriously affecting the lower classes—is erased. The friendly, chic, and stylish K-pop idol images obscure Gangnam's contentious history and controversial hegemony. Since urban branding operates as a "specific discursive formation and practice" (Mayes 2008, 126), local media coverage, mainly controlled by press releases from Gangnam-gu Office, reinforces this exclusive way of perceiving Gangnam.

Gangnam's image branding is not only contested, however; it also has no content. Obviously, the K-Star Road project puts K-pop idols in the forefront of place marketing. Idol-based place marketing is possible there due to the agglomeration of entertainment agencies in the area: there were 806 in total as of May 2017.[32] As discussed previously, the deliberate promotion of Gangnam and suppression of Gangbuk caused entertainment companies to concentrate there. For easy access to their workplaces, many celebrities actually live nearby. Gangnam, therefore, is where K-pop stars work, rest, and live their lives, which makes it a fantasy land for fans, where the chances of seeing idols are much higher than elsewhere. Yet the pilgrimage tours to Gangnam began even before the Gangnam Style boom and the K-Star Road project. These facts are also highlighted by a district official's promotional statement:

> The place is most-frequented by avid K-pop fans worldwide who visit Korea in hopes of seeing their idols in person. We hope this street becomes a landmark tourist attraction, especially with growing demands from K-pop fans who visit Korea for their concerts. We hope this street helps them have a unique cultural experience in a country of their beloved stars. Visitors to the street may want to really see Hallyu stars. So we'll hold autograph events regularly. The Korean entertainment industry is gaining worldwide recognition for its talented performers. The district will help support them by organizing events more frequently where they can interact with fans. We plan to further develop cultural content that can accommodate K-pop fan visitors to help them spend a memorable time while staying here.[33]

What Gangnam-gu Office is doing is merely capitalizing on both the already established cultural infrastructure in the area and the global fans' aspiration to meet K-pop stars. By giving a name, "K-Star Road," to the ambiguous geographical space where K-pop fans frequently hang out, the local government has made the growing phenomenon tangible and the exclusive property of that particular area.

Despite the power of its name, however, K-Star Road does not necessarily provide entertainment content to visitors, that is to say that fans cannot always see their idols or idol performances there. The mere physical clustering of management companies does not guarantee that any visitors actually experience K-pop; instead, fans sometimes experience the limited pleasure of expectation only. The idol-featuring art toys and bird symbols merely offer pseudo-idol experiences to K-pop fans. To supplement this vague and uncertain notion of "experience," the district office announced that it would organize more events such as Hallyu concerts and star–fan meetings (though not on a regular basis). Yet to what extent sporadic events of this kind will offer visitors sufficient and satisfactory K-pop experiences remains uncertain. The municipality does not engage in actual K-pop production at all; the actual cultural producers are the stars and entertainment agencies. Gangnam-gu is building its district image by simply appropriating the output of the cultural suppliers congregated within it. Thus, the idol-led place promotion is revealed as being image based rather than actually developing the cultural content of the area, in the same ways that K-pop idols are sold on the basis of their images rather than their actual cultural assets and talent. What the local government intends is a "celebrity transference" to the place, forging fictitious, rather than actual, links between K-pop idols and K-Star Road.

If the K-Star Road branding project does not provide any actual entertainment content, then what is the mechanism that will create and sustain the place's *brand*? What renders K-Star Road a truly Hallyu-filled place is fan-tourists' emotional investment in it. Seasoned fans share and disseminate the pleasure they got from expectation, connection, and knowledge accumulation about K-pop–related places among the fan communities. To give one example: "I really miss this place so much! I regretted that I didn't wait for a longer time in front of my idol's entertainment company. . . . I really wish to see him in real lifeeeeeeeeeeeee. . . . We headed to K-Star Road which located [sic] at Apgujeong Rodeo Station. I was soooooooooooo excited because I would be going to visit the place that my idol usually works! Inhaling the same air with him, walking through the places that he stepped before."[34] What truly advertises K-Star Road to an international audience, therefore, is not the district office's outpouring of media promotions, but fan-tourists' emotionally charged accounts of their own experiences of the place. The key to successful branding is to establish a relationship between brand and consumer; thus, there should be a close fit between the consumer's own physical and psychological needs and the brand's functional attributes and symbolic values (Hankinson and Cowking 1993). Likewise, city branding strategies aim to forge emotional links between a commodified urban space and consumers.[35] Thanks to the affective nature of popular culture, K-Star Road allows visitors to develop emotional connections with a celebrity-associated space. K-pop fans, particularly international fans, equate K-Star Road with K-pop idols; the urban space turns into an emotion-laden place brimming with expectation and yearning to meet the idols they admire in person. The above quotation demonstrates once again how passionate appreciation of K-pop idols is extended into affective consumption of place. The aim of the K-Star Road branding project, therefore, is to exploit the emotional resources that international K-pop fans invest in developing empathetic bonds with the place.

To complete the K-pop–focused urban branding project through its urban users' voluntary participation, the district office has come up with the idea of "storytelling." A notable feature of K-Star Road is its promotion of "Storyshops"—cafés, restaurants, and boutiques frequented by Hallyu stars. These star-associated businesses are scattered nuggets of K-pop acting as hidden magnets to draw in significant numbers of (foreign) tourists. Both domestic and international fan communities have shared enormous amounts of informal information about restaurants, cafés, and shops operated by K-pop idols and their families. Blogs and social media pages introduce the idol-run shops and include directions to them, menus, and even pointers about time slots that offer the best chances to spot the stars. Reviews of these shops display dazzling photos of their interiors and the dishes on offer, and describe in detail how celebrity families behave toward fans. For example: "Kamong Café is owned by the sister of one of the EXO members, Kai. K-pop fans, most especially EXO-Ls, have flooded this recently opened café because it's connected with one of the members of EXO. Her older sister has been gaining a lot of popularity these days by how she takes orders personally from her customers and fans would ask anything-under-the-sun questions about Kai and EXO."[36]

What Ganganm-gu Office has done is to publicly identify and brand those shops that are located within the district's boundary near K-Star Road. But neither the place marketers nor the designated shops themselves spread stories about Storyshops. The job of storytelling falls on consumers who visit K-Star Road, that is, mostly K-pop fans. Fans may spot their favorite idols on K-Star Road and circulate the story to online fan communities. Fans' accounts of their own experiences when visiting shops run by K-pop stars are always exciting for them and are likely to make fan communities jealous. Storytelling, therefore, requires consumers' proactive participation, in the form of a significant level of willingness to create stories. As in the drama-associated places, therefore, the essential advertiser of the place is devoted consumers. While regional municipalities show their particular interests in the number (itself) of tourists in boosting publicity, Gangnam devised an extra mechanism, via Storyshops, to encourage fan-tourists to voluntarily deliver their own stories about the place.

K-Star Road obviously aims to harness the global popularity of K-pop idols. Yet apart from the entertainment agencies, there are no local places that are directly associated with the stars. Idols are "made" in the transmedia circulation and by fans' discursive consumption. They are an intertextual commodity and thus not inherently associated with physical places. Stars are placeless; indeed, they are extremely mobile in visiting any places where there are demands for idols. Yet the K-Star Road project is an attempt to connect that place with stars. The Storyshops are those of a few places that could have, at least, some relations to celebrities by highlighting stars' memories. The shallow and fragmented star memories the Storyshops are trying to evoke serve to expose the project's lack of real content.

What, then, has been the outcome of the K-Star Road project? Because the project is relatively recent and still ongoing, it is too early to evaluate its success or failure. The number of foreign tourists visiting Gangnam has been continuously increasing since 2011.[37] Yet it is hard to tell what exactly attracts them in the context of the overall increase in inbound tourism to Korea; Gangnam's medical services, K-pop production, shopping centers, and other attractions all function as magnets. Thus, the particular impact of K-Star Road on foreign tourist numbers remains uncertain. Despite the ambiguous consequences of the policy, the branding project is not likely to wither in the near future. Capitalizing on the established cluster of entertainment agencies, the K-Star Road project is inherently different from the one-off sponsorship of drama production by regional cities. Since the area already has a settled cultural infrastructure, the branding power of K-Star Road is likely to be sustained for as long as the global popularity of K-pop lasts. Nevertheless, the K-pop–mediated branding practices are also speculative, because they entirely depend on K-pop's global popularity, whose duration is uncertain. Despite the rich infrastructure, the policy's short-term focus dovetails with the district governor's limited tenure, revealing the local nature of the policy extravaganza once again. Riding on the (probably temporary) K-pop craze, relying on preexisting cultural assets, and taking advantage of K-pop fans' emotional engagement, the K-Star Road branding project looks to be less expensive and more stable and sustainable than drama sponsorship.

It is difficult to think of Apgujeongro, where K-Star Road is located, as a "street." In reality, it is simply a road where car traffic is heavy and fast moving. Interactions between the road and nearby buildings are scant. Few people actually walk along the sidewalk, since upper-class customers mostly use cars to enter shops. Apgujeongro is densely dotted with designer brand shops, representing the superficial "lookism" nurtured by South Korea's compressed modernity. At the same time, these luxury shops embody the country's stratification, since they form an alienated and inaccessible enclave. The dazzling facades of the luxury shops, adorned with glittering glass and metal screens, offer in microcosm an image of the area's cold and impassive material urban evolution. Now, the hollow space has been decorated with K-pop images. The place marketers have chosen and promoted one particular fantasized and entertainment-led urban image, erasing the underlying material and spatial tensions the areas has. Moreover, what sustains and further develops the fantasized K-pop imagery of the place is not the place marketers' investment, but the emotional resources of consumers. The free labor of fan tourists who write personal accounts of this urban space is the mechanism used to advertise it and create brand value for it. The activities created for consumers' own pleasure are exploited as a means of generating surplus value from the commodified urban space. The superficial nature of this case of place branding is particularly well illustrated by its audience-led storytelling: the spectacle itself that audience has come to see has no substance, no content, and no investment. This is the naked reality of Gangnam. Gangnam's traditions have to be "engineered" by K-pop fans' proactive storytelling.

Chapter 5

# Cosme Road

## *K-Beauty and the Globalization of Myeong-dong*

This chapter[1] explores a case in which Korean popular culture sells a place associated with the cosmetics industry. While the cases in the previous chapters were about the local government's intervention to employ K-dramas and K-pop idols in place marketing, this chapter examines a casual process in which Hallyu has indirectly but greatly accelerated the globalization process of Myeong-dong, one of the biggest commercial districts in Korea. Although there is no drama and K-pop production centers aggregated in Myeong-dong, people can feel the Hallyu atmosphere more in this area than anywhere else through an urban landscape that is excessively decorated with K-star images. Employing K-pop idols as their brand models, cosmetics retail stores display the predominant Hallyu images. To consume both the Hallyu images and Hallyu-constructed Korean beauty, numerous foreign tourists are flowing into Myeong-dong, reconfiguring the area's retail landscape and place identity. Deciphering the triangular relations between Korean popular culture, Korean beauty ideals, and the cosmetics industry, this chapter offers detailed discussions about Myeong-dong's recent place reconfiguration associated with the projection of Hallyu desires and global flows. I argue that the multirealm global connections—the globalization of Korean pop culture, the construction of Korean beauty inspired by Hallyu, the global expansion of the Korean cosmetics industry, and the Hallyu-driven transnational tourism—complicate Myeong-dong's place meanings by turning the area into a site for the projection of Hallyu desires associated with capital accumulation.

## Myeong-dong: Brief History and Recent Globalization

Myeong-dong, now a commercial district in central Seoul, dates back to the Chosun dynasty (1392–1910), when it was called "Myeongryebang" (meaning "bright village") and was mostly a peripheral residential area where lower-level officials and merchants resided. The area was first open to outsiders around the late nineteenth century, when the peninsula emerged as a lion's share for contention among the neighboring powers. In 1882, to control the Imo Incident (a military revolt),[2] the Chosun government requested support, and in response, Qing sent three thousand troops and about forty merchants. These men did not return back to their country after the situation was subdued. In 1884, the Qing Office of General Affairs and Chinese Hall—the equivalent of the chamber of commerce for Qing merchants—was built in present-day Myeong-dong. In 1885, Japanese merchants were also granted legal residency. They mostly lived in southern Myeong-dong, at the foot of Nam Mountain, where the Japanese Consulate was located. As the number of foreigners residing in Seoul grew, the Chosun government made agreements with the diplomats of each country to restrict the areas where they could live. Present-day Myeong-dong was designated as the Chinese concession, while the area south of it in present-day Chungmuro became the Japanese settlement (Chun 2012). The presence of global forces seemed to create a cosmopolitan ambience in Myeong-dong: it was the space of the "Other" occupied by foreigners.

In the aftermath of the Sino-Japanese War (1894–1895), most Qing merchants returned home while the Japanese took over the Chinese concession. After Japan's victory in the Russo-Japanese War that broke out in 1904 and throughout Japanese colonial rule (1910–1945), Myeong-dong and Chungmuro became a hegemonic space through which Japanese colonial control was entrenched. Colonial administrative, commercial, and financial institutions—such as the Japanese General Government Building, the Bank of Japan, Chosun Commercial Bank, and Teikoku Life Insurance—were constructed in the area, visually asserting the colonial power there. Called "Honmanchi" in Japanese, on the other hand, Myeong-dong was transformed into the most bustling commercial district in Seoul and displayed colonial modernity. The modern urban space hosted Western-style buildings, public institutions, banks, and cafés, forming new urban visual spectacles. Four department stores (Mitsukoshi, Jojia, Minkai, and Hirata) opened there, launching the area's identity as a place of consumption and a mecca of fashion. Myeong-dong became a bustling hub of shoppers, strollers, people-watchers, and hustlers. The area was not a heterogeneous space where different kinds of crowds could mingle, however. Rather, Myeong-dong was a site in which the power lines between the colonizer and the colonized were constantly drawn.

After liberation from colonial rule, the Korean War (1950–1953) devastated Myeong-dong; nevertheless, the postwar recovery of the country centered around the area. Throughout the 1950s and 1960s, Myeong-dong established its position as *the* center of finance, commerce, fashion, and entertainment in South Korea. The DaeHan Stock Exchange Building, located at a connecting point between the Myeong-dong shopping district and the Eulji-ro office district, signified a burgeoning capitalism. On the flip side of material profit was the world of art and culture represented by Myeong-dong Theater and the UNESCO Building. Yet what turned Myeong-dong into a cultural place was its *dabang* culture. Literally meaning "tea house" but often translated as "coffee shop," *dabang* served as social hot spots where struggling musicians, poets, painters, and actors gathered, crafted their art, and dreamed of a better future.[3] Revolving around *dabang*, the postwar revitalization of Myeong-dong created a place of romance, culture, and pleasure. During the 1950s and 1960s, Myeong-dong also witnessed the proliferation of upscale shops, boutiques, and beauty parlors, transforming the area into the capital of fashion, trends, and stylish consumption. By the mid-1970s, the district had reached its position as "the premier shopping destination of Korea with the youthful and fashionable from all over the city visiting it not just to shop, but to see and be seen as fashion trends developed on the streets" (Chun 2012). The youth culture associated with drinking beer and folk guitar performances marked another aspect of the place in the 1970s.

Under the rule of the Yushin Constitution,[4] from 1972 through the 1980s, Myeong-dong was home to the heart of the democratic movement of Korea. As the hallowed ground of the prodemocracy movement, Myeong-dong Cathedral served as a shelter and base for protestors calling for democratization. On the other hand, the development of Gangnam fundamentally changed the nature of Myeong-dong since the 1980s. As many cultural facilities, entertainment shops, banks, and companies were relocated to Gangnam, the hegemony of Myeong-dong as the center of consumption was weakened. The most sophisticated consumption is no longer associated with Myeong-dong; it has moved to Gangnam and Myeong-dong has been demoted to an area of mass consumption. Fashion designers' conversion from tailored to ready-made clothes also contributed to Myeong-dong's decline. Shops began to carry low- and medium-priced, fast-fashion merchandise. While the land value of Myeong-dong was still the highest in the country, the customers at its shops and businesses were no longer the most fashionable or affluent. Yet Myeong-dong was still one of the most vibrant districts in Seoul, where thousands of brands were sold and innumerable passersby would gather and stroll.

Myeong-dong's rich history reveals that it has continuously constructed and reconstructed its distinctiveness. Starting from its origins as a foreign enclave through its destruction during the Korean War, to becoming the center of the prodemocracy movement, commerce, and fashion, Myeong-dong, as a place, has constantly reconfigured its meanings and identity. Historical, economic, political, and social conditions have contributed to its identity changes. Despite its identity mutations over time, what Myeong-dong has steadily held is its symbolic status in Korea, enabling the place go through the foremost transformation when there are any changes in the internal and external dynamics.

Myeong-dong is currently reshaping its identity, once again influenced by globalization. On a Saturday afternoon in 2014, when I was hanging around Myeong-dong, I accidentally overheard two young Korean women talking to each other. One of them said: "Are there still any Koreans in Myeong-dong? We might be the only ones." I soon found out that the remark was not an exaggeration. Myeong-dong is globalizing; foreigners comprise the majority of its shopping population. When I did fieldwork in 2014, Korean was not the most heard language in Myeong-dong. A street preacher was delivering speeches in multiple languages to cater to foreign passersby. It is hard to find store signboards written in Korean in the area: most are in Chinese, Japanese, and English. Almost all of its businesses—clothing stores, coffee shops, restaurants, and even small snack bars—have sales assistants who can speak more than two languages. All product names, prices, and menus are offered in four different languages: English, Chinese, Japanese, and Korean.

The recent reglobalization of Myeong-dong began with the inflows of Japanese tourists in the early 2000s when the unexpected popularity of Korean television dramas in Japan caused the emergence of drama tourism, typically centered on visiting shooting locations or efforts to meet Korean celebrities (see chapter 2). As Yukie Hirata (2005) explains, Japanese drama tourism is another form of the gendered travel comprising mainly of middle-aged women as cultural agency, distinguished from the previous male-oriented sex tour. Although Myeong-dong was not a popular destination for these drama-themed tours, the area was a significant part of "visiting Korea" for Japanese tourists because of its central location and symbolic position. Myeong-dong's physical proximity to the historical and cultural sites of Seoul such as Namdaemun, Insa-dong, and Gyeongbok Palace works perfectly to attract Japanese tourists, who want to explore traditional Seoul and enjoy shopping at lower prices simultaneously. The phenomenal strength of the yen (¥) during the period between 2009 and 2012 contributed to even more vibrant transborder tourism. The number of Japanese tourists, which remained steady at around 2.3 to 2.4 million during the five years from 2004 to 2008, suddenly soared to more than 3 million in 2009; it rose to more than 3.2 million in 2010 and 2011, and reached its peak at 3.5 million in 2012 (Korea Tourism Organization 2014). As Myeong-dong became a paradise for Japanese shoppers exploiting the strong yen, almost all businesses in the area, including hotels, duty-free shops, beauty clinics, nail shops, hair salons, and cosmetics stores, thrived. The successful business types also speak to the gendered composition of Japanese tourists—middle-class, middle-aged females who are increasingly empowered as consumers (Kim 2005). When I did my first fieldwork in spring 2011, *Irasshaimasei*! (Japanese, meaning "Welcome to the shop") was the most frequently heard word in the area; despite my obvious Korean look, I was always welcomed by the Japanese greeting at that time. The presentation of promotional products exclusively in Japanese signified both the predominance of Japanese customers and Japanese-targeted commercial operation in the area at that time.

Japan–Korea tourism, however, is strongly affected by the exchange rate, diplomatic relations between the two countries, and security issues in the Korean peninsula. When the ROKS *Cheonan* sinking occurred in 2010, for example, the number of inbound Japanese tourists significantly dropped for a while. When the value of the Japanese currency started to weaken in 2013, the number of Japanese tourists suddenly dropped to 2.7 million in 2013 (Korea Tourism Organization 2014). Yet that did not signify a downturn in foreign visitors to Myeong-dong. Rather, the number of international tourists has further escalated since 2012 thanks to Chinese tourists, commonly called *youkers* (a Chinese word meaning "tourists"), who now outnumber other nationalities and are rapidly increasing. According to the Korea Tourism Organization, around 2 million *youkers* visited Korea in 2011; the number surged to more than 4 million in 2013 and more than 6 million in 2014 (ibid.).[5] Albeit overshadowed in numbers by Japanese and Chinese, there are significant numbers of Southeast Asian tourists as well. The numbers from North America and Europe have also grown recently. Consisting of the mostly foreign tourists, over 1.5 million shoppers pass through the area each and every day, and the density of the shopping population in Myeong-dong is the world's highest.

In what sort of activities do these inflowing foreign tourists participate in Myeong-dong? Beside its traditional position as the center of commerce, exactly what recent aspect of Myeong-dong attracts these visitors? More than 80 percent of Chinese tourists picked shopping as a major activity during their visit to Korea; in 2013, the biggest shopping item in Korea was cosmetics for both Chinese (73.1 percent) and Japanese (43 percent) tourists (Korea Tourism Organization 2014). In a nutshell, the travelers from overseas visit Myeong-dong to engage in cosmetics shopping.

Myeong-dong boasts the country's highest land values and retail rents. Indeed, the top five most expensive lots in South Korea are located in Myeong-dong, and the area recorded the world's eighth-highest commercial rent in 2014, one rank up from ninth-highest in the previous year.[6] The economy of urban rent is driving retail transformation and reveals what is the "hottest" business at any particular time. While keeping its traditional reputation as a mecca of fashion, Myeong-dong has witnessed continuous changes in its predominant retail composition from designer brands, imported clothes, and flagship stores of domestic brands to global SPA (specialty store retailer of private label apparel) brands. These days, low-end or budget cosmetics (called *jeoga hwajangpum*) are among the few retail types that can afford the sky-high rents. Retail transformation is not simply a matter of new signboards on stores; it indicates a shift in the dynamics of the urban economy, the lived experiences of people, and their sense of place. Along with the retail transformation, Myeong-dong's primary identity is changing from "No. 1 Shopping District" to a beauty shopping, and more specifically, a cosmetics shopping area. Why and how have affordable cosmetics stores, selling items whose unit price ranges from only three to fifteen dollars, conquered the most expensive district in South Korea, while other types of businesses, including those selling luxury brand clothing and accessories, have ebbed away from the area? Understanding the mechanism underlying the emergence of the budget cosmetics industry and its growth helps us to grasp this process.

## The Growth of Budget Cosmetics

A truism in the cosmetics marketplace is that more expensive products sell better. By making their products appear to be exclusive via higher prices, luxury brands have carved out a class segment (Peiss 1990). Marketers' primary strategy for premium luxury brands lies in creating an aspirational product by appealing to social status rather than highlighting product quality. The atmosphere of luxury stores, where refined and disciplined shopping behaviors are implicitly requested, fortifies the exclusivity of price. Breaking with this received wisdom in the cosmetic industry, a Korean brand called Missha, launched by Able C&C in 2000, invented the concept of *budget cosmetics* by offering all their skin-care products, including toners, lotions, creams, and essences, at the unprecedentedly low price of 3,300 won (equivalent to around $3). Highlighting the fact that the actual production cost of cosmetics is small, Missha burst the price bubble by simplifying the previously complicated distribution process and stripping off the packing cost through the commercialization of cheap but well-designed plastic containers. The Missha revolution came from resistance to the market convention that stressed the lack of intrinsic product quality in cosmetics, thus emphasizing the importance of marketing and advertising. Missha has turned cosmetics into needed, everyday products and established its competitiveness through affordable prices, targeting volume sales at a low unit margin of profit.

Missha emerged from an online shopping mall, BeautyNet (www .beautynet.co.kr), that not only sells cosmetics products but serves as a community in which members exchange information about beauty items and skin care. BeautyNet has put great emphasis on two-way communication with customers and has actively reflected their opinions in production. Thanks to its consistent interactions with customers, Missha went viral among young women and garnered their loyalty. Backed by its online popularity, in 2002 Missha opened the first "brand store" or "road shop," a tailored retail store that sells only its own brand products. Countering the previous "multibrand shops" that deal in cosmetics from a variety of brands, the road shops function as a unique distribution channel (except for online sales). By eliminating several intermediaries, the road shops also contribute to lower pricing. Moreover, with its unique brand interior, the physical appearance of a road shop in itself represents the Missha brand, marking the strong identification of the retail stores with the brand name among customers. The proliferation of the road shops has further contributed to the consolidation of brand recognition. In just two years, the number of Missha brand shops passed 200, and as of 2013, Missha had 640 retail stores across the country. In carving out this distinctive market niche, Missha grew extraordinarily, recording $110 million in sales revenue in 2004 and $241 million in 2010.[7]

Missha's astonishing success led to the popularization of the budget cosmetics market. One of Korea's major companies, LG Household & Healthcare, followed the move to take over a growing low-end brand, THE FACE SHOP. As of 2015, THE FACE SHOP was operating 1,190 road shops across the country and recorded $610 million in sales revenue in 2014. Another cosmetics major, Amore Pacific, also established an affordable brand, *inisfree*, which achieved $457 million in sales revenue in 2014.[8] As of January 2015, the total number of low-end cosmetics brands has increased to more than fifteen, including Nature Republic, SKIN FOOD, Aritaum, It's Skin, Banila Co, holika holika, Todacosa, Tony Moly, and Etude House.[9] Rarely affected by fluctuations in the economy, even showing stronger performance during recessions, the budget cosmetics industry has continually run a growth trend, with more than 15 percent year over year in 2013, and 10 percent in 2014 (KDB Daewoo Securities 2014). Having dominated the cosmetics market in South Korea, the low-end segment is now actively carrying out overseas expansion.

The driving force behind budget cosmetics' growth is their reputation for great quality for the price. While insisting on low prices, the budget cosmetics companies have tried to establish a fine-quality image by promoting the "naturalism" of their products. THE FACE SHOP has highlighted the "pure vegetarian elements" in its products; under the slogan "Feed Your Skin," SKIN FOOD markets products made of fruit and vegetables; promising eco-friendliness, *inisfree* has launched several product lines made from natural ingredients such as "olive line products" and "green tea seed line products." Not a few of my interviewees verified the quality of the affordable brands: "At first, I was scared to use the 'cheap' products, fearing I would have skin problems. After trying them for several months, as strongly suggested by my friends, I realized that there's no quality difference between them and im-ported high-end cosmetics"; "My friends and I prefer imported luxury brands for perfume and makeup products, but absolutely domestic low-end ones for basic skin care because they are better."[10]

Some flagship products have propelled the popularity of affordable cos-metics. BB (blemish balm) cream, which provides everything from a light-weight, medium-coverage alternative to foundation to sun protection factor (SPF) properties, brought Korean low-end cosmetics into the spotlight. BB cream originated in Germany as an all-in-one product for patients to use postsurgery or after facial peels. The Korean budget cosmetics industry has made it the go-to face product, satisfying schoolgirls' eagerness to use cos-metics without flouting no makeup rules. Facial mask sheets, which are soaked with active ingredients such as fruit, grains, collagen, and green tea extracts, are also a megahit. Individual sheets are sold separately but neatly packed, costing around three dollars. Snail cream (made of snail secretion filtrate), aloe soothing gel, 3D mascara, and CC (color control) cream have also contributed to the creativity and buzz of the low-end brands. Recently, mainly stemming from industry efforts to target Chinese customers, more products are made of "indigenous" ingredients, including snail, horse oil, snake, bee venom, and donkey milk.

The majority of customers for low-priced cosmetics have turned out to be teenagers and women in their early twenties. Even with the advent of bud-get cosmetics, the industry had not realized the vast potential of the teenage market. The pocketbook friendly price, however, has turned young females into powerful purchasers, both sparking and fulfilling teenagers' desires to use cosmetics to improve their appearance. Moreover, the road shops have become places of entertainment and leisure where young customers can test various products at their ease. It is a form of play and leisure for young girls who come in twos and threes to test and talk about skin-care products with friends or experiment with combinations of various colors to create new looks. Eye-catching and whimsical product designs also captivate girls' minds. Even after customers have tested dozens of products, purchase is never coerced; rather, store assistants serve prospective customers by offering free samples, tailored advice, and a makeup service. Price affordability and friendly service have bridged the gap between customers and the low-priced brands.

The growth of affordable cosmetics has brought significant changes not only in the market share of the cosmetics industry but also in the urban landscape. The budget cosmetics boom caused mushrooming of the road shops across the country. Low-end cosmetics retail stores have crowded in major shopping districts, on neighborhood streets, and even inside grocery stores. As the competitiveness of brand shops still functions in their affordability, each store tries to carve out its own profitable boundary. The cosmetics retail stores, therefore, exist mainly in scattered forms, defending their own market area. The road shops in Myeong-dong these days, however, break the notion of the distribution of service. Multiple budget cosmetics stores suddenly appeared together and formed a cluster. Why have the low-end cosmetics retail shops aggregated and has the degree of concentration intensified over time in Myeong-dong?

## The Formation of Cosme Road

In Myeong-dong in the late 2000s, there was an intriguing interplay between the soaring numbers of tourists from overseas and the growth of the low-end cosmetics industry. Amid the steady economic recession since the 1990s, the affordability and perceived high quality of Korean budget cosmetics went viral among Japanese customers around the mid-2000s, causing those who visited Korea to consider them to be the best gift for friends and relatives. On the other hand, Myeong-dong already had the reputation of being the biggest shopping district in South Korea, which enabled the initial emergence of some flagship stores for budget cosmetics. Those two separate phenomena coincided in Myeong-dong: Japanese tourists discovered road shops in the area where they could purchase the low-priced cosmetics, and the budget cosmetics industry discovered the overseas customers who boosted sales.

Actually, those Japanese tourist-shoppers coined the term "Cosme Road" to refer to Myeong-dong's central street where the road shops are concentrated.

The strongest appeal of budget cosmetics results from consumers' perceptions of their high quality for the price. A store assistant said: "Affordability by itself does not lead to strong sales. They (foreign customers) actually love the quality." A Japanese woman in her thirties stated: "Korean essence products can be bought at less than half the price of Japanese ones, yet there isn't a big difference in quality." A female Chinese tourist in her twenties commented: "Korea has four distinct seasons for which Korean cosmetics firms have developed 'functional' products such as moisturizer and sunscreens. Korean cosmetics are better suited to Asian skin than Western imports."[11] Thus, many foreign customers that I observed in stores had specific and in-depth knowledge of Korean budget cosmetic brands and clear purchasing targets. In addition, the availability of variety products attracts overseas shopping tourists. The budget cosmetics brands have attempted to penetrate overseas markets. Currently, for example, THE FACE SHOP runs around 1,400 stores in 28 countries and *inisfree* operates 122 shops in foreign countries.[12] However, tourists verified that the overseas stores, mainly operated by local intermediaries, do not offer the same products as those in Korea and there are price differences for the products that are available. One Chinese customer suggested: "It is hard to find the same products in China. Although Beijing and Shanghai have some brand shops, they haven't permeated the more remote corners of China. Products introduced in fashion magazines, therefore, are actually not available in China." A store manager, who is ethnic Chinese, added: "China imposes heavy taxes on foreign businesses operating in China. That is why there are huge price differences between China and Korea."[13] Due to its clustering of cosmetics stores, Myeong-dong therefore became a primary destination for those shopping tourists.

The increasing tendency of budget cosmetics stores to settle in Myeong-dong has been obvious. There were around 21 cosmetics road shops in the area in 2008, but the number had increased to 35 in 2010 and almost quadrupled to 81 in 2012.[14] As of May 2014, around 100 brand cosmetic shops were doing business in central Myeong-dong, which stretches for only about 1,100 meters in total. The same brands have multiple shops in the area: Nature Republic operates 6 road shops in Myeong-dong alone; THE FACE SHOP, Etude House, *inisfree*, and Tony Moly each have 5 brand stores; Aritaum, Missha, and HolikaHolika run 4 shops; and another 7 brands have operated more than 2 stores.[15] These brand cosmetic shops are not simply concentrated in the same area but are also literally positioned next door to one another. In a mere 30-meter section of Cosme Road, 10 cosmetic shops are lined up together, with 6 shops on one side and 4 more on the other (see figure 5.1). The extreme degree of physical proximity of cosmetics shops offering similar products at almost the same quality and price forms an agglomeration.

The clustering of similar cosmetic stores attracts more customers, because it generates positive externalities such as customer interchange, overflow, and reciprocity that benefit retailers (Brown 1987). Consumers can also enjoy increased choice, greater ease in comparison shopping, and other conveniences that minimize the spatial and temporal cost of shopping. The economic logic of retail congregation is supported by my interviewees' descriptions. I asked storeowners (or managers) whether the extraordinary concentration of the same kinds of businesses in a small area would have a negative impact on each store. The answers were no: "To be honest, I do not care about other stores, because my store is doing really well"; "The opening of one more cosmetic store here does not hamper my profits at all. Rather, the formation of an identity as 'Cosmetic Road' has a strong advertisement effect"; "Even though Myeong-dong is one shopping district, due to the enormous size of its shopping population, each street in the area could be perceived as a separate commercial zone. An enormous crowd guarantees sufficient profits for all of them."[16] To synthesize the interview data, the agglomeration of budget cosmetics stores has the effect of bringing more customers to Myeong-dong; thus, many retailers dealing with similar products within a small area symbiotically coexist despite any internal competition. The data also reveal that sufficient consumer demand exists in the area to sustain the steady growth of the budget cosmetics stores despite the area's high rent.

The impacts of agglomeration are not confined to the economic realm. Allen Scott (2005) developed a theoretical framework regarding the relationship between agglomeration and place. Conceiving place as "not simply a passive receptacle of economic and cultural activity, but a critical source of successful system performance" (1), Scott suggests that the agglomeration of Hollywood producers and studios intensifies their place-specific competitiveness. If individual firms are densely gathered in one place, according to Scott, there are strong functional interdependencies and spillover effects allowing firms to tap into spatially concentrated labor markets and abundant

Figure 5.1. Scenes of Cosme Road. Photo by author.
Reprinted by permission from Oh 2017.

information flows.[17] Therefore, once an agglomeration is set up, it tends to generate benefit streams that reinforce each individual firm's competitive advantage. Agglomeration of firms also confers a strong sense of identity on a place, which attracts more firms, thus intensifying place-specific competitiveness. In this way, a virtuous cycle is formed that enhances competitive advantage for both industry and place.

Myeong-dong embodies the same synergetic transactions between the agglomeration of the same retail stores and the consolidation of place identity. As the No. 1 Shopping District, Myeong-dong originally had some flagship stores for budget cosmetics. Recently, the rapid rise in the number of foreign tourists has pushed the increase in the number of road shops selling affordable cosmetics. The sudden growth and clustering of the road shops have changed the area's identity, transforming it into a cosmetics shopping district. The newly formed place identity attracts more customers, who bring further fortunes to the clustered retailers. Thus, there has been mutual reinforcement of the concentration of cosmetics stores and the deepening of the area's place identity as Cosme Road. While the areas traditional function as a shopping hub was buttressed by the combination of overarching cutting-edge commercial ventures (e.g., fashion retail shops, beauty shops, coffee shops, and restaurants), present-day Myeong-dong reflects a significant departure toward an extremely narrowed retail use of low-end cosmetics. The monotonous retail landscape, however, does not indicate the entire disappearance of other commercial uses: they are now phased away to alleys where rent is more affordable, while the central street is predominantly conquered by cosmetics shops.

Myeong-dong's case about retail, however, critically differs from Scott's Hollywood case concerning production. In the production arena, the agglomeration of firms itself generates enough positive externalities that benefit individual companies, as Scott explains. In the consumption arena, however, sustaining the retail clustering requires steady flows of consumers. In present-day Myeong-dong, foreign tourists visiting in great numbers with continuous circulation sustain sales. The mobility of tourist-shoppers matters: they should not settle in the area but be constantly moving. Thus, different groups of tourists could continually frequent the area. In this way, tourists with extreme mobility, conventionally considered to be "out of place," become critical in constructing Myeong-dong's new identity and profitability. The cosmetics road shops have adopted various practices to quickly circulate the foreign customers. All the brand stores are located on the ground level, stretching the retail space into the streets. The extended retail spaces are filled with various types of promotional panels, brand model cutouts, and additional sales vendors (see figure 5.2). In each shop, at least one staff member stays in the street space in front of the store, trying to lure passersby inside. Handing out free samples (disposable facial mask, or boxes of cotton cosmetic pads), the sales assistants engage in proactive marketing through street solicitation. Once potential customers are persuaded to come inside the store, another sales assistant approaches them to offer product information and testers. After deciding on purchases, foreign customers face an electronic quotation board that displays the day's exchange rate. When customers offer Chinese or Japanese credit cards, clerks automatically calculate and display the product price in Chinese yuan or Japanese yen based on the day's exchange rate. For Chinese customers' convenience, most brands accept China UnionPay (an association representing China's bank card industry). After payment, store staff offer a map showing a center where foreign customers who have purchased goods worth more than thirty dollars can get a cash tax refund. All the practices are designed to facilitate shopping and payment, thus hastening customer circulation. The number of tourists and the pace of their mobility is crucial in the area's turnover rate.

Present-day Myeong-dong is distinct from the past "No. 1 Shopping District" to which customers flocked, not only to shop but to engage in leisure activities such as window shopping, wandering around, chatting, and relaxing on the bustling streets. The history of Myeong-dong suggests that it was a place to be seen, to stroll, and to socialize, with vitalizing mutual gazes among the anonymous public. Now, the dominant and privileged foreign shoppers move along in fast-shopping and fast-exit streams. Lots of carry-on baggage dotting the street exemplifies this quick movement. Although the numerical indicators—the number of customers, the size of sales revenues, and the level of retail rent—speak to the even more powerful status of the area, now the visitors have no time to engage with the "placenesss" of Myeong-dong, let alone with its layers of rich history. Although the destination of transnational tourists is place-based, reconfiguring the economic and cultural dynamics of Myeong-dong, the tourists are neither attracted by nor engaged with Myeong-dong's historical geography as a foreign enclave, a hub of fashion and commerce, or a symbolic center for the prodemocracy move-

Figure 5.2. Streetscapes of Myeong-dong. Photo by author.
Reprinted by permission from Oh 2017.

ment. Whereas the sizable numbers of foreign tourists and their quick mobility accelerates capital accumulation in the area, their circulation has reduced the social and cultural meanings of the place and has led to extreme commercialization. What, then, is the meaning of Myeong-dong to foreign tourists? How do we explain the transnational consumption of the urban place that is Myeong-dong?

## Hallyu, Myeong-dong, and Place

A deeper understanding of foreign tourists' congregation in Myeong-dong calls for a triangular connection among Korean popular culture, the construction of Korean beauty, and Korean budget cosmetics. As Korean popular culture has become the "face" of South Korea, Hallyu constructs a fantasy space for its audience that erects aspirational dreams about Korean beauty. Television dramas not only convey stories, but more important, represent and lead trends in fashion and lifestyle. Since K-pop is recognized more for its visual appeal than musical offerings, the images of K-pop idols also contribute to notions of "Korean beauty ideals." The idealized Korean look includes "big, sparkly eyes, button nose, delicate, pointed chins, light skin, a V-line facial shape, and S-line body." It is noteworthy that it is an international rather than domestic audience that has identified such distinctive physical characteristics in Korean celebrities, strengthening the notion of Korean beauty. Although these idealized looks bring to mind Caucasian-looking characters, the actual functioning of the beauty ideals is based on the notion of "racial proximity" (Erni and Chua 2005). Given the predominant presence of East and Southeast Asian audience members/tourists, a sense of Asianness makes them feel closer and related to the K-stars' physical characteristics (Kim 2007). In contrast to decidedly Western looks, the physical qualities of K-pop idols appear to be something achievable, prompting audience members to take action to reach goals that seem attainable. The prevalence of images of K-stars, who widely appear on television and in commercials, magazines, and music videos, further disseminates beauty standards and facilitates the consumption of notions about Korean beauty. It is now well known that international fans who are eager to emulate Korean celebrities travel to Korea to get plastic surgery.[18] With cosmetics use, perceived as an almost indispensable daily necessity among these consumers, using Korean cosmetics has become a way for foreign audience members to easily practice such Hallyu-oriented beauty ideals. In a personal interview in June 2014, a Chinese teenager remarked: "Watching Korean TV dramas, I've always thought Korean female actresses have very white and well cared–for skin. Many of my friends and I think it's because of the quality of Korean cosmetics."

The budget cosmetics industry has actively utilized the Korean Wave for its market expansion by hiring Hallyu stars, celebrities who are popular in East and Southeast Asia, in building their brand recognition. Actually, THE FACE SHOP, a relative latecomer in the low-end segment, has enjoyed extensive growth in sales by employing Hallyu stars such as Kwon Sang-woo, Bae Yong-jun, Won Bin, and Kim Hyun-jung. When Bae Yong-jun was a model for THE FACE SHOP in 2009, word among both industry marketers and Korean consumers was that Japanese tourists formed a long line simply to enter a store in Myeong-dong. Once when *innisfree* presented a life-size wax figure of Lee Min-ho, then the brand's model, it attracted numerous foreign customers who enjoyed taking pictures with it, turning the Myeong-dong retail store into a favored tourist destination. Nature Republic has also engaged Hallyu stars, including Jang Keun-suk and EXO, occasionally holding fan meetings at a road shop in the area. The power of star marketing is proved by the industry's extraordinary growth. One of my Japanese interviewees confirmed the ramification: "At first, I bought this brand only because my favorite star endorses it. Later, I came to like the quality of the products."[19]

Since 2011, when the globalization of K-pop was in full swing, the employment of idol groups and singers has become prominent in marketing affordable cosmetics. What is notable is the rise of male idol stars as endorsers of budget cosmetics: Nickun for It's Skin, G-Dragon for The SAEM, SHINee for Etude House, Superjunior for Tony Moly, and EXO for Nature Republic. Those male idols are particularly welcomed due to the sheer size of their (international) fandom. The recent rise of Korean "girl groups" has also shaped the advertising schemes of low-end cosmetics marketers. Dismantling the previous market orientation that valued top actresses' idealized beauty for cosmetics advertisements, the recent budget cosmetics lines emphasize the freshness, youthful energy, and trendy styles of young girls. Because idol group members are so admired by teenagers, hiring them as brand models sells well, especially considering the age segment of the major consumer groups for low-priced lines. Suzy (from Miss A) represents THE FACE SHOP; Krystal from f(x), Etude House; Yoona from Girls' Generation, *innisfree*; and Sandara Park from 2NE1, Club Clio.[20] Because the critical currency of K-pop idols is their appearance-oriented images, a straightforward connection between the idol's style and cosmetics as one of the critical elements of beauty has been formed. Lots of international fans have set up blogs and websites to introduce "K-beauty" in association with K-pop idols, posting articles such as "How to Look Like K-Pop Idols," "Beauty Tips for K-Pop Devotees," and "K-Pop Star Shares Secrets to Korean Dream Skin."[21] Due to the visually oriented consumption of K-pop idols, when they endorse cosmetics brands, a splendid correlation, beyond mere commercial sponsorship, is forged between idol models and brand products. The Korean cosmetics industry definitely benefits from the style-focused K-pop industry and its global popularity.

The purchase of Korean cosmetics endorsed by celebrities is deemed as the extension of consuming Korean popular culture. The cosmetics products that K-stars model are not distant from idol merchandise (see chapter 3). While *gihoeksa* sells idol-related products to fans, the cosmetics companies employ idols to advertise their products to consumers. In both, the image and aura of idols are capitalized on in marketing and the fan-consumers' desires are exploited in consumption. While *gihoeksa* pays little or no commission to idols, the cosmetics companies pay higher endorsement fees to idols to use their images in advertisements. Fans form affective connections between them and the products their favorite idols promote (Russell 1998); the connection blurs reality, leaving fans with the impression that having such products would actually make them feel closer to their idols. More fanatical fans do not care what the product is; as long as their beloved idol endorses the product, they are willing to buy it. Buying the idol-endorsed products, therefore, is an embodiment of affection. While I was in a Nature Republic store, a couple of Japanese girls entered and bought a promotional product packaged with a huge photograph of EXO. The girls explained: "We came to Korea to go to the EXO concert yesterday and we only visited this store to get the photograph (not a cosmetic product)."[22] Around thirty minutes later, Chinese women bought a bulk mask pack, costing around $300, which also came with EXO photos. "They (fans) don't hesitate to buy 'special products' that are bundled with photographs of EXO despite their higher price. And we do know who [among EXO's then twelve members] are the particularly popular ones and they are strategically promoted."[23] Mentioning this, a store manager pointed to a huge photo cutout of one EXO member displayed outside of the store.

Myeong-dong's landscapes represent the ways popular culture representations intersect with consumer practices. Almost all the road shops display huge screen-size pictures of their brand models, mostly K-pop idols. As seen in figure 5.1, the size of the model photos easily exceeds that of the name boards, as they are a more effective means of appealing to customers. Exhibited right outside each store, the life-size cardboard photos of Hallyu stars are also critical parts of streetscape configurations. Images and representations draw customers, in exactly the same way that the production of idol personas and groups is more about producing desirable bodies, stylish images, and lifestyles than it is about musical content. Myeong-dong's image-dominated landscape reveals that foreign tourists there carry out the instant consumption of Hallyu imaginaries, are motivated by Hallyu-inspired beauty aspirations, and are drawn to cheap consumer products. To the foreign travelers, Myeong-dong represents a materialized proxy space of the Korean Wave. Their flash consumption of the image-based place reflects again the area's fast-shopping and fast-exit streams. It discloses the place's intense mode of commercialization: popular imaginaries prompt beauty aspirations among their audiences and draw them to consume both the cultural images and beauty products; the massive arrival of the Hallyu-inspired overseas tourists creates the monotonous retail landscapes in which only those retail uses that can generate fast and higher turnover rates survive; the retail environment creates various measures to quickly circulate the customers for more profits; and the image-dominated landscape urges customers to engage in the immediate consumption of both the Hallyu aesthetic and the place.

Myeong-dong's recent transformation is not the result of government intervention as discussed in the previous chapters; rather, it is shaped by the economic logic of place. Myeong-dong is a subadministrative unit that belongs to Jung-gu. Unlike Gangnam-gu's proactive place-marketing practices, Jung-gu does not initiate any place projects around Myeong-dong. The district office briefly introduces the area as part of the "Myeong-dong/Namdaemun/Bukchang Special Tourist Zone."[24] Jung-gu's place-promotion policies focus more on the revitalization of the inner city area, introducing "Eulji-ro Urban Industry Special Zone," where the industrial facilities that modernized Korea are gathered: lighting, tools, sewing, tiles, pottery, shoes, sculptures, furniture, and more. Amid the inner alleys of Eulji-ro, which have experienced both decline and gentrification, the district's policies are directed toward supporting a few remaining old-fashioned shops.[25] The place selling of Myeong-dong, by contrast, is layered on the place's preexisting symbolic power and the ongoing economic logic that eliminates unprofitable uses.

## The Politics of Difference

With the growth of foreign tourists since 2008, Myeong-dong has become a site in which the supply and demand of budget cosmetics is unexpectedly but perfectly matched. The increasing presence of Japanese and Chinese shoppers who are passionate about Korean cosmetics has sparked the proliferation of cosmetics retail shops in Myeong-dong. The burgeoning of the cosmetics road shops has transformed the area's identity into a beauty shopping district, or "Cosme Road," and the newly shaped place identity is further attracting more foreign customers, accelerating the globalization of Myeong-dong. The steady inflows of sizable volumes of foreign tourists have become imperative in sustaining the retail economies in Myeong-dong. The budget cosmetics stores in the area are therefore carrying out diverse practices to cater to the prized foreign customers.

The simultaneous presence of multiple languages is apparent in the affordable cosmetics stores. Indeed, all cosmetics road shops employ staff members who are fluent in Chinese, Japanese, or English. Ethnic Chinese (Korean minorities in China) make up the majority of store staff, and mostly serve Chinese tourists and Korean customers. Salespeople at Nature Republic stores wear a name badge displaying the national flags of the countries whose languages they speak. For example, an ethnic Chinese person who is fluent in both Korean and Chinese has a badge with Korean and Chinese flags on it. Special delivery services are also offered to foreign customers: stores deliver purchased products to nearby hotels for consumers who spend more than $200; for customers who buy more than $500 worth of goods, products are mailed to their home countries via international Express Mail Service free of charge.

Spatial practices that distinguish foreign customers also exist. The biggest Nature Republic store, located on the most expensive lot in South Korea[26] near a primary entrance to Myeong-dong, uses its first floor as a general shopping space but reserves the second floor as a space for foreign customers only. The foreigner-only space enables international customers to enjoy more relaxed and comfortable shopping free from the density, noise, and congestion elsewhere. It also offers comfortable seating, free drinks, and a free gift-wrapping service. One Etude House store in Myeong-dong runs a (foreign) customer lounge that exhibits photos of the brand's overseas stores; the store also contains the "Global TOP5 Zone," in which products popular with foreign customers are collected, so that they can easily find their favorites.

The creation of difference based on race and ethnicity is also verified by the interview data from salespeople: "It is not an exaggeration to say that Myeong-dong is basically for tourists. Around 80 percent of the customers are Japanese or Chinese tourists, and they contribute most of the sales"; "We definitely prefer foreign customers for two reasons. First, Chinese and Japanese tourists are volume purchasers, showing no reluctance to buy several mask-pack sets, each consisting of 100 individual sheets and priced at 550,000 won (around $550). There's no comparison between revenues from tourist buyers and those from local customers"; "Korean customers often complain about our lack of fluency in Korean [yet this interviewee definitely spoke perfect Korean with very little accent]. I feel much more comfortable serving foreign customers."[27]

The data indicate that because foreign customers account for most of the sales revenue and profits, the preferential treatment that retailers offer to them, including exclusive services and spaces, is required in the accumulation process. As Gangnam particularly welcomes foreign tourists that will engage with the area's conspicuous consumption and entertainment images, in the consumption arena in Myeong-dong "other Asians" also become highly valued customers to whom retailers devote special attention. Because tourists from overseas have purchasing power and their sheer size and extreme mobility promise more profits, Myeong-dong has become a site in which the distinction between the domestic and the foreign is constantly checked, produced, and reproduced. The hierarchy formed along ethnicity is critically associated with the very material processes of urban economies and place selling.

The previous chapters addressed the limitations of pop culture–associated place marketing based on creating pseudo place images and meanings that are not necessarily related to actual local histories, thus distorting/reducing socioeconomic realities. The production of place images for external consumption tends to exclude local communities and residents, forcing them to deal with inflowing tourists and the discrepancy between fantasy and realities. Myeong-dong's new regime of capital accumulation based on both the implicit and explicit exclusion of local customers in favor of foreigners embodies similar limitations of pop culture–driven place selling. Preferential treatment of foreign over local customers is associated with the accelerated commercialization of Myeong-dong. I discussed the ways Korean municipalities harness the presence of foreign tourists in second-round place promotion, constructing the narrative that the place is worthy to visit evidenced by the inflows of foreign tourists. In Myeong-dong, the arrival of pioneering overseas shoppers has led to further streams of foreign tourists resulting from consolidation of the place's identity as a beauty shopping district. Previous chapters also show how drama- and K-pop–associated place marketing requires consumers' emotional commitment to sustaining the affective power of the advertised place. With Myeong-dong's recent accumulation regime sustained by the continuous flow of foreign tourists, the selling of Myeong-dong entails the user-exploitative nature.

## Global Flows and Place

Myeong-dong's recent development is marked by a constellation of global forces: the globalization of Korean popular culture, the global flows of tourists, and the global expansion of the beauty industry. Myeon-dong's reconfiguration caused by global movements provides insights into the discussion of place that is contested in globalization. Place is marginalized in globalization discourses that highlight mobility such as travel, border crossing, diaspora, migration, displacement, and deterritorialization. Similarly, the global flows of people, commodities, media, information, and technology seem to imply the decreasing relevance of place (Appadurai 1996; Escobar 2001). For Manuel Castells (1996), this is the rise of a "space of flows" and the erosion of a "space of place." Anthropologist Marc Augé (1995) coined the term *nonplace* to refer to places such as railway and bus stations, motorways, airports, hotel rooms, and supermarkets that facilitate motion and hold less significance as places. Yet place preserves its continuing salience in a mobile world since what is mobile is also material and must emerge in a place to be spread (Cresswell 2004). Anna Tsing (2005) shows that the global spread of science, capital, and political ideologies that seems to flow freely actually engages with the particularities of place, encountering "the friction of place." Place, therefore, is not elusive in the mobile world. Rather, place becomes critical for flows, that is, for their actual movement toward every corner of the globe.

This chapter can be a good addition to the "place-based" studies of globalization (see, e.g., Dirlik 2001; Kim 2004; Woods 2007) arguing that place does not become less significant in the globalized and mobile world.[28] Rather, globalization is a "source of the reproduction of geographical uneven development, and thus of the uniqueness of place" (Massey 1991, 29). Myeong-dong's case shows how global flows transform place and reconstruct place identity. In discussing the ways global flows affect place, Massey's conceptualization of place is critical. In contrast to Augé's conceptualization of "nonplace," in which place is formed by boundaries, and through which people develop meanings and attachments, Massey sees the notion of place as authentically rooted in history and having a singular and essential form of identity as problematic (Cresswell 2004). Massey raises questions about delineating place in terms of fixity, stability, and noncontradictory identity. Place is not about boundaries for Massey (1993) because "boundaries make distinction between 'them' and 'us' and therefore contribute to a reactionary politics" (in Cresswell 2004, 73). Rather, she explores senses of place as a process marked by outside flows and connections. As the uniqueness of a place is determined by its openness, permeability, and constant interactions, place becomes a site in which multiple identities and histories are constantly (re) formed and challenged.

Despite rich theoretical discussions about the "global sense of place" (Massey 1991), there have been surprisingly few studies to empirically engage with the question of place identity and its changing nature in the global environment. If a place is constituted through its particular linkage to outside flows (Massey 1994), how does the process actually take place? If the specificities of place are constantly reproduced, how does such transformation develop? Myeong-dong's case can provide the theoretical debates with empirical analysis and enrich the theory by identifying specific spheres and directionality of global flows. First, Myeong-dong's case shows how its changing place characteristics represent and mediate the multiple directions and realms of global connections. The ever-increasing numbers of inbound foreign tourists have actually been caused by the global popularity of Korean popular culture. The tourists' obsession with Korean cosmetics is also influenced by Korean beauty ideals represented in K-dramas and embodied in K-pop idols. Thus, Myeong-dong's recent dynamic entails interactions among the imaginaries of Hallyu, the cosmetics industry employing Hallyu, and Hallyu-driven transnational tourism. The Korean Wave is conventionally understood as the outbound spread of Korean entertainment. Yet the outward circulation of Korean popular culture has spawned inbound global flows by drawing an audience of tourists and shoppers. More important, these multidirectional flows convene at a specific place, Myeong-dong, causing the transformation of its economy, culture, and urban landscape. While Massey's case demonstrates how global economic restructuring in general affects a local place, this chapter identifies specific spheres and directionalities of global connections, whose interactions reshape place distinctiveness.

Second, Myeong-dong's case can contribute to Massey's argument that what constitutes place is the connections with outside flows by focusing more on the mobility of global flows. The volumes of foreign tourists who have specific shopping aspirations have narrowed the retail composition in Myeong-dong to the dominance of low-end cosmetics. When the tourist-shoppers are in constant circulation, the cosmetics retailers do better, leading to a more intense clustering of cosmetics shops and the deepening of the place's identity as Cosme Road. Thus, global tourists' mobility is critical to the area's turnover rates. The Myeong-dong shops, therefore, have practiced various measures to speed up tourist circulation and implicitly restrict domestic customers, redefining the social and cultural meanings of the place. This chapter demonstrates the ways not only globalization in general but also the very mobility of the global flows themselves reconfigure place identity in association with capital accumulation.

Myeong-dong's place identity has continuously mutated over time due to political, economic, and social conditions. Myeong-dong's complex and contested place identity is undergoing a drastic shift once again in the era of globalization. Along with the global popularity of Korean popular culture, Myeong-dong's recent transformation mediates the global connections in multiple realms: popular culture, beauty, tourism, and the cosmetics industry. The global circulation of pop culture, the global dissemination of beauty ideals, and the global flows of tourists intermingle in Myeong-dong, transforming its material and cultural meanings. The very mobility of tourist flows has substantial power to alter the place's economy, creating the monotonous retail landscape. As this mobility plays a critical role in the area's both customer and profit turnover rate, diverse spatial and cultural measures are practiced to expedite customer circulation in the area. During this process, Myeong-dong's place meanings are changing from activities associated with leisure, sociability, and politics toward an intense mode of capital accumulation. Massey develops the notion of a progressive sense of place by asserting that global connections reconstitute a place through which multiple and contested identities emerge. This chapter adds a more nuanced and critical perspective to her open-ended claims by showing that the global flows associated with image-dominated popular culture, beauty aspirations, and the consumer market leads to the extreme commercialization of a place. This materialism, however, should be differentiated from global capital's invasion of a local place. Rather, it should be understood that the global streams formulate the complex contours of the place's identity.

# Conclusion

In the 1980s, South Korea witnessed a sudden boost in the number of cultural spectacles created out of political necessity on the part of the then–military dictator, Chun Doo-hwan, whose military regime began with a coup after Park Chung-hee's assassination in 1979. Chun's consolidation of his authoritarian power involved the merciless suppression of the Gwangju Democratic Movement in 1980. To divert the nation's attention away from politics, Chun promoted the so-called 3S (screen, sports, and sex) policy. Accordingly, a professional baseball league was established in 1982, and Chun himself threw the first pitch at the opening game. Professional sports events were aired on color television, a medium that was then being disseminated nationwide. In 1981, Seoul won the right to host the 1988 Summer Olympics and the 1986 Asian Games. A vast number of erotic films were produced in the 1980s since, ironically, state censorship actually promoted sexually suggestive cinema. Sexually explicit posters and banners were displayed at movie theaters and elsewhere so that nudity even dominated the urban landscape. The sex industry boomed, with a mushrooming of bars and red-light districts. The abolition of the nightly curfew drove people to so-called places of amusement.

Since the development of Gangnam, real estate speculation (*budongsan tugi*) has become a prominent secondary mode of wealth accumulation for the upper classes. The continuing influx of people to Seoul from the rest of the country has yielded multiple rounds of creative destruction in the metropolis's residential spaces. The restructuring of residential neighborhoods is conducted through the wholesale demolition of obsolete districts and the construction of high-rise apartment complexes on a gigantic scale. As the bulldozing of existing houses is accompanied by the large-scale displacement of tenants, the lower classes bear the brunt of redevelopment. Property owners enjoy an increase in the value of their properties through the heightened density, improved physical conditions, and beautified surroundings that result from the redevelopment process. Since the incessant movement of the population to the greater Seoul area sustains the demand for housing, surplus value can be created merely by engaging in rounds of property selling, thus leading to rampant real estate speculation. Urban restructuring in the Seoul metropolitan area since the 1980s, therefore, has taken the form of reducing the life span of apartment complexes, thereby further advancing the redevelopment process. With only a few exceptions,[1] government policies have worked to aggravate real estate bubbles by relaxing regulations and increasing reconstruction densities. Speculative urban development has been a main feature of South Korea's urbanization (Shin 2016).

In the Korean Wave era, cultural spectacles shifted from being state organized to being industry driven and instigated by global demand. While the speculative real estate market still thrives, local municipalities now tend to practice speculative urbanization to advertise their areas. The combination of pop culture spectacles and speculative urban promotion has led to the proliferation of splendid sites throughout the country.

I have discussed how the globalization of Korean popular culture has changed the Korean urban landscape by creating fantasized images attached to places. Beyond the merely accidental spatial consequences of the Korean Wave, I highlight the coproduction of culture and place: how cultural content is produced by inserting places into it or by utilizing spatial agglomeration, and how the images and meanings of a place are created by television dramas or K-pop idols. The linkages between popular culture and cities have grown out of the needs of both the culture industry and municipalities. While the two pursue different goals—financial capital in the case of the industrial players and political capital in that of the urban players—both share the same speculative nature. The pop culture industry is innately speculative because audiences use cultural commodities in highly volatile ways, causing some products to garner more or less profit than expected. The Korean Wave, however, has rendered the Korean pop culture industry more speculative still, driving the industrial players to gamble on the probable overseas popularity of their products. Despite its inherent uncertainty, the global rise of Hallyu seemed to guarantee the success of every Korean commercial entertainment venture, prompting numerous people to jump into the industry and gamble on the ostensibly attainable prospect of achieving a megahit. I have discussed the speculative character of the industry by examining (1) supply-driven, small-sized independent drama producers and their spontaneous, improvised practices in creating dramas, and (2) the profit-diversification strategies of pop music agencies. Due to their risk-taking and short-term profit-seeking tendencies, Korean pop culture producers require greater financial sources, leading them to launch the new practice of inviting cities to act as sponsors. The cultural sponsors—Korean municipalities—are also engaging in speculative efforts as they seek instant popularity and run risks with their culture-associated place marketing. The reason speculative projects among Korean cities are in vogue lies in their urban aspirations and the political ambitions of their urban governors. In the context of the country's decentralization and the globalization of Korean popular culture, the profit-seeking practices of the culture industry have neatly dovetailed with the desires of Korean cities for sensational promotion.

The speculative ventures by both the industry and the municipalities, however, require the continuing global popularity of Korean popular culture. Only a steady global demand for Korean pop culture can absorb the oversupply of cultural content. For culture-mediated place marketing to succeed, the cultural hype needs to be translated into actual inbound tourism. Thus, the efforts to gain material and political capital by Korean cultural producers and cities can only be successful when there are steady commitments from global fans. Since the mid-2000s, triangular transactions have been taking place that involve the profit-seeking culture industry, the passionate desires of fans, and cities' branding strategies. Both the Korean culture industry and municipalities have utilized fan-tourists' affective and participatory engagement with Korean popular culture and culture-associated places.

The appropriation of consumer desires and commitments is what lies behind the adventurous moves by producers and municipalities to speculate on future forms of popularity. Thus, the continuous growth of the Korean culture industry and the sustainability of culture-mediated place promotion rely on maintaining the alluring charm of Korean dramas and K-pop music and idols to ensure global fans' constant devotion and loyalty. In this book, I suggest that the globalization of Korean popular culture has resulted in local impacts that interact with changes in urban governance and the urban political economy. Conversely, the prospects for culture-associated urban policy trends in Korea hinge on the future performance of Korean popular culture in the global market.

In early March 2017, a critical incident occurred that adversely affected the constant overseas demand for Korean entertainment and steady stream of foreign tourists—that is, the U.S. government's deployment of the U.S. Terminal High Altitude Area Defense (THAAD) missile system.[2] While the United States and the Park Geun-hye administration insisted that this action was a countermeasure to North Korea's continued provocations, China is uncomfortable with the radar's proximity to its soil, viewing THAAD as an extension of U.S. strategic interests in the region. Criticizing the South Korean government for undermining bilateral relations by hosting the missile system, the Chinese state encouraged its citizens to boycott South Korean products and companies (Mullany and Gordon 2017). Chinese authorities recently called for the closing of retail stores owned by Lotte, Korea's eighth largest conglomerate, because of its agreement to make land owned by the company available to the THAAD program. As anti-Lotte sentiment grew, the conglomerate is on the verge of entirely withdrawing its retail business from China, while it is also suffering from drastic sales decreases in its duty-free business (70 percent of which comes from Chinese travelers) (Premack 2017). Beginning on March 15, 2017, the Chinese government (unofficially) instructed travel agencies to stop selling group package tours to South Korea. Chinese people, among whom a sense of nationalism is strong, are supportive of the state's action; for instance, 3,400 Chinese tourists refused to disembark when they arrived at Jeju via a cruise ship on March 5, 2017, while tour guides and the drivers of 80 tour buses waited to transport them around the island. From March to May 2017 alone, the number of Chinese tourists in Korea plunged to around 800,000, a decrease of more than 55 percent from the year before.[3] Korean entertainment has been another affected area. Many K-pop concerts were canceled altogether and Korean celebrities were barred from doing endorsements in China. The case of Song Joong-ki, who garnered huge stardom across Asia by appearing in the drama *Descendants of the Sun*, exemplifies this phenomenon. While the megahit drama brought him several endorsement deals in China where appearance fees are several times higher than in Korea, the ban led advertisers to replace their product endorsers.

At a time when the negative consequences of such international disputes fall primarily on the tourism and commercial entertainment sectors, Korean municipalities' pop culture–led place selling is also threatened directly. One representative example is Incheon's sponsorship of *Goblin: The Lonely and Great God* (*Seulpeugo Chanranhan Sin Dokkaebi* 2016), as the Incheon Film Commission (IFC) paid part of the production cost and supported the on-location shooting. The sponsorship is part of the "Inspiring Location Incheon" project, according to which IFC invites cultural creators to the city and helps them with location scouting, under the motto "Infusing imagination onto space by filling it with diverse stories." Written by *the* top drama writer, Kim Eun-sook,[4] and casting top celebrities including Gong Yoo, the drama series was packed with commercial potential. As the television series became *the* talk of the nation, Incheon's many previously ordinary places that were featured in the drama (e.g., an old bookstore) emerged as romantic places. As a promotion measure, the city runs a blog exclusively dedicated to the *Goblin* tour and posted a self-produced short video in which a young couple hangs around the *Goblin* filming locations in Incheon. IFC also engaged in interactive communications with audience-tourists via social media by posting weekly quizzes to allow people to guess the drama locations in the city. Those who uploaded their "proof photo" showing that they had visited the drama locations were also awarded small gifts. The drama series particularly struck the fashion industry through product placement. Gong Yoo, a model-turned-actor who performed as the protagonist "Kim Shin," received multiple sponsorships from high-end luxury brands—including Givenchy, Burberry, Lavin Paris, and Tom Ford—and all of the clothes that Gong wore in the drama were eventually sold off despite their exorbitant prices.

Although multiple indicators, including its ratings, demonstrate that *Goblin* was a commercial success,[5] it remains in question whether the drama producer and city sponsor, who primarily targeted the larger Chinese market, were fully satisfied with the outcome. The drama series' overseas promotion encountered trouble due to timing. When the domestic airing of *Goblin* ended in late January 2017, the producers and sponsors were busy with the overseas promotion. Even without the official distribution in China, the drama series already garnered huge popularity among Chinese and the title-role actor Gong Yoo was listed in the top ranks of search words on Weibo, China's largest social media site. When the deployment of THAAD was announced and the Chinese government responded with highly critical voices, however, all *Goblin*-related content, as well as other Korean pop culture content, suddenly disappeared from Weibo except for the short official preview video.[6] China's travel boycott of South Korea exacerbated the situation at the most critical time to promote *Goblin*-inspired tourism to Korea. Having enjoyed megasuccess in the drama-induced tourist inflows from China by sponsoring *My Love from the Star*,[7] the city of Incheon's expectations regarding *Goblin* were extremely high. The sponsorship and promotion of *Goblin* is part of the city's attempt to transform itself from a port city into a "city of media and culture" (*yeongsang munhwa dosi*). The mayor proactively supported the media creators and actually visited *Goblin*'s shooting sites to deliver meals and snacks to the director, staff, and actors.[8] Against Incheon's all-out efforts, the THAAD turmoil was entirely unexpected and dealt critical blows to the city's *Goblin*-related place promotion. In response to China's travel boycott, not only the city of Incheon but also the Korean Tourism Organization in general have hastily shifted the target area from China to Southeast Asia by holding more information sessions in the region about traveling to Korea while also increasing the number of flights. Efforts to cultivate new markets, however, will take years to bear significant fruit.

The aftermath of THAAD obviously speaks to the vulnerability of "soft power."[9] Despite the Korean state's proactive efforts to utilize the Korean Wave to cultivate positive images of the country and develop new markets, audience reception is not always positive, particularly in foreign markets. As the anti-Hallyu movements in Japan, Taiwan, China, and other areas show, the reception of popular culture can be a contested site of negotiation (Nye and Kim 2012). Moreover, it remains questionable how the breezy, superficial, style-oriented Korean popular culture might work in actual and specific international relations. As much as popular culture can operate as a powerful tool to touch and lure audiences, the THAAD storm indicates that it is also vulnerable to shifts in issues of diplomacy, security, and nationalism. I mentioned above how Korean municipalities attempt to address local problems of fiscal deficiency and low recognition status through transnational means by attracting foreign tourists. The aftermath of THAAD, however, demonstrates how local policies can be rendered impotent in the face of national disputes and policies.

Despite such risks of fragility, more and more Korean municipalities are practicing pop culture–related place selling. Not only Incheon but many other cities are fostering a "media city" image by establishing local media commissions, encouraging place placements in films and drama series, or constructing film-shooting complexes. Utilizing the now-established Busan International Film Festival (BIIF), Busan has promoted its "Cineport Busan Plan" since 2004; Bucheon announced its plans to develop the Bucheon Film and Culture Complex in 2014, which will function as an infrastructural complement to Bucheon International Fantastic Film Festival (BiFan);[10] capitalizing on its extraordinary natural scenery, Seoguipo City has also been promoting itself as a "media city" since 2015; and Cheongju established the city's media commission in 2017, also as part of a "media city" project. As discussed in detail in chapter 2, Cheongju City has been embroiled in conflicts with residents who were excluded from the decision-making process and have thus suffered from various problems caused by the city's drama sponsorship. Remarking on the more frequent cases of drama shooting in the area, however, one local news channel conveyed the state's perspective by saying, "Despite the inconvenience citizens and students would experience, the city government is promoting the media city project because of its contribution to the local economy and publicity."[11] Despite its uncertainty, vulnerability, and limited sustainability, popular culture still dominates the urban policies of Korean municipalities in the decentralized era.

It is intriguing to note the differences in urban practices between Korean municipalities and those in Japan and China, which are also experiencing decentralization these days. Japan's historical and spatial development trajectory is very similar to that of South Korea; however, it would be more accurate to claim that South Korea imitated Japan's development practices in its post–Korean War economic development. Japan's post–World War II development path entailed uneven geographies that benefited only selected regions, the Tokyo-Yokohama region in particular. Given the center–periphery disparity, rural problems became even more acute in the decentralization era that coincided with the burst of the bubble economy in the

1980s, constant economic recession since the 1990s, and population decline and the aging of its society. Japanese regions have carried out various efforts to achieve greater autonomy and self-reliance. Locality studies, a form of community mapping, emerged as a popular technique "as part of a larger boom in agrotourism, heritage food, and other initiatives designed to reinvigorate regional localities" by awakening rural places' unique resources (Love 2013, 113). Although these practices are sometimes criticized as neoliberal decentralization efforts to shift the responsibility of rural socioeconomic decline to individual municipalities, they can also empower and unite local communities (ibid.). Place branding based on product promotion is another popular practice to promote a region's agricultural/fishery/forestry products and to attract tourists, such as the Japan Brand Development Assistance Program's promotion of registering trademarks consisting of "name of a local area" plus "name of product" (Rausch 2008). Although there are elements of selling places and attracting tourists, the measures to *practice* decentralization in Japan basically involve a protection of industry that requires local residents' participation. The balanced mutual cooperation between the local state and local society in the Japanese model reveals contrasts to Korean municipalities' state-dominated place-selling efforts. In chapter 2, I briefly discussed some Japanese municipalities' place-promotion tactics, mainly sponsoring Korean television dramas in the hopes of attracting drama fans both from Japan and the rest of Asia. Even in those cases, community support was critical because multiple local groups and residents in general provided part of the funding, accommodated the on-location shooting, and provided psychological support.

In China, decentralization is more tightly interlocked with urban projects. Exercising its exclusive power of land ownership, local states have emerged as the most active developers in China and urban development has manifested new accumulation regimes in the transition from a socialist to a capitalist economy. You-tien Hsing's (2010) research suggests that China's decentralization is intertwined with local states' capacity to consolidate their power through land ownership and the control of various development projects. Urban development projects include multiple forms, from infrastructure installation to image creation, most of which undertake commercial and residential development through the state's control of land, which entails massive evictions and displacement of residents and tenants. By hosting China's new, massive numbers of middle-class, as well as international tourists, the construction of houses, condominiums, hotels, and consumption spaces provide local states with both political and economic capital. Given the state's legal ownership of land, local governments at multiple levels—provincial, municipal, township, and village—engage in fierce competition among themselves and other state institutions/agencies to "represent the state." Local state building configures, and is configured by, its territorial authority through initiating development projects.

Japanese local governments' community-centered policies and the Chinese state's use of land ownership as powerful resources contrast with Korean municipalities' state-dominated, image-oriented, and tourist-focused place selling via Korean popular culture. Such differences elucidate the particular lack of resources Korean local states can mobilize despite their developmental aspirations, even though all three countries confronted decentralization within a context of significant urban–rural, center–periphery disparities. While Korea's decentralization ignited pervasive place selling, its actual practices have taken place together with the globalization of Korean popular culture. Initially, the prearranged transactions[12] between the cultural producers and cities were developed to utilize popular culture's ability to construct and advertise place images through its affective, sensational, and increasingly global power. Over time, however, Korean municipalities have recognized and harnessed the highly skilled and devoted labor provided by passionate fans, in the form of sharing personal experiences about pop culture–featured places, as a critical means to internationally publicize their areas. Despite the risks involved, due to its cost-saving but sensation-creating nature this user-appropriating mechanism of place selling will further spark the cities' interests and utilizations of media entertainment content.

# Notes

## Introduction

1. Throughout this book, Korea refers to South Korea.

2. See, among others, Cho 2005, Joo 2007, Chua and Iwabuchi 2008, Kim 2013, Kim and Choe 2014, and Lee and Nornes 2015. These works use Korean popular culture as a lens through which to contemplate nationalism, transnationalism, and postindustrial consumer modernity in Korea and East Asia. For the detailed textual analysis of Korean television dramas, see Heo 2002, Ho 2011, and Lee 2012.

3. These refer to the Park Chung-hee (1961–1979) and Chun Doo-hwan regimes (1980–1988).

4. In 2003, the Roh Moo-hyun administration passed a special bill on decentralization that granted more rights and responsibilities to local governments, thus further increasing the degree of decentralization.

5. For the discussion of the developmental state, please see Amsden 1989, Castells 1992, Wade 2003, and Oh 2016.

6. U.S. aid and grants from Japan (given in exchange for signing the Normalization Treaty in 1965) accounted for the majority of state investments. Around half of the foreign aid received between 1959 and 1969 was spent on building infrastructure facilities. Thus, South Korea might be said to be a site that absorbed surplus capital

from advanced countries in the form of foreign aid, what David Harvey (1981) calls "spatial fix."

7. The three rounds of the Comprehensive National Physical Plan were the First Comprehensive National Physical Plan (1972–1981), the Second Comprehensive National Physical Plan (1982–1991), and the Third National Comprehensive Physical Plan (1992–2001).

8. See chapter 4 for the details of Land Adjustment Development.

9. In 1987, a nationwide civil uprising (the June Democratic Uprising [*yuwol minju hangjaeng*]) occurred that called for the end of the military dictatorship and promotion of democracy. Nationwide prodemocracy struggles led to the pronouncement of the June 29 declaration that brought about the resignation of Chun Doo-hwan. By the end of 1987, South Korea had experienced its first direct presidential election, which gave birth to the Roh Tae-woo administration and launched a substantive form of democracy in the country.

10. South Korea witnessed an annual economic growth rate of 10 percent during the 1980s. This economic boom resulted in a flood of money into the real estate market, which pushed up property values. In fact, property values quadrupled during the 1980s. In the aftermath of the 1988 Olympics in particular, the rate of increase went up sharply, from 18 percent in 1988 to 38 percent in 1990. The housing price hikes contributed to an increase in workers' expenditures on housing, thus fueling wage increases (Oh 2016).

11. In 1987, before the inauguration of the Roh administration, South Korea had built a total of 645,000 housing units, satisfying only 56 percent of the housing demand in Seoul and 69 percent of nationwide demand. During the five-year period from 1988 to 1992, a grand total of 2,720,000 housing units were generated in the five newly developed towns. This form of rapid and massive construction of houses and cities was unprecedented in South Korea (Oh 2016).

12. In the presidential election of 2002, twenty years after the FNT project, candidate Roh Moo-hyun highlighted the uneven conditions of the country's rapid growth as an election issue. Pointing out the excessive concentration of people, resources, and power in the SMA, the liberal presidential candidate attacked the greater Seoul area's privileged power. He called for "Balanced National Development" (*gukga gyunhyeong baljeon*), which became the Roh administration's policy priority during his presidential tenure (2003–2007). To actually achieve balanced development, President Roh argued, an active governmental role in spatial planning would be paramount. From its inception, the Roh administration promoted several development policies to attenuate uneven development. The major intervention was the construction of a new administrative city (now called Sejong City) outside of the Seoul metropolitan region, in the hope that population movement would follow the transfer of central administrative functions to the new city. Following the completion of the city's construction, as of 2014, nine ministries, two agencies, two services, two presidential offices, twenty subordinate institutions, and sixteen government-funded research institutions had moved to Sejong City. In addition, the Roh administration also developed "Innovation Cities" (*hyeoksin dosi*) and "Business Cities" (*gieop dosi*) across the country, to which state corporations and private firms would be relocated, which aimed at drawing people away from the greater Seoul area to the rest of the

country. A total of 161 state corporations have been relocated to Innovation Cities located across the country. Detailed information can be accessed at http://innocity.molit.go.kr/.

13. South Korea is made up of seventeen first-tier administrative divisions: six metropolitan cities (*gwangyeoksi*), one special city (*teukbyeolsi*), one special self-governing city (*teukbyeol jachisi*), and nine provinces (*do*), including one special self-governing province (*teukbyeol jachido*). These are further subdivided into a variety of smaller entities, including cities (*si*), counties (*gun*), districts (*gu*), towns (*eup*), townships (*myeon*), neighborhoods (*dong*), and villages (*ri*).

14. Robert Oppenheim's book (2008) provides in-depth ethnography of the place making in Kyungju using its cultural heritages, discussing the complexities around the notion of agency, locality, and subjectivity.

15. For the research on tourism and the construction of urban spectacles, please see Cartier 2005 and Gotham 2007.

16. Hallyu is not the first case of the globalization of Asian popular culture; there was a boom in Hong Kong cinema in the 1980s (Lo 2005) and the Japan Wave in the 1990s (Iwabuchi 2002; Allison 2006). What differentiates the Korean Wave from these earlier phenomena is that: first, it has garnered a much broader audience via both formal (dissemination through a greater number of broadcasting channels through active exporting) and informal (such as the Internet and DVD piracy) distribution routes; and second, it has instigated massive pop culture-driven international tourism involving visits to the K-places. Using the concept "Inter-Asian Referencing," Iwabuchi (2013) discusses how the Korean Wave has opened a field through which Asians encounter and discover neighbors and selves.

17. Scholars have discussed how the Korean Wave has sparked the previously restrained gendered desires to be exploded among East and Southeast Asian females and pointed out the contemporariness in such desires (Kim 2001; Lee 2008).

18. To advertise the new brand, the state corporation employed top Hallyu stars such as Big Bang, Krystal from f(x), and Lee Min-ho, and produced multilanguage television ads featuring these stars. The promotional movies can be found at http://www.imagineyourkorea.com/.

19. According to Pile (2010) and Bondi (2005), Thrift (2004, 2007) also uses emotion and affect interchangeably. Greco and Stenner's work (2008) also adopts the interchangeable concept of emotion and affect.

20. See Pile (2010) for the distinction between affective geography and emotional geography.

21. See chapter 2 for the audience groups having varied degrees of interest and commitment.

22. There are rich studies about the film-induced pilgrimage and the pilgrims' perception of the film location sites. See Torchin 2002, Beeton 2005, Hudson and Ritchie 2006, Macionis and Sparks 2009, Roesch 2009, and Tzanelli and Yar 2016.

23. Drawing on Schumpeter, however, Jessop claims that the economic risks involved reflect the nature of capital not entrepreneurship.

24. Garnham defines culture as "the production and circulation of symbolic meanings," and conceives a culture industry as involving "a material process of production

and exchange, determined by the wider economic process of society with which it shares many common features" (1990, 155).

25. At the same time, digitization also means the loss of audience markets due to the development of pirated products and informal distribution routes.

26. Exporting requires marketing costs, yet it is negligible compared with the benefits that the export markets bring. Moreover, thanks to the already existing Korean Wave, Korean exporters did not need to expend much effort on marketing during the 2000s.

27. See the conclusion for discussion of the aftermath of THAAD.

28. Unevenness operates at different scales: "in the organization of the global economy (e.g. the categories of first and third worlds), at regional scales within most countries (e.g. heavily industrialized or finance-centered regions versus 'laggard' or persistently poor rural areas), within metropolitan areas (e.g. 'inner cities' versus suburbs), and within many cities at neighborhood and block-by-block scales" (Gregory et al. 2009, 780). Thus, there are multiple centers and peripheries at each scale.

29. See South Korean Ministry of Land, Infrastructure and Transport, http://www.molit.go.kr.

30. Actually, the construction of the Five New Towns in the SMA exacerbated this spatial unevenness because construction of more than two million new houses attracted people not only from Seoul but from the rest of the country as well, reinforcing the concentration of national resources and population in the SMA. The urban projects, therefore, caused long-term externalities in deepening the country's uneven development. The main social cost of the development projects was charged to the rest of the country, as rural areas faced increasing poverty and isolation (Oh 2016).

31. An alternative term for cultural industries is "creative industries," defined by UNESCO as "sectors of organized activity whose principal purpose is the production or reproduction, promotion, distribution and/or commercialization of goods, services and activities of a cultural, artistic or heritage-related nature." http://www.unesco.org/new/en/santiago/culture/creative-industries/. In this book, I will use the cultural industry, the creative industry, and the entertainment industry exchangeable.

## Part I

1. Please see chapter 1 on live production for why they were always pressed for time.

2. All amounts have been converted into U.S. dollars for the sake of accessibility and the conversion from Korean won to U.S. dollars is made at a rate equivalent to $1 = 1,000 won throughout this book.

3. There are four terrestrial broadcasting stations that use public waves in South Korea: KBS (Korean Broadcasting System), MBC (Munhwa Broadcasting Corporation), SBS (Seoul Broadcasting System), and EBS (Educational Broadcasting System). Since EBS focuses on educational content, the other three compete against one another for ratings in dramas, entertainment shows, and news.

## 1. Speculative Producers

1. SBS's first commercial success was achieved through the drama *Sandglass* (*Morae Sigye*, 1995), a twenty-four-episode series depicting the Gwangju Uprising (Gwangju Democratic Movement) of 1980 and the political oppression later in that decade. This epic modern history series recorded stunning 64.5 percent ratings at its peak and is still in fifth place in the all-time rankings of Korean television dramas, with average ratings of 46.7 percent (Russell 2008). *Sandglass* thrust SBS forward, making it a competitive player in the industry. Since then, the ratings battles have seriously intensified among networks, especially over prime-time dramas.

2. The ratio was originally set for a minimum of 3 percent of total broadcasting hours and was gradually raised at a rate of up to 5 percent annually, so that, as of 2015, the ratio stands at 35 percent on MBC, 35 percent on SBS, 24 percent on KBS 1, and 40 percent on KBS 2 (Korea Creative Content Agency 2015).

3. *What Is Love All About* was first aired on Channel 1 of China Central Television (CCTV) from June to December 1997 and took second place in viewer ratings (average 4.2%) among all foreign programs. Following audience requests for a rerun, the series was rebroadcast in 1998 on Channel 2.

4. The term *hallyu*, meaning the Korean Wave, was first coined in Taiwan around 1997. The Taiwanese replaced the Chinese character *han* in the term *hanliu* (meaning "cold wave") with another Chinese character *han* (meaning "Korean"), which has the same pronunciation. Thus, the term was not initially invented to show appreciation of Korean popular culture. Rather, in creating the term, the local media were warning the Taiwanese entertainment industry that it had to fend off the formidable competitiveness of Korean television dramas (Lee 2011).

5. As daytime two-hour dramas were reduced or phased out during the 2000s, Japanese broadcasters became desperate to fill the time slots. They found Korean dramas much less expensive to air than reruns of previous Japanese dramas and it was easier to handle the copyright issues, too. These market conditions opened the floodgates, allowing Korean television dramas to flow into Japan, which later witnessed an enormous and unexpected rise in their popularity.

6. As of 2008, total exports had reached around $11 million (KOFICE 2008).

7. As the next section explains, most independent producers are small and frequently go bankrupt due to their financial instability. Some bankrupt firms later reappear but with different names.

8. The biggest telecommunication company, SK Telecom, is a heavy shareholder in Sidus HQ and the second biggest communication mogul, KT, controls one of the major production firms, Olive 9.

9. Listed companies include Sidus HQ, Pan Entertainment, Olive 9, Chorokbaem Media, DSP E&T, JS Pictures, Yellow Entertainment, and Eight Pics. Kim Jong Hak Production carried out a backdoor listing by merging with an existing listed technology firm, Pure Nanotech.

10. Broadcasters do not calculate the total production cost and pay exactly 70 percent of it; rather, conventionally, until 2011, when I did my field research, the price was more

or less fixed at around $100,000 per episode. In more recent practices, the amount differs in terms of casting, profit-distribution schemes, and dealing with copyrights.

11. Until the late 1990s, when actors were still employed by and thus belonged to broadcasting firms, their appearance fees were paid by the in-house rating system: broadcasters established eighteen categories based on career and work experience, and restricted the fees to $300 to $1,500 per episode. A few top-tier actors played as free contract agents, but even their fees per episode did not exceed the maximum of $3,000. Very recent practices, however, show clear departure from the 2000s. No tacit regulations are applied and sheer market principles determine the compensation for top celebrities, who usually earn $100,000 to $150,000 per episode.

12. The weak financial capability of most drama production firms has been revealed by several scandals over unpaid appearance fees. In 2010, the labor union of the nation's broadcasting industry representing staff, actors, and singers claimed that there were overdue appearance fees and other unpaid wages totaling $3.7 million. As a result, the union decided to boycott the filming of outsourced dramas at all three major broadcasting companies. The unionists stopped appearing in dramas for days and abandoned their collective action only after the broadcaster promised to devise measures to prevent payment delays. What is notable is that the union strikes targeted the broadcasters rather than independent producers, with representatives saying: "Although the subcontractors are in the first instance responsible for the unpaid salaries, the broadcasting companies should also take responsibility. The major broadcasters have abandoned their social and ethical duties." A similar incident occurred in 2011, when the Korea Entertainment Management Association disclosed a list of companies, responsible for thirty-two dramas and films, which had failed to pay actors, and announced that actors belonging to the association would not appear in dramas and movies made by the named production companies. A director from the association stated: "Heads of the production companies failed to pay performance fees, but kept making dramas by setting up other production firms or changing their names. Therefore, the overdue payment problem is getting bigger. Broadcasting companies know this, but they keep outsourcing, saying the payment delay is an issue between producers and actors, and not their business." This time again, the union criticized broadcasters as much as the producers who failed to make payments. These two incidents indicate the unreliable financial conditions of small-sized independent producers and the critical role of broadcasters, who can control delinquent independent firms. More information can be found at "Entertainers' Union and KBS Reached Agreement," *Korea Times*, September 1, 2010, http://koreatimes.co.kr/www/news/nation/2010/09/113_72392.html.

13. Revenues from selling in overseas markets generally make up 40 percent of income in ordinary independent production firms (Korea Creative Content Agency 2009).

14. Television dramas broadcast via cable channels have only recently begun to be exported. These include *Shut Up Flower Boy Band* (*Dakchigo Kkoccminam Baendeu*, tvN, 2012), *I Need Romance* (*Romaenseuga Piryohae*, tvN, 2011, 2012), *Queen In-Hyun's Man* (*Inhyeonhwanghuui Namja*, tvN, 2012), *Yellow Boots* (*Noran Boksucho*, tvN, 2012), *Vampire Prosecutor*, Season 1, 2 (*Baempaieo Geomsa*, OCN [Orion Cinema Network], 2011, 2012), *Special Affairs Team TEN* (*Teuksusageonjeondamban Ten*, OCN, 2012), *God's Quiz*, Season 1, 2, 3 (*Sinui Kwijeu*, OCN, 2010, 2011, 2012), *Girl K* (*Sonyeo Kei*, Channel

CGV, 2011), *Incomplete Life* (*Misaeng*, tvN, 2014), *Bad Guys* (*Nappeun Nyeoseokdeul*, OCN, 2014), and *Cheese in the Trap* (tvN, 2016).

15. Because of the uncertainty of a show making it onto a television channel and the precarious financial backing, stars have become a critical factor in attracting investment rather than a mere element in the drama. Independent producers have established a system whereby they monopolize high-profile writers and cast celebrity actors first, then win a slot on a channel, and later scrape up the investment money, using the actors' star power. Capitalizing on the name value of stars as *the* critical route to funding the production signifies that they rely on future success with no tangible source of security for financial backing. On the other hand, there is no system for verifying whether the money invested is being used wisely. Broadcasting networks, which buy the final product (television dramas), never concern themselves with the sources and uses of the investment money. These capital flows subject the major players in the drama industry to great uncertainty, as they are always gambling on the success of their shows.

16. Author interview with a project manager at a small-sized drama production firm, March 2011.

17. Author interviews with industry insiders, March 2011.

18. Parts of this section were published in Oh 2015.

19. "The Final Twist in the Drama *Sign* was the Broadcasting Accident," [In Korean.] *Chosun Ilbo*, March 12, 2011, http://news.chosun.com/site/data/html_dir/2011/03/12/2011031200059.html.

20. "Strike Aftermath? *The Equator Man*'s Broadcasting Accident," [In Korean.] *Media Today*, May 25, 2012, http://www.mediatoday.co.kr/news/articleView.html?idxno=102726.

21. Author interview, February 2011.

22. "Mo PD's So What!," [In Korean.] *Pressian*, August 23, 2011, http://www.pressian.com/article/serial_article_list.asp?series_idx=460.html.

23. Actually, three dramas that started their first episodes on the same date recorded viewer ratings proportionate to the running times of their second episodes: *Witch's Romance* (*Manyeoui Yeonae*, SBS, 80 minutes), *Thank You* (*Gomawoyo*, MBC, 72 minutes), and *The Devil* (*Mawang*, KBS, 71 minutes) recorded 16.3 percent, 14.6 percent, and 8.7 percent, respectively. Cited from "Ratings Proportional to Running Time," [In Korean.] *Nocut News*, March 23, 2007, http://www.nocutnews.co.kr/show.asp?idx=468765.

24. "Actors Pull All-Nighters, Tragic Reality," [In Korean.] *Newsen*, August 25, 2011, http://www.newsen.com/news_view.php?uid=201108250009101001&search=title&searchstring=%B9%E3%BB%F9%20%B1%E2%B7%CF%B0%E6%C0%EF.

25. Author interview, March 2011.

26. Author interview with a scriptwriter, April 2011.

27. For the interactive nature of television series, please see Hand and Varan 2007.

28. "The Production Processes in *The King of Dramas* Synchronized 100% with Reality," [In Korean.] *Entertainment Today News*, December 24, 2012, http://www.tvj.co.kr/news/articleView.html?idxno=2359.

29. Parts of this analysis draw on the 2011 report by Korea Creative Content Agency, *Product Placement in TV Drama and Storytelling: An Analysis of Cases in the "Secret Garden."*

30. "A Well-Made Drama, *Secret Garden*, Laid a Golden Egg of $30 Million +α," [In Korean.] *Weekly Donga*, January 17, 2011, http://weekly.donga.com/docs/magazine/weekly/2011/01/17/201101170500023/201101170500023_1.html.

31. In *simple placement*, brands are featured in three primary ways: first, the product itself can be seen either in the background or, more desirably, while actually being used; second, a corporate logo, insignia, trademark, or other identifying feature may be shown; third, an advertisement, such as a billboard or television commercial, may be placed in a scene as ambiance in the background (Smith 1985).

32. Lukaćs (2010a) examines how lifestyle-driven trendy dramas effectively targeted the young female audience in Japan in the 1990s.

33. Exceptions include *Sign* (*Ssain* 2011), *Golden Time* (*Goldeun Taim* 2012), *The Chaser* (*Chujeokja* 2012), *Punch* (*Peonchi* 2014), and *The Village: Achiara's Secret* (*Maeul Achiaraui Bimil* 2015). While the prime-time series on terrestrial channels were dominated by commercial Cinderella stories, cable channels successfully experimented with genre series such as *God's Quiz*, *Gap-dong* (*Gapdongi*, tvN, 2014), and *Signal* (*Ssigeuneol*, tvN, 2014). Critics reckon that production conditions on the cable channels, which are less affected by sponsorship because commercials are allowed in the middle of a show, have created more room for creativity and freshness.

34. Cited from the public board Audience Opinion on the drama's official web page, http://wizard2.sbs.co.kr/w3/template/tpl_iframetype.jsp?vVodId=V0000347780&vProgId=1000649&vMenuId=1013331.

35. Ibid.

36. Author interview, March 2011.

37. Author interview, February 2011.

38. "The World of Idols in Drama," [In Korean.] *Herald Economy*, May 7, 2013, http://isplus.live.joinsmsn.com/news/article/article.asp?total_id=11442093.

39. Such comments are prevalent on drama web pages and online drama discussion forums, and in general discourse on social media.

40. "Why Do Dramas Prefer Idol Singers?," [In Korean.] *News Tomato*, May 9, 2013, http://www.newstomato.com/ReadNews.aspx?no=361976.

41. Author interview, April 2011.

42. See chapter 2 for discussion of spatially organized story development.

43. "'Low-Cost, High-Efficiency' . . . Nothing Can Match Remaking," [In Korean.] *Sports Kyung Hyang*, June 6, 2012, http://sports.khan.co.kr/news/sk_index.html?cat=view&art_id=201306062035196&sec_id=540201.

44. Ibid.

45. Criticisms have also arisen regarding the industry's lack of long-term creative development; when writers only process existing stories, the scope of their creativity is bound to be narrowed.

46. Historical grudges originated from the Japanese colonial rule of Korea. There were no cultural exchanges between the two countries until 1998, when South Korea lifted its ban on Japanese pop culture. Since then, South Korea has phased in Japanese cultural products; however, this has so far not included an opening of terrestrial channels to Japanese broadcasting programs. Yet Japanese television dramas enjoy a broad

Korean audience, which mainly experiences them via cable television, online, or on DVDs (Koreanfilm.org).

47. Among these, *Saimdang, Memoir of Colors* received a significant amount of investment from Emperor Group, a Hong Kong–based company, and *Descendants of the Sun* has already sold its transmission rights to iQiyi.

## 2. Spectacular Places

1. Parts of this chapter were originally published in Oh 2014.

2. Another spatial aspect of cultural production is the agglomeration of cultural producers in place, forming the synergetic relationship between the industry and place. Please see chapter 5 and Scott 2004, 2005.

3. I am referring here to dramas set in premodern dynastic eras such as Chosun (1392–1910), Goryeo (918–1392), United Silla (676–935), and the Three Kingdoms Period (57 BC–668 AD) in which Goguryeo, Baekje, and Silla coexisted.

4. This is similar to docudrama in that actual historical events are dramatically depicted. Consequently, these dramas were rarely shot outside established indoor studios; outdoor scenes were mainly filmed at Gyeongbok Palace (the Chosun dynasty royal palace) or the Korean Folk Village.

5. Historical dramas usually consist of more than fifty episodes that are broadcast over a period of six months to a year.

6. For example, *Queen Sundeok* (*Seondeog Yeowang* 2009), featuring the Silla period, was mainly filmed at the Kyungju Millenium Park in Kyungju City, the capital of the Silla dynasty.

7. Sometimes broadcasters try to find sponsors. In the case of Yongin City, the city government smoothed administrative procedures to turn the land owned by MBC into a drama-filming site and funded parts of the construction cost. In the case of *Kim Soo Ro* (*Kimsooro* 2010), Kimhae City contracted with a broadcaster, MBC.

8. Author interview, February 2011.

9. Considering the fact that the average viewer rate for television dramas in Korea is around 15 percent, this number indicates the staggering popularity of the drama.

10. "Golden Goose vs. White Elephant: While Munkyung Becomes a Mecca for Filming Historical Dramas, Jecheon and Jangsung Witness Their Drama Sets in Ruins after a Short-Term Success," [In Korean.] *Seoul Newspaper*, January 16, 2015, http://www.seoul.co.kr/news/newsView.php?id=20150117005004.

11. Wando County offered $4 million and the provincial government gave a grant of the same amount. In addition, the private sector in the area contributed $10 million. The sponsorship amount was about 8 percent of the total annual budget ($184 million).

12. "New Tourism Brand, Wando," [In Korean.] *Hankooki*, September 22, 2008, http://economy.hankooki.com/ArticleView/ArticleView.php?url= estate/200809/e2008 092218085469550.htm&ver=v002.

13. Author interview, May 2011.

14. The term *destination placement* is inspired by the term *product placement* (see Bala-subramanian 1994). See chapter 1 for a discussion of the practice of product placement in Korean television dramas.

15. While most Korean cases are the states' projects and are entirely driven by local government, community members (including Village Youth Groups) participated in the drama sponsorship to a greater extent in these two Japanese cases by providing money or free on-site labor. A crisis mentality reigned throughout both prefectures. They con-sidered drama sponsorship to be their last chance to enhance material conditions in their areas and raise outsiders' awareness of their area.

16. See http://blog.naver.com/odk1956/100037040735.

17. Through the county's drama sponsorships, the same places are also featured in *Seoyoung, My Daughter* (*Nae Ttal Seoyeongi* 2012), *49 Days* (*Sasipguil* 2011), and *A Man Called God* (*Sinira Bullineun Sanai* 2010).

18. Sponsored by *Shinsun Seolleongtang* (Beef Broth Soup Firm), the aging CEO's company is set to run Seolleongtang business and one of the sponsor's branches was actually used as a major filming location.

19. As discussed in chapter 1, production sponsorship is often contracted while a series is actually being aired. Particularly series that show sharp ratings increases in the first few episodes attract late-coming sponsors. In *Shining Inheritance*, textual notices of Donghae City's sponsorship appear only from episode 7 (out of a total of 28 episodes), implying that Donghae City joined late as a sponsor.

20. For the study on the melodramatic narrative, please see Keating 2006 and Newman 2006.

21. "Goyang Spent $1 Million to Advertise the City via *Dream High* . . . Wasting Money?," [In Korean.] *Yonhap News*, February 22, 2011, http://www.yonhapnews.co.kr/bulletin/2011/02/22/0200000000AKR20110222156700060.HTML.

22. Author interview, June 2011.

23. Author interview, May 2011.

24. Author interview, March 2011.

25. Author interview, April 2011.

26. "Korean TV Show Sparks Chicken and Beer Craze in China," *Wall Street Journal*, February 26, 2014, http://blogs.wsj.com/chinarealtime/2014/02/26/korean-tv-show-sparks-chicken-and-beer-craze-in-china/.

27. Rephrased from http://www.dramabeans.com/2014/01/you-from-another-star-episode-7/.

28. "Mixed Tourism Products Are Rising: Getting Beauty Services after Visiting the Film Locations of *My Love from the Star,*" [In Korean.] *DongA Ilbo*, March 12, 2015, http://news.donga.com/3/all/20150311/70076454/1.

29. Hirata Yukte (2004) explains the phenomenon of Korean drama tourism as middle-aged Japanese women indulging themselves in Korea, a different form of gen-dered travel from the earlier male-oriented sex tour. See also chapter 5.

30. During my fieldwork period in spring 2011, I never encountered Japanese fan-meeting groups in Korea. The data presented here were collected through interviews with tour guides, translators, travel agency staff, or on-site set managers, who all had more than one experience with Japanese fan groups.

31. Author interview with a then-interpreter, March 2011.

32. Author interview with the civil official, May 2011.

33. *SBS News*, March 27, 2016, [In Korean.] http://news.sbs.co.kr/news/endPage.do ?news_id=N1003490383.

34. *Chosun Ilbo*, March 29, 2016, [In Korean.] http://news.chosun.com/site/data/html _dir/2016/03/29/2016032900244.html.

35. *Money Today*, March 27, 2016, [In Korean.] http://news.mt.co.kr/mtview.php ?no=2016032718332185402.

36. *Chosun Ilbo*, March 28, 2016, [In Korean.] http://news.chosun.com/site/data/html _dir/2016/03/28/2016032803114.html. *Youker* refers to Chinese tourists.

37. Author interviews with officers in multiple municipalities, spring 2011.

38. Author interview, May 2011.

39. Author interview, May 2011.

40. For studies on the gendered nature of television audience fandom, see Modleski 1982, Nochimson 1993. Nancy Baym's research (2000) examines the formation of online community among mostly female television fans.

41. Tokyo, 175; Osaka, 25; Nagoya, 23; Sendai, 15; and Fukuoka, 11 (Korea Tourism Organization 2005, 2006).

42. "Youngyang County Wasted Tax Payer's Money to Sponsor Drama Production," [In Korean.] *J-news*, August 9, 2010, http://www.j-news.co.kr/news/view.html?section =1&category=7&page=131&style= title&no=919.

43. "Municipalities Gamble for Drama Sponsorship," [In Korean.] *Kyeonin.com*, February 29, 2012, http://www.kyeongin.com/news/articleView2.html?idxno=637602.

44. The extensive remodeling that established sets for multiple historical periods has attracted the production of new drama series, including *The Great Seer* (*Daepungsu* 2012), *The Kings' Daughter, Soo Baek-hayng* (*Jewangui Ttal, Subaekhyang* 2013), and *Six Flying Dragons* (*Yukryongi Nareusya* 2015).

45. The $50 million were split into $20 million for set construction and $30 million for the production. This is an extraordinarily large amount because the sponsorship was promoted at a provincial level.

46. The drama production firm, Chungam Entertainment, bought the land, valued at KRW 16,900 (around $17) per 3.3m², at the appraised price of KRW 11,000 (around $10).

47. "Local States' Flames of Desire Left a Heap of Ashes," [In Korean.] *The Hankyoreh*, October 21, 2012, http://h21.hani.co.kr/arti/special/special_general/33122 .html.

48. Of course, local residents are not universally opposed to the state's projects. Active local participation in Wando County is a good example. Having witnessed the explosive power of drama sponsorship through the so-called *Haeshin* set, local residents collected money to help the county sponsor the drama *Gourmet* (*Sikgaek* 2008), in which the local specialty, Wando abalone, was strategically featured. Resident participation was possible because the drama sponsorship was directly related to the livelihood of the locals.

49. Author interview with a tour guide who described the Japanese tourists' experiences, March 2011.

50. Author interview, May 2011.

51. "Youngdeok, 'Concerned with Money' for a Drama Sponsorship," [In Korean.] *Maeil Ilbo*, June 4, 2004, http://www.imaeil.com/sub_news/sub_news_view.php?news _id=20379&yy=2004.

52. "Anseong City Is Promoting the Nine Million Dollars of Drama Sponsorship," [In Korean.] *Anseong News*, July 27, 2009, http://assm.co.kr/sub_read.html?uid=5669&section = sc2.

53. "Local Politicians Send Out Negative Messages about the Baudeogi Drama Sponsorship," [In Korean.] *Anseong News*, October 6, 2009, http://m.assm.co.kr/a.html?uid =5885.

## Part II

1. For the history of Korean music before the domination of idol music, see Lie 2015.

2. Elsewhere I have discussed the operational structure of DC Inside and how that prompts the discursive consumption of popular culture; see Oh 2015. For the in-depth anthropological research on DC Inside, please see Lee, Gil-ho 2012.

## 3. Image Producers

1. Aoyagi (2005) and Galbraith and Karlin (2012) provide in-depth research about the Japanese idol system.

2. Young talents who debut as actors and actresses, for instance, are not labeled *idols*. For more detailed research on the Korean idol system, please see Lee 2010, Kim and Yoon 2012, and Won and Kim 2012.

3. For more information about the *jimusho* system, please refer to Marx 2012.

4. Shin and Kim (2013) stress the role of large Korean entertainment houses in the evolution of the current global visibility of K-pop.

5. These days, the contracted trainees belonging to major management agencies are already elite groups; many young children spend extra tuition on singing and dancing lessons at private institutions simply to pass an audition by one of the entertainment agencies. As the K-pop industry has prospered, the number of private institutions has also mushroomed to nurture idol wannabes. See Ho 2012.

6. Lee Soo-man, a founder of SME, introduced the concept of CT (cultural technology) to explain the in-house training system. According to him, "CT is the driving force behind the development of SM's pop culture into global *Hallyu*. One of the elements of CT is our training system. Through auditions, we discover hidden talent and put them through three to seven years of music, dance, and acting training in order to create a star that's close to perfection. It's through this unique system that the Hallyu wave was created." "Lee Soo Man Outlines SM Entertainment's Three Stages of Globalization," *Allkpop*, June 13, 2011, http://www.allkpop.com/article/2011/06/lee-soo-man -outlines-sm-entertainments-three-stages-of-globalization.

7. While performers who leave their initial management company find themselves blacklisted and unwelcome within the entertainment industry in Japan (Marx 2012), the recruitment of dropped-out trainees by smaller agencies is a common practice in Korea. Given their lack of an established training system, as a way of saving on development costs smaller companies prefer to scout those who have already experienced training at a major firm. Quite a few K-pop idol stars who currently belong to medium- or small-sized management agencies were previously trainees at one of the three majors: for example, Soyeon of Tiara is an ex-trainee at SME and Lee Gi-kwang of Beast was originally trained at JYPE.

8. "The Utopia and Reality of the Idol Industry," [In Korean.] *Ten Asia*, February 5, 2015, https://storyfunding.daum.net/episode/381.

9. In July 2009, Jaejoong, Yoochun, and Junsu attempted to split from SME, claiming that their thirteen-year contract was excessively long, schedules were extended without the permission of the band members, and profits were unfairly distributed. In October 2009, the Seoul Central District Court granted the trio a temporary contract injunction, and TVXQ's group activities in Korea ceased. TVXQ returned as a duo in 2011. Keith Negus' book (1999) discusses the uneasy relations between production firms and artists in the music industry.

10. "Three Things K-Pop Trainees Should Stay Away From," [In Korean.] *Sports Chosun*, August 19, 2011, http://news.chosun.com/site/data/html_dir/2011/08/19/2011081901024.html.

11. The unique feature of *K-Pop Star*, an audition program aired by SBS, is that it provides some participants who pass through a certain number of rounds with the opportunity to get training at three major management companies: SME, JYPE, and YGE. The on-the-spot training scenes also display the interiors of major agency buildings, which are decorated with photos of leading K-pop idols.

12. Girls' Generation started as a nine-member group in 2007, but Jessica departed from the group in 2014 and three other members (Sooyoung, Tiffany, and Seohyun) left the group in 2017.

13. K-pop fans play a game of pretending to be SM creator Lee Soo-man, saying, "We included everybody in the hope that you can find at least one or two boys or girls to suit your own taste from the large groups."

14. One market approach that the major *gihoeksa* have adopted is to acquire public recognition for a new group during its predebut stage. SME has been operating the "SM Rookies" system through which the SM trainees get to face the public. Under the slogan, "Idols and fans grow together," SME aims to establish a substantial fan base before the official launch of a new group. YGE and JYPE have also actively used television programs to obtain public recognition for their newly launched idol groups. In 2006, YG Entertainment released *Real Documentary: Big Bang*—a survival reality program in which trainees competed against each other to be selected as a member of Big Bang—on GOM TV (an Internet-based television channel). The program clocked up more than a million viewings within only two weeks and was reaired via tvN (a cable channel) as *Big Bang: The Beginning*. Enjoying the enormous publicity generated by the program, in 2013 on MNet YGE launched another one called *Who Is Next: WIN*. The show dealt with multiple rounds of a competition between "Team A" and "Team B," both formed from trainees within YGE. "Team A" won all three rounds of public

voting, and made its debut as WINNER. The next year, YGE released another reality survival program, called *Mix & Match*, to select members of iKON, a seven-member boy band. The program featured the six members of Team B in *Who is Next: Win* and three new trainees. JYP Entertainment released a documentary, *Blood Men*, via MNet in 2007 that shows the predebut audition and training days of the group One Day, which later split into 2AM and 2PM. By revealing the brutal realities of the debut process, the reality programs plant the idea among audiences that the selected members went through rigorous training and finally achieved their dreams. The commercial exploitation of the debut process for idol groups has generated enormous publicity; not only are the newly formed groups and their members widely known to the public but fandom is established even before the debut. Such practices, however, are limited to major *gihoeksa* with powerful influence over broadcasting stations.

15. For the discussions of idols' sexuality and the gendered nature of idol production, please see Kim 2011 and Jung 2013.

16. Some idols are trained to be able to compose music and allowed to produce their own albums. Representative examples of this include G-Dragon in Big Bang, B.I in iKON, Jung Yong-hwa in CNBLUE, and Yong Jun-hyung in BEAST. Only recently, agencies have begun to nurture the artistic production skills among trainees; BTS and Stray Kids were created upon such creative autonomy.

17. Retrieved from https://www.reddit.com/r/kpop/comments/3bqlb2/park_jin_young_harshly_criticizes_sixteen_jihyos/.

18. "1 vs. 100" aired on August 18, 2015, on KBS.

19. For discussions of neoliberal human capital in contemporary Korea, please refer to Song 2009 and Elena Kim 2012. Joo-hyun Cho's article (2009) discusses the construction of neoliberal women and beauty in postfinancial-crisis Korea.

20. "Apink's Showtime Will Reveal Members' Private Lives and Bare Faces," [In Korean.] *Newspim*, August 6, 2014, http://www.newspim.com/view.jsp?newsId =20140806000409.

21. For the studies on fandom, please see Lewis 1992 and Jenkins 1992b. For the celebrity studies, please see Gamson 1994.

22. I have explored the discursive consumption of Korean television dramas elsewhere (Oh 2015). In the web 2.0 era, the reception process of television shows goes far beyond passive watching to embrace collective consumption and collaborative reproduction among the anonymous public.

23. Cited from *Music Industry Blog*, https://musicindustryblog.wordpress.com/tag /cd-sales/.

24. Ibid.

25. Moreover, easy access to free digital copies of music files further eats away at the profitability of the pop music business.

26. "How Has the Ever-Expanding Idol Business Been Made?," [In Korean.] *Cine 21*, July 26, 2012, http://www.cine21.com/news/view/mag_id/70551.

27. A few idol groups that have megasize fandom, such as EXO and BTS, still sell their music albums well. EXO is a quadruple-million seller as its four albums (*XOXO*, *Exodus*, *Ex'Act*, and *The War*) have sold more than one million copies. Such very rare cases do not necessarily render music a primary currency in the K-pop industry.

28. "Suzy Appears on Twenty-Two TV Commercials, Total Revenue Reached $10," [In Korean.] *Herald Economy*, April 19, 2013, http://biz.heraldcorp.com/view.php?ud=20130419000456.

29. Marx (2012) discusses how the Japanese *jimusho* system promotes "created" performers over talented ones. Against the backdrop of a dwindling music market and the decline of television viewership, *the* top channel for the creation of revenue streams is corporate/product sponsorship and promotion. In the *jimusho* system, this commercial logic leads to emphasis on attractive looks over artistic talent where idols are concerned and results in industry players devoting more time to securing advertising deals than producing entertainment content. Thus, the Japanese idols that the *jimusho* system prefers are those with general talent rather than those who are too specialized.

30. "How Far Would You Travel to See Girls' Generation?," *CNN Travel*, October 29, 2011, http://travel.cnn.com/seoul/play/how-far-would-you-travel-see-girls-generation-317566/.

31. In the holographic performance hall, screens are transparent, tilting at forty-five degrees. When the holographic video is projected on the tilted screens, it creates 3D holographic projections floating in midair.

32. As regards hologram performances, my informants reported: "They are quite realistic, and therefore afford audiences a semblance of what a true concert experience could be, only without all the high-pitched screaming"; "These showings are ideal for tourists who are visiting Seoul and may never have the opportunity to see their biases [favorite idols] in the flesh." Author interviews, June 2016.

33. Although the majority of them were fan girls, I spotted fan boys and fan adults as well. In my personal interviews, many fan girls interpreted K-pop places such as the Artium as public spaces in which their identity as fans would not necessarily be disclosed, as the following interview quotes suggest: "The Artium is a space I would feel safe to go to for my own interests. It is not like waiting in a long line at a fan-meeting venue. When you are shopping and looking around here you won't be glared at much by other people. In here, I could be just a shopper, as far as the public is concerned, rather than a fan, and that is a great relief"; "It is totally possible to enjoy the Artium without spending a single penny; entry is free and a good majority of the interactive activities are free as well. Hanging around is not discouraged in spaces like the LIVErary either"; "While I'm still intimidated by public fan culture, there is something comforting about walking into a space knowing that you will not be judged for the things you enjoy." Author interviews, June 2016.

34. Author interview, June 2016.

35. "COEX, Holograms, and the Ever-Expanding SM Empire," *Seoulbeats*, January 21, 2015, http://seoulbeats.com/2015/01/coex-holograms-ever-expanding-sm-empire/.

36. "Lee Soo Man Outlines SM Entertainment's Three Stages of Globalization," *Allkpop*, June 13, 2011, http://www.allkpop.com/article/2011/06/lee-soo-man-outlines-sm-entertainments-three-stages-of-globalization. For the study on hybridity, please see Kraidy 2005.

37. "Wonderful K-Pop, But . . . . ," [In Korean.] *Sports Donga*, June 16, 2011, http://sports.donga.com/3//20110615/38062625/3.

38. Foreign fans have tried to enhance their visibility by urging entertainment agencies to create English-language websites for overseas audiences and increase the number

of overseas concerts. It is common for global fans to organize flash mobs in prominent public areas via Facebook, performing and dancing to the latest K-pop songs.

39. For the discussion of K-pop fandom in Southeast Asia, please see Jung 2011.

40. Cited from http://beyondhallyu.com/k-pop/how-youtube-helped-create-the -k-pop-international-fan-community-a-timeline/.

41. Uploaders can also adjust the settings to disallow any comments on their videos.

42. Cited from https://thelittleshopofdonuts.wordpress.com/2014/06/06/a-case-for -k-pop/.

43. Author interview, April 2015.

44. Dance practice videos display idols' in-house choreography practice wearing ordinary clothes. Filmed from the front and uninterrupted by the busy camerawork of music shows, the practice videos plainly reveal the overall choreography. They are thus used as dance tutorials by fans. Ardent fans eagerly wait for these unofficial videos because they find watching their idols going through ordinary rehearsals in their not-so-sparkly outfits surprisingly entertaining.

45. The number of views generates revenues to YouTubers. If the view count reaches ten million, the estimated revenue is between $13,600 and $34,000. See http:// youtubemoney.co/.

46. A microblog differs from a traditional blog in that its content is typically smaller in both actual and aggregated file size. Cited from Wikipedia, https://en.wikipedia.org /wiki/Tumblr.

47. When celebrities appear at an airport for overseas schedules, fans have opportunities to take photos of them in an off-stage ordinary outfit.

48. Cited from http://kpoprealitycheck.tumblr.com/post/6866500026/10-how-true -are-otps, accessed in October 2015.

49. Actually, the term "cannon goddess" originated from the SHINee fan club. SHINee members often remark, "Our fans take pictures of us using cameras that are used to take pictures of the moon."

50. Cited from http://www.allkpop.com/forums/discussion/238594/pann-shinee -s-cannon-goddesses.

51. Cited from http://www.huffingtonpost.kr/2015/10/06/story_n_8248868.html.

## 4. K-Star Road

1. This does not necessarily mean that all Gangnam residents are part of the upper class: many young parents with school-age children have opted to be tenants in the area to enjoy the better educational opportunities.

2. Park seized power in a military coup in 1961; the military dictatorship continued until 1979, when he was assassinated.

3. See also the MBC Documentary *I Can Tell Now* (*Ijeneun Malhal Su Issda*), episode 79, "The Roots of Speculation: The Republic of Gangnam (*Tugiui Ppuri: Gangnam Gonghwaguk*)," which aired on April 10, 2004. At that time, an apartment condo of around 2,000 square feet located in central Seoul cost around $11,000; thus, $2 million in illegal political funds was an unimaginable amount.

4. To pacify individual landowners' complaints, the state exempted them from real estate transfer tax in the Gangnam development site.

5. School District 8 is known to have the best public schools in the country and is also a mecca of private education.

6. Valérie Gelézeau (2007) interprets the appearance of large-scale apartment areas in Korea as the result of deliberate government policy, especially the allotment system (*bunyang jedo*). Through the *bunyang* system, would-be home owners bought apartments at below-market prices before they were even built; then, when construction was complete, they found themselves suddenly wealthy because values had already soared. At the same time, apartments became a symbol of social recognition for a new stratum that had lost its traditional sense of identity based on birthplace (*kohyang*).

7. The currency depreciation affected the price of imported oil, causing price hikes for every single manufactured product. Skyrocketing interest rates also aggravated household debt.

8. The interview data are excerpted from the following news article: "Why Entertainment Agencies Cannot Leave Gangnam," [in Korean.] *OSEN*, February 8, 2013, http://news.joins.com/article/10639415.

9. Gangnam-gu is one of the twenty-five *gu* (districts) that make up the metropolitan area of Seoul; Gangnam-gu Office is the district government. As stated above, Gangnam, broadly speaking, refers to the three wealthy *gu* located south of the Han River: Seocho(-gu), Gangnam(-gu), and Songpa(-gu). Although Gangnam-gu is only one part of broader Gangnam (sometimes referred to as the greater Gangnam area), the district office is trying to make the symbolic status of Gangnam apply only to the area within its district boundaries.

10. The original data can be accessed at the following site: http://gangnam.go.kr /portal/bbs/selectBoardList.do?bbsId=B_000031&menuNo=200097.

11. Although such efforts to be global face criticism in terms of the normalization of the global city and the exacerbation of sociospatial polarization, particularly among "developing" cities, *playing the global* has been a desperate initiative for emerging cities and legitimized "the entrepreneurial turn" of urban governance. See also Robinson (2002) and Dupont (2011).

12. Medical tourism is nothing but a euphemism for plastic surgery tourism. The overseas marketing of Korean popular culture has constructed an image of Korean beauty that fuels fans' aspirations to emulate the appearance of Korean stars (see chapter 5). Given the growing boom in "plastic surgery tours" to Korea, Gangnam-gu Office is trying to capitalize on this "medical" demand by exploiting the density of beauty clinics in the area. A discussion of plastic surgery tourism, however, goes beyond the scope of this study.

13. Multicultural (*damunhwa*) policies are designed to provide an alternative to Korea's historic ethnic homogeneity by acknowledging and endorsing the diverse cultural origins of migrant brides, foreign investors, and migrant workers. The policy originally intended to embrace "Otherness." Ironically, however, it has created a dichotomy between the multicultural and the nonmulticultural (i.e., the "Korean").

14. In my attempt to interview district officials, I was asked to, first, reveal my perspective on their place-promotion policies: "If your research intends to criticize our

policies, we cannot do any interviews. If there is criticism only, city officials cannot do anything." Personal phone call with a district officer, June 2016.

15. Seriously underestimating actual demand, SM Entertainment scheduled one single concert; all tickets were sold in less than fifteen minutes. Those who did not get a ticket took to the streets, urging SM Entertainment to add more dates. French fans picketed the main courtyard of the Louvre Museum, waving signs and banners saying, "Please hold the concert on another day" and "We want a second SM Town Live in Paris." The demonstration lasted for about an hour. The protestors staged a flash mob performance, and sang and danced to a number of K-Pop songs. This incident was turned into a huge national media spectacle back home in Korea to show how K-pop was gaining worldwide recognition even in the West.

16. The quotation is taken from a British journalist's interview with a twenty-two-year-old Italian woman. Jennifer Cox, "Seoul Searching: On the Trail of the K-Pop Phenomenon," *Guardian*, December 28, 2012.

17. This quotation is from Gem Muzones's blog (www.travelswithahobo.com), a founder and author of the budget travel blog *Travels with a Hobo*.

18. This was posted as a "Reply" to the following: http://www.allkpop.com/article/2014/07/what-its-like-going-to-a-k-pop-concert.

19. "The Ultimate Guide to K-Star Road," *(x)clusive*, August 24, 2015, http://x-clusive.sg/2015/08/24/travel-the-ultimate-guide-to-k-star-road/.

20. Author interview, March 2011.

21. Blog posting by Wanderlust Yeoja, "Seoul: Kpop-Filled Trip," https://wanderlustyeoja.wordpress.com/.

22. The data is drawn from Kpop United, a group that organized to bring K-pop fans together and to also teach them about the culture behind K-pop. They created their first tour called "Dream Tour Korea!" in 2012. The blog posting can be found at http://kpoptamago.blogspot.com/2013/04/kpop-united-dream-tour-korea-day-1.html, accessed in October 2015.

23. "What It's Like Going to a K-Pop Concert," *Allkpop.com*, July 29, 2014, http://www.allkpop.com/article/2014/07/what-its-like-going-to-a-k-pop-concert.

24. Wanderlust Yeoja, "Seoul: Kpop-Filled Trip."

25. In an effort to make inroads into overseas markets, some major agencies have held overseas concerts. For example, under the aegis of the "SMTOWN Live World Tour," in which all SM artists collaborate and perform together, SM Entertainment has regularly held overseas concerts in many different countries. Big groups such as Big Bang, Shinhwa, and 2PM are often on an Asia tour or a world tour. Yet such opportunities do not come along often—only a few times a year in Japan and China, which are major markets for K-pop, and at best once a year in other smaller markets. Minor agencies do not have the capacity to launch overseas concerts on their own. Lack of opportunities to see their idols in their own countries, however, is not the only reason that hungry and tantalized foreign fans are driven to visit Korea. Korea has a unique concert culture that can be experienced only in the mecca of K-pop.

26. Called *dreame* (meaning "dream rice"), these rice stacks are a type of charitable activity engaged in by fans in the names of their idols. It is now common practice among

K-pop fans to send *dreame* mock-ups to show support for their stars rather than sending flowers. This activity has become a representative form of activism within K-pop fandom; once largely driven by consumerism, fan culture has become socially aware (Jung 2012).

27. Author interview, June 2014.

28. The following YouTube pages introduce K-pop–related places, including K-Star Road: https://www.youtube.com/watch?v= DBw-vXLlGp0, https://www.youtube.com /watch?v=pUZEWd_DfLc, and https://www.youtube.com/watch?v=K8rUfa6ayDQ, https://www.youtube.com/watch?v=-0TLblF85tc, https://www.youtube.com/watch ?v= SA-OcgbD_cI.

29. Wanderlust Yeoja, "Seoul: Kpop-Filled Trip."

30. In addition to K-Star Road, the K-ROAD project is envisioned as encompassing "K-Fashion Road," a remodeling of a neighborhood where fashion shops and studios are clustered; "K-Beauty Road," an area where beauty shops and clinics are concentrated; "K-Gourmet Road," which is lined with quality restaurants; and "K-Riverside Road," which connects Gangnam with the nearby Han River Park.

31. The brand of a product embodies a set of physical and sociopsychological attributes as well as beliefs that are associated with the product. See Simoes and Dibb (2001).

32. Korea Creative Content Agency 2017.

33. "K-Star Road in Gangnam Lures K-Pop Fans," *Korea Times*, April 15, 2015, http://www.koreatimes.co.kr/www/news/nation/2015/04/116_177179.html.

34. http://chlospace.blogspot.com/2015/07/korea-trip-summer-2015-k-star-road-and .html.

35. Building affective connections between a city and its users can be done by a variety of means: by appealing to the aesthetic sensibilities and cultural tastes of the so-called new middle class (young, high-income professionals), who would like to live in gentrified neighborhoods (Zukin 1995; Smith 1996; Florida 2002); through consumer lifestyle magazines that encourage readers to aspire to particular lifestyles and brand names (Greenberg 2000, 2008); and through cultural stories that construct cities' images (Jensen 2007). These affective strategies, which mainly target a particular (upper middle) class, have, however, also been the object of contestations over privatization, exclusion, and displacement (Ley 1996; Smith 1996).

36. Wanderlust Yeoja, "Seoul: Kpop-Filled Trip."

37. The numbers of inbound foreign tourists to Gangnam-gu have been reported by the Statistic Portal of the South Korean Ministry of Culture, Sports, and Tourism as follows: 334,255 in 2013, 342,331 in 2014, and 342,636 in 2015. http://culturestat.mcst .go.kr/StatisticsPortal/McstPortal/index.jsp, accessed in November 2016.

## 5. Cosme Road

1. Parts of this chapter was originally published in Oh 2017.

2. "Imo" is the nineteenth year in the sexagenarian cycle, corresponding to the year 1882. The Imo Incident was a revolt by some units in the military against the government's

discriminatory policies favoring the new Special Skill Force organized by the Japanese advisory.

3. The writing of the poem/song "As Time Goes By" (*Sewori gamyeon*) is a famous story. One night in 1956, a group of artists gathered together at the famous Gyeong Sang Do House (a drinking place) in Myeong-dong. As the group sat drinking, the poet Park In-hwan began scribbling down a poem. Composer Lee Jin-seob looked at it and created a musical score to go along with the poem on the spot. The actress Nah Ae-sim began to sing it, and when the group was joined by tenor Yim Man-seob, it became a full-fledged performance.

4. The Fourth Republic (1972–1979) was established under the new constitution called *Yushin* (meaning "Revitalization" or "Reform") in 1972. The reform created an authoritarian institution called the National Conference Unification (NCU). NCU was essentially an electoral college whose main task was to choose the president through a nonpopular voting mechanism. Park Chung Hee was elected without opposition in 1972 and 1978. This system remained in effect until after Park's assassination in 1979. Establishing the presidency as a self-perpetuating and highly autocratic position in the South Korean government, the Yushin Constitution was little more than a legal mechanism for institutionalizing Park's dictatorial rule.

5. Deployment of the US Terminal High Altitude Area Defense (THAAD) caused significant declines in inbound Chinese tourists in Korea. See the conclusion for discussion of the aftermath of THAAD.

6. "Rent in Myeong-dong, World's Eighth," [In Korean.] *Asia Economy*, November 19, 2014, http://www.asiae.co.kr/news/view.htm?idxno=2014111917194537275.

7. "The Revival of Missah, the Low-End Cosmetics Brand," [In Korean.] *Kyung-Hyang Biz*, August 22, 2011, http://bizn.khan.co.kr/khan_art_view.html?artid=2011 08212206435&code=920401&med=khan.

8. "THE FACE SHOP vs. *inisfree* . . . Who Is Number 1?," [In Korean.] *Asia Economy*, February 4, 2015, http://www.asiae.co.kr/news/view.htm?idxno=20150204094355 98463.

9. For brand name spellings, I referred to their own logo images.

10. Author interviews, May 2014.

11. Author interviews, May 2014.

12. "THE FACE SHOP vs. *inisfree*."

13. Author interviews, May 2014.

14. "Highest Myeong-dong Rent: $250,000 Monthly. . . . How Much They Earn," [In Korean.] *Hankook Ilbo*, March 4, 2015, http://www.hankookilbo.com/v/bad72b189f 3447a8af87b9c1276435ea.

15. The road shops may be either directly operated by a cosmetics firm or by franchising agreement.

16. Author interviews, June 2014.

17. Despite the advantages of agglomeration, measures to reduce production costs have led companies to form outsourced satellites that rely upon inexpensive labor costs, for example, in Vancouver, British Columbia (Coe 2000; Scott 2007).

18. Gangnam is a primary destination for such "medical tourism," but discussion of the Hallyu-driven plastic surgery tours much exceeds the scope of this book.

19. Author interview, June 2014.

20. These modeling examples are as of 2015 and the brands frequently change their models over time.

21. In comparison, there are few blogs that discuss the musical styles of K-pop.

22. Author interview, June 2014.

23. Author interview with a store assistant at Nature Republic, June 2014.

24. Detailed information about the Special Tourist Zone can be accessed at http://www.junggu.seoul.kr/tour/eng/content.do?cmsid=10249.

25. Detailed information about the Eulji-ro Urban Industry Special Zone can be accessed at http://www.junggu.seoul.kr/content.do?cmsid=984.

26. As of December 2014, the official appraised land value for the site was around $200,000 per square meter; it had held the number-one position for ten straight years. Land value data is from the Korea Land Information System, https://www.realtyprice.kr:447/notice/gsindividual/siteLink.htm, accessed on April 29, 2018.

27. Author interview, May 2014.

28. Eun-Shil Kim's (2014) research on Itaewon, Seoul, convincingly delivers the significance of place in globalization.

## Conclusion

1. One example is the Roh Moo-hyun administration's Comprehensive Real Estate Tax (*jonghap budongsan segeum*), which imposed an additional 1 to 3 percent of property tax on real estate whose value exceeded 600 million won (about $600,000). The policy was intended to redistribute wealth and prevent speculative bubbles.

2. The initial agreement between the United States and South Korea was made on July 7, 2016.

3. Korea Tourism Organization Data from http://kto.visitkorea.or.kr/kor.kto, accessed on April 29, 2018.

4. The screenwriter achieved great commercial success through her works, including *Descendants of the Sun*, *The Heirs*, and *Secret Garden*.

5. Its final episode recorded an 18.680 percent nationwide audience share, an indication of exceptional success for a drama series aired via a cable channel, making it the second highest rated drama in Korean cable television history.

6. "Goblin Disappeared . . . China's Erasure of Hallyu," [In Korean.] *Maeil Business Economy*, March 3, 2017, http://news.mk.co.kr/v2/economy/view.php?sc=30000001&cm=%C0%AF%C5%EB%BE%F7%B0%E8+%B5%BF%C7%E2&year=2017&no=147918&selFlag=&relatedcode=.

7. See chapter 2 for details.

8. "Goblin Appears in Incheon . . . the Drama Filming Locations Turned into Tourist Destinations," [In Korean.] *donga.com*, January 7, 2017, http://news.donga.com/BestClick/3/all/20170116/82418670/1.

9. I draw on Joseph Nye's (2004) conceptualization of soft power as a form of power that arises from the attractiveness of a country's cultural values. This entails the ability to get what one wants by seduction rather than coercion. See also Lukács 2010b.

10. For the relationship between international film (festival) and cities, see Stenger 2001 and Stringer 2001.

11. "Envision the 'Media and Culture City' Based on Local Places," *MBC Chungbuk News*, May 16, 2017. The news video clip can be watched at https://www.youtube .com/watch?v=O7XdNEfkO4k.

12. Cities in other parts of Asia have been endeavoring to tap into the popularity of certain media content: for example, the Japanese National Tourist Organization's effort to enhance international tourism to Tokyo by capitalizing on the popularity of *Lost in Translation*, and Taipei City's efforts to develop the historic district of Bopiliao by appropriating the representations and meanings of the hit film *Monga* (Chen and Mele 2017). In contrast to such postproduction efforts, my focus in this book is on the precontracted placement of places in media content.

# Reference List

Adorno, Theodor. 1991. *The Culture Industry: Selected Essays on Mass Culture*. New York: Routledge.

Adorno, Theodor, and Max Horkheimer. 2002. *Dialectic of Enlightenment*. Translated by Edmund Jephcott. Stanford, CA: Stanford University Press.

Ahmed, Sara. 2010. *The Promise of Happiness*. Durham, NC: Duke University Press.

Ahn, Changmo. 2010. "Gangnamgaebalgwa gangbugui hyeongseonggwajeong gochal" [The birth of Gangbuk in the process of making Gangnam]. *Seoulhak yeongu* [Journal of Seoul Studies] 41: 79–91.

Aitken, Stuart, and Leo Zonn, eds. 1994. *Place, Power, Situation and Spectacle: A Geography of Film*. Lanham, MD: Rowman and Littlefield.

Allen, Robert. 1985. *Speaking of Soap Operas*. Chapel Hill: University of North Carolina Press.

———, eds. 1995. *To Be Continued . . . Soap Operas around the World*. London: Routledge.

Allison, Anne. 2006. *Millennial Monsters: Japanese Toys and the Global Imagination*. Berkeley: University of California Press.

Amsden, Alice. 1989. *Asia's Next Giant: South Korea and Late Industrialization*. New York: Oxford University Press.

Aoyagi, Hiroshi. 2005. *Islands of Eight Million Smiles: Idol Performance and Symbolic Production in Contemporary Japan*. Cambridge, MA: Harvard University Press.

Appadurai, Arjun. 1996. *Modernity at Large: Cultural Dimensions of Globalization.* Minneapolis: University of Minnesota Press.

Ashworth, Gregory. 2009. "The Instruments of Place Branding: How Is It Done?" *European Spatial Research and Policy* 16 (1): 9–22.

Augé, Marc. 1995. *Non-Places: Introduction to an Anthropology of Supermodernity.* London: Verso.

Balasubramanian, Siva. 1994. "Beyond Advertising and Publicity: Hybrid Messages and Public Policy Issues." *Journal of Advertising* 23 (4): 29–46.

Baym, Nancy. 2000. *TUNE IN, LOG ON: Soaps, Fandom, and Online Community.* Thousand Oaks, CA: Sage.

Beeton, Sue. 2005. *Film-Induced Tourism.* Clevedon, U.K.: Channel View.

Bilton, Chris. 1999. "Risky Business: The Independent Production Sector in Britain's Creative Industries." *International Journal of Cultural Policy* 6 (1): 17–39.

Bolin, Göran. 2009. "Symbolic Production and Value in Media Industries." *Journal of Cultural Economy* 2 (3): 345–361.

Bollhöfer, Björn. 2007. "Screenscapes: Placing TV Series in Their Contexts of Production, Meaning and Consumption." *Tijdschrift voor Economische en Sociale Geografie* [Journal of Economic and Social Geography] 98: 165–175.

Bondi, Liz. 2005. "Making Connections and Thinking Through Emotions: Between Geography and Psychotherapy." *Transactions of the Institute of British Geographers* 30 (4): 433–448.

Bourdieu, Pierre. 1977. *Outline of a Theory of Practice.* Cambridge: Cambridge University Press.

——. 1984. *Distinction: A Social Critique of the Judgment of Taste.* Cambridge, MA: Harvard University Press.

——. 1993. *The Field of Cultural Production.* New York: Columbia University Press.

Brenner, Neil, and Roger Keil. 2006. *The Global Cities Reader.* New York: Routledge.

Broudehoux, Anne-Marie. 2004. *The Making and Selling of Post-Mao Beijing.* New York: Routledge.

——. 2007. "Spectacular Beijing: The Conspicuous Construction of an Olympic Metropolis." *Journal of Urban Affairs* 29 (4): 383–399.

Brown, Stephen. 1987. "A Perceptual Approach to Retail Agglomeration." *Area* 19 (2): 131–140.

Browne, Meredith. 2013. "What Is South Korean Tourism without K-Pop?" *POLYGRAFI.* http://polygrafi.com/2013/04/29/what-is-south-korean-tourism-without-k-pop/, accessed on October 15, 2015.

Carruth, David. 2009. "Global COO of Korea's Largest Ad Agency, Cheil Worldwide; Bruce Haines." *10 Magazine Korea,* November 30, 2009. http://10mag.com/bruce-haines/, accessed on October 15, 2015.

Cartier, Carolyn. 2005. "Introduction: Touristed Landscapes/Seductions of Place." In *Seductions of Place: Geographical Perspectives of Globalization and Touristed Landscapes,* edited by Carolyn Cartier and Alan Lew, 1–20. New York: Routledge.

Castells, Manuel. 1992. "Four Tigers with a Dragon Head: A Comparative Analysis of the State, Economy, and Society in the Asian Pacific Rim." In *States and Development in the Asian Pacific Rim*, edited by Richard Appelbaum and Jeffrey Henderson, 33–70. London: Sage.

———. 1996. *The Rise of the Network Society*. Vol. 1 of *The Information Age: Economy, Society, and Culture*. Oxford: Blackwell.

Cha, Frances. 2012. "Harnessing K-Pop for Tourism." *CNN*. April 17, 2012. http://travel.cnn.com/seoul/visit/harnessing-k-pop-tourism-386868.

Chancellor, Edward. 1999. *Devil Take the Hindmost: A History of Financial Speculation*. New York: Farrar, Straus and Giroux.

Chaney, Keidra. 2014. "YouTube and International Music Fan Communities: K-Pop." *The Learned Fangirl*, April 28. http://thelearnedfangirl.com/2014/04/youtube-and-international-music-fan-communities-k-pop/.

Chang, Ha-Joon. 1998. "Korea: The Misunderstood Crisis." *World Development* 26 (8): 1555–1561.

Chen, Fuwei, and Christopher Mele. 2017. "Film-Induced Pilgrimage and Contested Heritage Space in Taipei City." *City, Culture and Society* 9: 31–38.

Cho, Hae-Joang. 2005. "Reading the 'Korean Wave' as a Sign of Global Shift." *Korea Journal* 45 (4): 147–182.

Cho, Joo-hyun. 2009. "Neoliberal Governmentality at Work: Post-IMF Korean Society and the Construction of Neoliberal Women." *Korea Journal* 49 (3): 15–43.

Cho, Myung-rae. 2004. "Yongmanggwa jayeonui sangpumhwawa singaebaljuui" [Developmentalism and the commodification of desire and nature]. *Hwangyeonggwa saengmyeong* [Environment and Life] 41: 26–39.

Choe, Youngmin. 2008. "Affective Sites: Hur Jin-ho's Cinema and Film-Induced Tourism in Korea." In *Asia on Tour: Exploring the Rise of Asian Tourism*, edited by Tim Winter, Peggy Teo, and T. C. Chang, 109–127. London: Routledge.

———. 2016. *Tourist Distraction: Traveling and Feeling in Transnational Hallyu Cinema*. Durham, NC: Duke University Press.

Choo, Hae Yeon. 2016. *Decentering Citizenship: Gender, Labor, and Migrant Rights in South Korea*. Stanford, CA: Stanford University Press.

Chua, Beng Huat, and Koichi Iwabuchi, eds. 2008. *East Asian Pop Culture: Analysing the Korean Wave*. Hong Kong: Hong Kong University Press.

Chun, Wooyong. 2012. "Myeong-dong through History." *The Place* 17.

Coe, Neil M. 2000. "On Location: American Capital and the Local Labour Market in the Vancouver Film Industry." *International Journal of Urban and Regional Research* 42 (1): 79–94.

Cresswell, Tim. 2004. *Place: A Short Introduction*. Malden, MA: Wiley Blackwell.

Debord, Guy. 1994. *The Society of the Spectacle*. Translated by Donald Nicholson-Smith. Brooklyn, NY: Zone Books.

De Certeau, Michel. 1984. *The Practice of Everyday Life*. Berkeley: University of California Press.

De Chernatorny, Leslie, and Francesca Dall'Olmo Riley. 1998. "Defining A 'Brand': Beyond the Literature with Experts' Interpretations." *Journal of Marketing Management* 14 (5): 417–443.

DeSouza, Megan E. 2013. "A Case of the Red Pants Mondays: The Connection between Fandom, Tumblr, and Consumption." Major Papers by Master of Science Students, paper no. 3, University of Rhode Island.

Dirlik, Arif. 2001. "Place-Based Imagination: Globalism and the Politics of Place." In *Places and Politics in the Age of Globalization*, edited by Roxann Prazniak and Arif Dirlik, 15–52. Lanham, MD: Rowman and Littlefield.

Duffett, Mark. 2013. *Understanding Fandom: An Introduction to the Study of Media Fan Culture*. London: Bloomsbury Academic.

Du Gay, Paul. 1997. *Doing Cultural Studies: The Story of the Sony Walkman*. London: Sage.

——, eds. 1998. *Production of Culture/Cultures of Production*. London: Sage.

Dupont, Véronique D. N. 2011. "The Dream of Delhi as a Global City." *International Journal of Urban and Regional Research* 35 (3): 533–554.

Edensor, Tim. 2000. "Staging Tourism: Tourists as Performers." *Annals of Tourism Research* 27 (2): 322–344.

Epstein, Stephen, and James Turnbull. 2014. "Girls' Generation? Gender, (Dis)Empowerment, and K-pop." In *The Korean Popular Culture Reader*, edited by Kyung Hyun Kim and Youngmin Choe, 314–336. Durham, NC: Duke University Press.

Erni, John Nguyet, and Siew Keng Chua. 2005. "Introduction: Our Asian Media Studies?" In *Asian Media Studies: Politics of Subjectivities*, edited by John Nguyet Erni and Siew Keng Chua, 1–15. Oxford: Blackwell.

Escobar, Arturo. 2001. "Culture Sits in Places: Reflections on Globalism and Subaltern Strategies of Localization." *Political Geography* 20: 139–174.

Fiske, John. 1987. *Television Culture*. London: Methuen.

——. 1989. *Understanding Popular Culture*. London: Unwin Hyman.

Fletchall, Ann, Chris Lukinbeal, and Kevin McHugh. 2012. *Place, Television, and the Real Orange County*. Stuttgart: Franz Steiner Verlag.

Florida, Richard. 2002. *The Rise of the Creative Class: And How It's Transforming Work, Leisure, Community and Everyday Life*. New York: Basic Books.

Freeman, Caren. 2011. *Making and Faking Kinship: Marriage and Labor Migration between China and South Korea*. Ithaca, NY: Cornell University Press.

Galbraith, Patrick. 2016. "The Labor of Love: On the Convergence of Fan and Corporate Interests in Contemporary Idol Culture in Japan." In *Media Convergence in Japan*, edited by Patrick Galbraith and Jason Karlin, 232–264. Tokyo: Kinema Club.

Galbraith, Patrick, and Jason Karlin, eds. 2012. *Idols and Celebrity in Japanese Media Culture*. London: Palgrave Macmillan UK.

Gamson, Joshua. 1994. *Claims to Fame: Celebrity in Contemporary America*. Berkeley: University of California Press.

Garnham, Nicholas. 1990. *Capitalism and Communication: Global Culture and the Economics of Information*. London: Sage.

Gelézeau, Valérie. 2007. *Apateu gonghwaguk* [The republic of apartments]. Seoul: Humanitas.

Gotham, Kevin Fox. 2005. "Theorizing Urban Spectacles: Festivals, Tourism and the Transformation of Urban Space." *City* 9 (2): 225–246.

——. 2007. "(Re)Branding the Big Easy: Tourism Rebuilding in Post-Katrina New Orleans." *Urban Affairs Review* 42 (6): 823–850.

——. 2011. "Resisting Urban Spectacle: The 1984 Louisiana World Exposition and the Contradictions of Mega Events." *Urban Studies* 48 (1): 197–214.

Gottdiener, Mark. 2001. *The Theming of America: Dreams, Media Fantasies and Themed Environments.* Boulder, CO: Westview Press.

Greco, Monica and Paul Stenner, eds. 2008. *Emotions: A Social Science Reader.* New York: Routledge.

Greenberg, Miriam. 2000. "Branding Cities: A Social History of the Urban Lifestyle Magazine." *Urban Affairs Review* 36 (2): 228–263.

——. 2008. *Branding New York: How a City in Crisis Was Sold to the World.* New York: Routledge.

Gregory, Derek, Ron Johnston, Geraldine Pratt, Michael Watts, and Sarah Whatmore. 2009. *The Dictionary of Human Geography.* Oxford: Wiley-Blackwell.

Gupta, Pola, and Stephen Gould. 1997. "Consumers' Perceptions of the Ethics and Acceptability of Product Placements in Movies: Product Category and Individual Differences." *Journal of Current Issues and Research in Advertising* 19 (1): 38–50.

Hae, Laam. 2017. "Traveling Policy: Place Marketing and the Neoliberal Turn of Urban Studies in South Korea." *Critical Sociology* 44 (3): 533–546.

Hall, Stuart. 1980. "Encoding/Decoding." In *Culture, Media, Language,* edited by Stuart Hall, Doothy Hobson, Andrew Lowe, and Paul Willis, 117–127. London: Hutchinson.

——. 1997. "The Work of Representation." In *Representation: Cultural Representations and Signifying Practices,* edited by Stuart Hall, 13–74. London: Hutchinson.

Hall, Tim, eds. 1998. *The Entrepreneurial City: Geographies of Politics, Regime and Representation.* New York: John Wiley and Sons.

Hand, Stacey, and Duane Varan. 2007. "Exploring the Effects of Interactivity in Television Drama." In *Interactive TV: A Shared Experience: 5th European Conference, EuroITV 2007, Amsterdam, the Netherlands, May 24–25, 2007, Proceedings,* edited by Pablo Cesar, Konstantinos Chorianopoulos, and Jens Jensen, 57–65. Berlin: Springer.

Hankinson, Graham, and Philippa Cowking. 1993. *Branding in Action: Cases and Strategies for Profitable Brand Management.* London: McGraw-Hill.

Hannigan, John. 1998. *Fantasy City: Pleasure and Profit in the Postmodern Metropolis.* London: Routledge.

——. 2003. "Symposium on Branding, the Entertainment Economy and Urban Place Building: Introduction." *International Journal of Urban and Regional Research* 27 (2): 352–360.

Hardt, Michael. 1999. "Affective Labor." *Boundary* 26 (2): 80–100.

Harvey, David. 1978. "The Urban Process under Capitalism: A Framework for Analysis." *International Journal of Urban and Regional Research* 2: 101–131.

——. 1981. "The Spatial Fix: Hegel, von Thünen and Marx." *Antipode* 13 (3): 1–12.

——. 1989a. "From Managerialism to Entrepreneurialism: The Transformation of Urban Governance in Late Capitalism." *Geografissker Annaler. Series B, Human Geography* 71 (1): 3–17.

——. 1989b. *The Condition of Postmodernity: An Inquiry into the Origins of Cultural Change.* Oxford: Wiley-Blackwell.

——. 1990. "Flexible Accumulation through Urbanization. Reflections on 'Post-Modernism' in the American City." "Theater, Theatricality, and Architecture," *Perspecta* 26: 251–272.

——. 1996. *Justice, Nature and the Geography of Difference.* Oxford: Blackwell.

——. 2001a. *Spaces of Capital: Towards a Critical Geography.* New York: Routledge.

——. 2001b. "Globalization and the 'Spatial Fix.'" *Geographische Revue* 2: 23–30.

——. 2002. "The Art of Rent: Globalization, Monopoly and the Commodification of Culture." In *A World of Contradictions: Socialist Register,* edited by Leo Panitch and Colin Leys, 93–110. New York: Monthly Review Press.

Heo, Jin. 2002. "Junggugui hanryu hyeonsanggwa hanguk tibi deurama suyonge gwanhan yeongu" [The "Hanliu" (Korean Syndrome) phenomenon and the acceptability of Korean TV dramas in China]. *Hanguk bangsong hakbo* [Korean Broadcasting and Telecommunications Studies] 16 (1): 496–529.

Herwitz, Daniel. 2008. *The Star as Icon: Celebrity in the Age of Mass Consumption.* New York: Columbia University Press.

Hesmondhalgh, David, and Sarah Baker. 2008. "Creative Work and Emotional Labour in the Television Industry." *Theory, Culture & Society* 25: 97–118.

——. 2011. *Creative Labour: Media Work in Three Cultural Industries.* London: Routledge.

Hirata, Yukie. 2005. *Hangugeul sobihaneun ilbon: hanryu yeoseong deurama* [Japan consuming Korea: *Hallyu*, women, and drama]. Seoul: Chaeksesang.

Ho, Swee Lin. 2011. "Old Texts, New Desires: How the Korean Television Drama *Daejanggeum* Evokes Reflexivity, Renewal and Resistance among Japanese Women." *Review of Korean Studies* 14 (2): 91–113.

——. 2012. "Fuel for South Korea's 'Global Dreams Factory': The Desires of Parents Whose Children Dream of Becoming K-pop Stars." *Korea Observer* 43 (3): 471–502.

Hoffman, Lily, Susan Fainstein, and Dennis Judd. 2003. *Cities and Visitors: Regulating People, Markets, and City Space.* Oxford: Wiley-Blackwell.

Hopkins, Jeff. 1994. "Mapping of Cinematic Places: Icons, Ideology and the Power of (Mis)representation." In *Place, Power, Situation and Spectacle: A Geography of Film,* edited by Stuart Aitken and Leo Zonn, 47–67. Lanham, MD: Rowman and Littlefield.

Hsing, You-tien. 2010. *The Great Urban Transformation: Politics of Land and Property in China.* Oxford: Oxford University Press.

Hudson, Michael. 1998. "Financial Capitalism v. Industrial Capitalism." Paper presented at The Other Canon Conference on Production Capitalism vs. Financial Capitalism, Oslo, September 3–4. http://michael-hudson.com/1998/09/financial-capitalism-v -industrial-capitalism/.

Hudson, Simon, and Brent Ritchie. 2006. "Promoting Destinations via Film Tourism: An Empirical Identification of Supporting Marketing Initiatives." *Journal of Travel Research* 44 (4): 387–396.

Hwang, Sok-yong. 2010. *Gangnam mong* [Dream of Gangnam]. Seoul: Changbi.

Iwabuchi, Koichi. 2002. *Recentering Globalization: Popular Culture and Japanese Transnationalism.* Durham, NC: Duke University Press.

——. 2013. "Korean Wave and Inter-Asian Referencing." In *The Korean Wave: Korean Media Go Global,* edited by Youna Kim, 43–57. New York: Routledge.

Jenkins, Henry. 1992a. *Textual Poachers: Television Fans and Participatory Culture*. New York: Routledge.

——. 1992b. "'Strangers No More, We Sing': Filking and the Social Construction of the Science Fiction Fan Community." In *The Adoring Audience: Fan Culture and Popular Media*, edited by Lisa Lewis, 208–236. New York: Routledge.

——. 2006. *Convergence Culture: Where Old and New Media Collide*. New York: New York University Press.

Jenkins, Henry, Sam Ford, and Joshua Green. 2014. *Spreadable Media: Creating Value and Meaning in a Networked Culture*. New York: New York University Press.

Jensen, Ole B. 2007. "Culture Stories: Understanding Cultural Urban Branding." *Planning Theory* 6 (3): 211–236.

Jessop, Bob. 1998. "The Enterprise of Narrative and the Narrative of Enterprise: Place Marketing and the Entrepreneurial City." In *The Entrepreneurial City: Geographies of Politics, Regime and Representation*, edited by Tim Hall and Phil Hubbard, 77–99. Chichester: Wiley.

Ji, Joo-Hyoung. 2016. "Gangnam gaebalgwa gangnamjeok dosiseongui hyeongseong: bangong gwonwijuui baljeongukgaui gongganjeok seontaekseongeul jungsimeuro" [The development of Gangnam and the formation of Gangnam-style urbanism: On the spatial selectivity of the anti-communist authoritarian developmental state]. *Hangukjiyeokjirihakoeji* [Journal of the Korean Association of Regional Geographers] 22 (2): 307–330.

Jin, Dal Yong. 2011. *HANDS ON/HANDS OFF: The Korean State and the Market Liberalization of the Communication Industry*. New York: Hampton Press.

——. 2015. *Digital Platforms, Imperialism and Political Culture*. New York: Routledge.

Joo, Young-ha. 2007. *Ilbon hallyu, hankuk kwa ilbon eseo boda* [*Hallyu* in Japan from the perspectives of Japan and Korea]. Seoul: Academy of Korean Studies.

Jun, Gang-Soo. 2012. "1970 nyeondae bakjeonghui jeonggwonui gangnamgaebal" [Gangnam development by the Park Chung-hee regime in the 1970s]. *Yeoksamunjeyeongu* [Critical Studies on Modern Korean History] 28: 9–38.

Jung, Eun-Young. 2013. "K-pop Female Idols in the West: Racial Imaginations and Erotic Fantasies." In *The Korean Wave: Korea Media Go Global*, edited by Youna Kim, 106–119. London: Routledge.

Jung, Sun. 2011. "K-Pop, Indonesian Fandom, and Social Media." Special issue, "Race and Ethnicity in Fandom," edited by Robin Anne Reid and Sarah Gatson, *Transformative Works and Cultures*, no. 8. http://dx.doi.org/10.3983/twc.2011.0289.

——. 2012. "Fan Activism, Cyber Vigilantism, and Othering Mechanisms in K-Pop Fandom." Special issue, "Transformative Works and Fan Activism," edited by Henry Jenkins and Sangita Shresthova, *Transformative Works and Cultures*, no. 10. http://dx.doi.org/10.3983/twc.2012.0300.

Kang, Myounggu. 2015. "Gangnamgaebalgyehoek" [Gangnam development plan]. *Seoul Archive*. https://www.seoulsolution.kr/ko/node/3072.

Kaplan, Andreas, and Michael Haenlein. 2010. "Users of the World, Unite! The Challenges and Opportunities of Social Media." *Business Horizons* 53 (1): 59–68.

KDB Daewoo Securities. 2014. "Cosmetics Survival Game," *2014 Outlook Report*.

Keating, Patrick. 2006. "Emotional Curves and Linear Narratives." *Velvet Light Trap* 58: 4–15.

Kim, Andrew Eungi, Fitria Mayasari, and Ingyu Oh. 2013. "When Tourist Audiences Encounter Each Other: Diverging Learning Behaviors of K-Pop Fans from Japan and Indonesia." *Korea Journal* 53 (4): 59–82.

Kim, Changwook. 2008. "Labor Flexibility and Subjectivity in the Korean Independent Broadcasting Production Sector." Master's thesis, Seoul National University.

Kim, Eleana. 2012. "Human Capital: Transnational Korean Adoptees and the Neoliberal Logic of Return." *Journal of Korean Studies* 17 (2): 299–328.

Kim, Eun-Shil. 2004. "Itaewon as an Alien Space within the Nation-State and a Place in the Globalization Era." *Korea Journal* 44 (3): 34–64.

Kim, Hoyoung, and Tae-Jin Yoon. 2012. "Hanguk daejungmunhwaui aidol siseutem jakdong bangsik" [How the IDOL system in Korean pop culture works: An explorative study on the dual structure of production/consumption of idol culture]. *Bangsonggwa keomyunikeisyeon* [Broadcasting and Communication] 13 (4): 45–82.

Kim, Hyun Mee. 2001. "*Yongmang-ui dongsiseong*" [Coevalness of desire]. *Hankyoreh 21*, October 30, 282.

———. 2005. *Geullobeol sidaeui munhwa beonyeok: Jendeo, injong, gyecheungui gyeonggyereul neomeo* [Cultural translation in the global age: Beyond the barriers of gender, race, and class]. Seoul: Tto hanaui munhwa.

Kim, Jeongmee. 2007. "Why Does Hallyu Matter? The Significance of the Korean Wave in South Korea." *Critical Studies in Television* 2 (2): 47–59.

Kim, Kyung Hyun, and Youngmin Choe, eds. 2014. *The Korean Popular Culture Reader.* Durham, NC: Duke University Press.

Kim, Sangkyun. 2012. "Audience Involvement and Film Tourism Experiences: Emotional Places, Emotional Experiences." *Tourism Management* 33: 387–396.

Kim, Sun-Woong. 2015. "Tojiguhoekjeongnisaeop" [Land readjustment project]. *Seoul Archive*. https://seoulsolution.kr/ko/content/%ED%86%A0%EC%A7%80%EA%B5%AC%ED%9A%8D%EC%A0%95%EB%A6%AC%EC%82%AC%EC%97%85.

Kim, Yeran. 2011. "Idol Republic: The Global Emergence of Girl Industries and the Commercialization of Girl Bodies." *Journal of Gender Studies* 20 (4): 333–345.

Kim, Youna, eds. 2013. *The Korean Wave: Korean Media Go Global.* New York: Routledge.

KOFICE (Korea Foundation for International Culture Exchange). 2008. *Hanryupoebeo: Hanryuui hyeonjusowa gyeongjejeok hyogwa bunseok.* [*Hallyu* forever: Current situation of Hallyu and its economic effects]. Seoul: KOFICE.

Kong, Lily. 2007. "Cultural Icons and Urban Development in Asia: Economic Imperative, National Identity, and Global City Status." *Political Geography* 26: 383–404.

Korea Communication Commission. 2007. *Hanguk deurama saengsan siseutem gaeseoneul wihan yeongu* [A study on improvement measures in the Korean drama production system].

———. 2005–2015. *Bangsong saneop siltae josa bogoseo* [Reports on the condition of the broadcasting industry]. Seoul: Korea Communication Commision.

Korea Creative Content Agency. 2009. "Bangsongkeontencheu hwalseonghwareul wihan oejujejak gaeseonbangan" [Guidelines for improving the independent production system for content diversification]. *KOCCA Focus*, no. 9. Seoul: Korea Creative Content Agency.

——. 2011. "Deurama ganjeopgwanggowa seutori telling" [Product placement in TV drama and storytelling: An analysis of cases in the *Secret Garden*]. *KOCCA Focus*, no. 4. Seoul: Korea Creative Content Agency.

——. 2015. "Bangsong oejujejak 25nyeonui seonggwawa gwaje" [Outcomes and issues: A 25-year review of the independent production system]. *KOCCA Focus*, no. 4. Seoul: Korea Creative Content Agency.

——. 2017. *Daejungmunhwayesulgihoegeop jijache deungrok hyeonhwang* [Entertainment agencies registered in municipal governments]. http://www.kocca.kr.

Korea Culture and Tourism Institute. 2006. *Hanguk jiyeokchukje josapyeongga mit gaeseonbanghyang yeongu* [Evaluation of Korean local festivals and policy suggestions]. Seoul: Korea Culture and Tourism Institute.

Korea Tourism Organization. 2005. *Haeoe hanryu hanryu gwangwang donghyang* [*Hallyu* overseas and *Hallyu* tourism trends in 2005]. Seoul: Korea Tourism Organization.

——. 2006. *Haeoe hanryu hanryu gwangwang donghyang* [*Hallyu* overseas and *Hallyu* tourism trends in 2006]. Seoul: Korea Tourism Organization.

——. 2011. *Munhwahanryueseo gyeongjehanryuroui doyageul wihan geullobeol hanryu donghyang mit hwaryong jeonryak* [Global *Hallyu* trends: From cultural *Hallyu* to economic *Hallyu*]. Seoul: Korea Tourism Organization.

——. 2012. *Hanryu gwangwang janggihwa bangan maryeoneul wihan yeongu: keipap konseoteu chamgajareul jungsimeuro* [How to sustain long-term *Hallyu* tourism: Focusing on K-pop concert attendants]. Seoul: Korea Tourism Organization.

——. 2014. *2013 banghan gwangwangsijang bunseok* [Inbound tourism statistics in 2013]. http://kto.visitkorea.or.kr.

Korean Ministry of Public Administration and Security. 2016. "Jibangjachidanche jaejeong hyeonhwang." [Revenue Summary of Local Governments.]

Kraidy, Marwan. 2005. *Hybridity, or The Cultural Logic of Globalization*. Philadelphia: Temple University Press.

Langdale, John. 1997. "East Asian Broadcasting Industries: Global, Regional, and National Perspectives." *Economic Geography* 73 (3): 305–321.

Lee, Dong Yeun. 2010. "Aidol pabiran mueosinga? jinghujeok dok hae" [What is idol pop? Signature analysis]. *Munhwa hyeonsil bunseok* [Analysis of Cultural Reality] 62: 210–227.

——, eds. 2011. *Aidol: H.O.T. eseo sonyeosidaekkaji aidol munhwa bogoseo* [Idol: The idol culture reports from H.O.T. to Girls' Generation]. Seoul: Imagine.

Lee, Gil-ho. 2012. *Woorineun dissi: DC, ingyeo, geurigo saibeospeiseui inryuhak* [We, the DC: DC Inside, surplus, and anthropology of cyberspace]. Seoul: Imagine.

Lee, Jenghoon, and Eunhee Park. 2008. "Oejujejakjeongchaek doip ihu jisangpa deurama jejak siseutem byeonhwa" [Changes in the condition for nurturing the TV station's producing crew since the introduction of the independent production quota]. *Bangsongmunhwayeongu* [Studies of Broadcasting Culture] 20 (2): 31–58.

Lee, Sangjoon, and Abé Mark Nornes. 2015. *Hallyu 2.0: Korean Wave in the Age of Social Media*. Ann Arbor: University of Michigan Press.

Lee, Soojin, Daivd Scott, and Hyounggon Kim. 2008. "Celebrity Fan Involvement and Destination Perceptions." *Annals of Tourism Research* 35 (3): 809–832.

Lee, Sooyeon. 2008. *Hallyu deuramawa asia yeoseongui yokmang* [Korean Wave television serials and Asian women's desires]. Seoul: Communication Books.

——. 2012. "The Structure of the Appeal of Korean Wave Texts." *Korea Observer* 43 (3): 447–469.

Lee, Yang-Su. 2011. "Liu Ming-liang: Korea Is the Only Country Worth Making Friends With; So I Have Learned." *Korea Focus*, July 17, 2011. http://www.koreafocus.or.kr /design2/layout/content_print.asp?group_id=103687.

Lewis, Lisa, eds. 1992. *The Adoring Audience: Fan Culture and Popular Media*. New York: Routledge.

Ley, David. 1996. *The New Middle Class and the Remaking of the Central City*. Oxford: Oxford University Press.

Lie, John. 2015. *K-Pop: Popular Music, Cultural Amnesia, and Economic Innovation in South Korea*. Berkeley: University of California Press.

Lo, Kwai-Cheung. 2005. *Chinese Face/Off: The Transnational Popular Culture of Hong Kong*. Champaign: University of Illinois Press

Love, Bridget. 2013. "Treasure Hunts in Rural Japan: Place Making at the Limits of Sustainability." *American Anthropologist* 115 (1): 112–124.

Lukács, Gabriella. 2010a. *Scripted Affects, Branded Selves: Television, Subjectivity, and Capitalism in 1990s Japan*. Durham, NC: Duke University Press.

——. 2010b. "Iron Chef around the World: Japanese Food Television, Soft Power, and Cultural Globalization." *International Journal of Cultural Studies* 13 (4): 409–426.

Macionis, Nicole, and Beverley Sparks. 2009. "Film-Induced Tourism: An Incidental Experience." *Tourism Review International* 13 (2): 93–101.

MacLeod, Gordon. 2002. "From Urban Entrepreneurialism to a 'Revanchist City'? On the Spatial Injustices of Glasgow's Renaissance." *Antipode* 34 (3): 602–624.

Marx, David. 2012. "The *Jimusho* System: Understanding the Production Logic of the Japanese Entertainment Industry." In *Idols and Celebrity in Japanese Media Culture*, edited by Patrick Galbraith and Jason Karlin, 35–55. London: Palgrave Macmillan UK.

Massey, Doreen. 1991. "A Global Sense of Place." *Marxism Today* 38: 24–29.

——. 1993. "Power-Geometry and a Progressive Sense of Place." In *Mapping the Futures: Local Cultures, Global Change*, edited by J. Bird, B. Curtis, T. Putnam, G. Robertson and L. Tickner, 59–69. London: Routledge.

——. 1994. *Space, Place and Gender*. Minneapolis: University of Minnesota Press.

Massumi, Brian. 2002. *Parables for the Virtual: Movement, Affect, Sensation*. Durham, NC: Duke University Press.

Mathews, Vanessa. 2010. "Set Appeal: Film Space and Urban Redevelopment." *Social and Cultural Geography* 11 (2): 171–190.

Mayes, Robyn. 2008. "A Place in the Sun: The Politics of Place, Identity and Branding." *Place Branding and Public Diplomacy* 4: 124–135.

McCracken, Grant. 2005. "'CONSUMERS' OR 'MULTIPLIERS'?" *Spreadable Media*. http://spreadablemedia.org/essays/mccracken/#.WaLv6JOGPq0.

Modleski, Tania. 1982. *Loving with a Vengeance: Mass Produced Fantasies for Women*. Hamden, CN: Archon.

Mullany, Gerry, and Michael Gordon. 2017. "U.S. Starts Deploying Thaad Antimissile System in South Korea, after North's Tests." *New York Times*, March 6.

Mullins, Patrick. 1991. "Tourism Urbanization." *International Journal of Urban and Regional Research* 15 (3): 326–342.

Nagaike, Kazumi. 2012. "Johnny's Idols as Icons: Female Desires to Fantasize and Consume Male Idol Images." In *Idols and Celebrity in Japanese Media Culture*, edited by Patrick Galbraith and Jason Karlin, 97–112. London: Palgrave Macmillan UK.

Negus, Keith. 1999. *Music Genres and Corporate Cultures*. New York: Routledge.

Newman, Michael. 2006. "From Beats to Arcs: Toward a Poetics of Television Narrative." *Velvet Light Trap* 58: 16–28.

Nochimson, Martha. 1993. *No End to Her: Soap Opera and the Female Subject*. Berkeley: University of California Press.

Nye, Joseph. 2004. *Soft Power: The Means to Success in World Politics*. New York: Public Affairs.

Nye, Joseph, and Youna Kim. 2013. "Soft Power and the Korean Wave." In *The Korean Wave: Korea Media Go Global*, edited by Youna Kim, 31–42. London: Routledge.

Oh, Youjeong. 2014. "Korean Television Dramas and the Political Economy of City Promotion." *International Journal of Urban and Regional Research* 38 (6): 2141–2155.

——. 2015. "The Interactive Nature of Korean TV Dramas: Flexible Texts, Discursive Consumption, and Social Media." In *Hallyu 2.0: Korean Wave in the Age of Social Media*, edited by Sangjoon Lee and Abé Mark Nornes, 133–153. Ann Arbor: University of Michigan Press.

——. 2016. "The Developmental State in Urban Modernity: Two State-Led Urban Developments in South Korea." In *The Changing Role of the Korean State: In the Post Developmental Era*, edited by Hong Yung Lee and Sunil Kim, 39–47. Berlin: Logos Verlag Berlin.

——. 2017. "Global Flows and the Changing Place Identity of Myŏng-dong." *Journal of Korean Studies* 22 (1): 177–195.

Oppenheim, Robert. 2008. *Kyŏngju Things: Assembling Place*. Ann Arbor: University of Michigan Press.

Otmazgin, Nissim, and Irina Lyan. 2013. "Hallyu across the Desert: K-Pop Fandom in Israel and Palestine." *Cross-Currents: East Asian History and Culture Review* 9: 68–89.

Paddison, Ronan. 1993. "City Marketing, Image Reconstruction and Urban Regeneration." *Urban Studies* 30 (2): 339–350.

Park, Bae-Gyoon. 2008. "Uneven Development, Inter-scalar Tensions, and the Politics of Decentralization in South Korea." *International Journal of Urban and Regional Research* 32 (1): 40–59.

Peiss, Kathy. 1990. "Making Faces: The Cosmetics Industry and the Cultural Construction of Gender, 1890–1930." *Genders* 7: 143–169.

Pile, Steve. 2010. "Emotions and Affect in Recent Human Geography." *Transactions of the Institute of British Geographers* 35 (1): 5–20.

Premack, Rachel. 2017. "A Row with China over U.S. Missiles Is Devastating South Korea's Tourism Industry." *TIME*, April 10, 2017.

Rausch, Anthony. 2008. "Place Branding in Rural Japan: Cultural Commodities as Local Brands." *Place Branding and Public Diplomacy* 4 (2): 136–146.

Robinson, Jennifer. 2002. "Global and World Cities: A View from Off the Map." *International Journal of Urban and Regional Research* 26 (3): 531–554.

Roesch, Stefan. 2009. *The Experiences of Film Location Tourists*. Bristol, U.K.: Channel View.

Roy, Ananya, and Aihwa Ong, eds. 2011. *Worlding Cities: Asian Experiments and the Art of Being Global*. Malden: Wiley-Blackwell.

Russell, Cristel A. 1998. "Toward a Framework of Product Placement: Theoretical Propositions." In *Advances in Consumer Research*, edited by Joseph Alba and J. Wesley Hutchinson, 25: 357–362. Provo, UT: Association for Consumer Research.

Russell, Mark James. 2008. *POP Goes Korea: Behind the Revolution in Movies, Music, and Internet Culture*. Albany, CA: Stone Bridge Press.

Sassen, Saskia. 1991. *The Global City*. Princeton, NJ: Princeton University Press.

Schiller, Herbert. 1969. *Mass Communications and American Empire*. Boulder, CO: Westview Press.

Scott, Allen. 2004. "Cultural-Products Industries and Urban Economic Development: Prospects for Growth and Market Contestation in Global Context." *Urban Affairs Review* 39 (4): 461–490.

———. 2005. *On Hollywood: The Place, The Industry*. Princeton, NJ: Princeton University Press.

———. 2007. "Hollywood, Vancouver, and the World: Employment Relocation and the Emergence of Satellite Production Centers in the Motion Picture Industry." *Environment and Planning A* 39 (6): 1364–1381.

Selby, Martin. 2004. "Consuming the City: Conceptualizing and Researching Urban Tourist Knowledge." *Tourism Geographies* 6 (2): 186–207.

Shim, Doobo. 2008. "The Growth of Korean Cultural Industries and the Korean Wave." In *East Asian Pop Culture: Analysing the Korean Wave*, edited by Beng Huat Chua and Koichi Iwabuchi, 15–32. Hong Kong: Hong Kong University Press.

Shim, Sungeun. 2008. "Behind the Korean Broadcasting Boom." *NHK Broadcasting Studies* (Tokyo) 6.

Shin, Hyun Bang. 2012. "Unequal Cities of Spectacles and Mega-events in China." *City* 16 (6): 728–744.

———. 2016. "The Developmental State, Speculative Urbanisation and the Politics of Displacement in Gentrifying Seoul." *Urban Studies* 53 (3): 540–549.

Shin, Solee, and Lanu Kim. 2013. "Organizing K-Pop: Emergence and Market Making of Large Korean Entertainment Houses, 1980–2010." *East Asia* 30 (4): 255–272.

Shon, Jung-mok. 2003. *Seoul dosigyehoek iyagi: seoul gyeokdongui 50nyeongwa naui jeungeon* [The story of Seoul urban planning: Turbulent 50 years in Seoul and my testimony]. Vol. 3. Seoul: Hanul.

Simoes, Claudia, and Sally Dibb. 2001. "Rethinking the Brand Concept: New Brand Orientation." *Corporate Communications: An International Journal* 6 (4): 217–224.

Smith, Bob. 1985. "Casting Product for Special Effect." *Beverage World* 104 (March): 83–91.

Smith, Neil. 1994. *Uneven Development: Nature, Capital and the Production of Space*. Oxford: Blackwell.

———. 1996. *The New Urban Frontier: Gentrification and the Revanchist City*. London: Routledge.

Song, Jesook. 2009. *South Koreans in the Debt Crisis: The Creation of a Neoliberal Welfare Society*. Durham, NC: Duke University Press.

Stenger, John. 2001. "Return to OZ: The Hollywood Redevelopment Project, or Film History as Urban Renewal." In *Cinema and the City: Film and Urban Societies in a Global Context*, edited by Mark Shiel and Tony Fitzmaurice, 59–72. Oxford: Blackwell.

Stringer, Julian. 2001. "Global Cities and the International Film Festival Economy." In *Cinema and the City: Film and Urban Societies in a Global Context*, edited by Mark Shiel and Tony Fitzmaurice, 134–144. Oxford: Blackwell.

Takeyama, Akiko. 2010. "Intimacy for Sale: Masculinity, Entrepreneurship, and Commodity Self in Japan's Neoliberal Situation." *Japanese Studies* 30 (2): 231–246.

Thrift, Nigel. 2004. "Intensities of Feeling: Towards a Spatial Politics of Affect." *Geografiska Annaler* 86 (B): 57–78.

———. 2007. *Non-Representational Theory: Space, Politics, Affect*. London: Routledge.

Torchin, Leshu. 2002. "Location, Location, Location: The Destination of the Manhattan TV Tour." *Tourist Studies* 2 (3): 247–266.

Trigg, Stephanie. 2014. "Introduction: Emotional Histories—Beyond the Personalization of the Past and the Abstraction of Affect Theory." *Exemplaria* 26 (1): 3–15.

Tsing, Anna. 2005. *Friction: An Ethnography of Global Connection*. Princeton, NJ: Princeton University Press.

Tzanelli, Rodauthi, and Majid Yar. 2016. "Breaking Bad, Making Good: Notes on a Televisual Tourist Industry." *Mobilities* 11 (2): 188–206.

Ursell, Gillian. 2000. "Television Production: Issues of Exploitation, Commodification and Subjectivity in UK Television Labor Markets." *Media Culture Society* 22 (6): 805–825.

Wade, Robert. (1990) 2003. *Governing the Market: Economic Theory and the Role of Government in East Asia's Industrialization*. Princeton, NJ: Princeton University Press.

Wenner, Lawrence. 2004. "On the Ethics of Product Placement in Media Entertainment." *Journal of Promotion Management* 10 (1–2): 101–132.

Won, Yong-jin, and Ji-man Kim. 2012. "Sahoejeok jangchiroseoui aidol hyeonsang" [Inventing a new social apparatus: Idol stars and entertainment agencies]. *Daejungseosayeongu* [Mass Narrative Research] 29 (18): 319–361.

Woods, Michael. 2007. "Engaging the Global Countryside: Globalization, Hybridity and the Reconstitution of Rural Place." *Progress in Human Geography* 31 (4): 485–507.

Yeoh, Brenda S. A. 2005. "The Global Cultural City? Spatial Imagineering and Politics in the (Multi) Cultural Marketplaces of Southeast Asia." *Urban Studies* 42 (5–6): 945–958.

Zillmann, Dolf. 1995. "Mechanisms of Emotional Involvement with Drama." *Poetics* 23 (1–2): 33–51.

Zukin, Sharon. 1995. *The Cultures of Cities*. Oxford: Blackwell.

# INDEX

Note: Page numbers in italics indicate illustrations; those with a *t* indicate tables.